The Actor's
SURVIVAL KIT

Fourth Edition

The Actor's
SURVIVAL KIT

Miriam Newhouse and Peter Messaline

SIMON & PIERRE
A MEMBER OF THE DUNDURN GROUP
TORONTO

Design: Alison Carr
Printer: Marquis

Library and Archives Canada Cataloguing in Publication

Newhouse, Miriam, 1944-

    The actor's survival kit / Miriam Newhouse and Peter Messaline. -- 4th ed.

Includes bibliographical references.

ISBN: 978-1-55002-678-8

    1. Acting--Vocational guidance--Canada. I. Messaline, Peter, 1944- II. Title.

PN2055.N48 2007   792.02'802371   C2006-906914-X

1 2 3 4 5   11 10 09 08 07

    Conseil des Arts du Canada   Canada Council for the Arts   Canadä   ONTARIO ARTS COUNCIL CONSEIL DES ARTS DE L'ONTARIO

We acknowledge the support of the Canada Council for the Arts and the Ontario Arts Council for our publishing program. We also acknowledge the financial support of the Government of Canada through the Book Publishing Industry Development Program and The Association for the Export of Canadian Books, and the Government of Ontario through the Ontario Book Publishers Tax Credit program, and the Ontario Media Development Corporation.

Printed and bound in Canada.
Printed on recycled paper.

www.dundurn.com

Dundurn Press	Gazelle Book Services Limited	Dundurn Press
3 Church Street, Suite 500	White Cross Mills	2250 Military Road
Toronto, Ontario, Canada	High Town, Lancaster, England	Tonawanda, NY
M5E 1M2	LA1 4XS	U.S.A. 14150

The Actor's
SURVIVAL KIT

Table of Contents

Introduction

This is a book about being an actor in Canada. It's not about how to act — there are plenty of ways to learn that — and it's not about working in the States — plenty of people have written about that. *The Actor's Survival Kit* is about the problems of being an actor, but it is mainly a celebration of the fact that so many people overcome those problems. If you are interested in being a professional actor in Canada, we are talking to you.

We have made all the mistakes it is possible to make, and we aren't afraid to pass them on to you as Awful Warnings. We have both worked in the United States, England, and Canada. Teaching Acting as a Business across the country, we have listened to the questions and concerns of hundreds of people in just your situation. Most important, we have survived almost forty years in the business.

There is no one way of getting into the business. Later on you'll read about the options that are open to you.

This book won't make you a success. What it will do is help you discover what success is. We have a friend who can't walk down the street without being recognized because of his television series. We know actors who work nine to five, doing commercial voice-overs and earning six-figure incomes in complete obscurity. An ex-student who was determined to be a stage actor now finds himself deep in the producing side of the film industry. Who is a success? All of them, of course. Deciding what you want is your first step to success. If you don't know where you're going, how will you know when you get there?

We're not offering you a miracle method. If you are at the beginning of your career, we can save you some time. Instead of making all your own mistakes, you can read about ours. If you are further along, you can bounce your ideas off ours and perhaps get ammunition for a specific problem.

There are no easy answers here. But there are some hard questions you should be asking yourself. We can't take legal or moral responsibility for your career — that's your job. We can show you some problems and offer some advice, but the solutions are up to you.

We can only talk about what we know. Unfortunately, that means we have had to ignore the francophone side of the business. We hope that someone with knowledge and experience in that area will fill the gap.

Writers have yet to solve the he/she/they hassle. We try to steer clear of the problem where possible, but we've decided to call directors "he" and agents and stage managers "she" because that has been the usual pattern in our experience. "Actor" is generic. Indeed, many female actors will not be called anything else.

We try to avoid jargon, but the business is full of it — if the meaning of anything isn't clear, you should find it in the Glossary.

With each edition of this book, the larger picture both changes and remains the same. In theatre, there has been an upswing in modest commercial productions, with a few large commercial ventures on one side and small artist-driven projects on the other. Film and television work is well established in the Maritimes and is on the increase in the Prairies; agents are part of the picture outside Toronto, Montreal, and Vancouver. On the other hand, women and visible minorities are still treated unfairly; actors as a group still contribute most to producers' funds, still remain some of the worst paid professionals — and still consider themselves blessed in their career choice.

We were blessed by the generosity of the hundreds of people we interviewed and by the support of Marian Wilson and Jean Paton of Simon & Pierre. Twenty years ago, they welcomed our audition speech collections and we discovered we couldn't have chosen a better home for our work. The first edition of *The Actor's Survival Kit* followed, and when Kirk Howard and his Dundurn Group adopted S&P and us, we were delighted to find another warm supporter, wildly different in style, but just as interested in Canadian theatre.

Without people like these, producing Canadian material and keeping Canadian culture alive, we would all be the poorer. As long as they are ready to work harder and longer, and for less money, than in for-profit ventures, the south's cultural imperialism will not take us over.

A rich man would never give anything to panhandlers. He would lend them a dollar and say, "Pass it on when you see someone who needs it." In the early days we had people who were our mentors, whom we can never really thank. This is our way of paying forward what we have been given. Take what you know and pass it on in your turn.

CHAPTER ONE

Taking Charge

"You can't hope to be lucky — you have to prepare to be lucky."
Timothy Dowd, NYPD

In a profession where employment depends so much on other people's tastes and biases, it is easy to feel that we have no control over our own affairs. We do have control — not much, but some — and the sooner we start using it, the better.

Acting is not only an art; it is also a business. When we wrote the first edition, we were leading the minority promoting this idea. That minority has grown, but even now, too many drama students and their teachers feel that actors are artists and should not have to deal with mundane realities. Rubbish. Andy Warhol as quoted in the *New Yorker*: "Making money is art and working is art and good business is the best art." There is no point in being an artist if you cannot practise your art. No matter how good you are, if you aren't working, who cares?

Certainly the actual execution of our craft demands an artistry and a sensitivity that is at odds with the grown-up world of business. Eve Brandstein writes in *The Actor*: "Performing is childlike and joyous. Being an actor is a profession. You act from the Child. You do business from the Adult." Being an adult means doing things you'd rather someone else did. It also means knowing what has to be done. The business side of acting involves three main responsibilities, and not one of them is any fun: decision-making, marketing, and self-discipline.

Decision-Making

Throughout your career, you will have choices to make. Every time you make a choice, you open one door and leave another closed. You will never find out what was really behind that closed door. Whatever opportunities you might have had will be lost to you. How do you choose? How will you know if your choice was right? Who do you blame if your choice was wrong?

How do you choose? Find out as much as you can about the problem. Talk to people with knowledge and experience, but consider the sources. Many of your mentors from drama school have not kept up with the changes in the business and are out of touch with the profession as it today. And beware: people on the cutting edge also make assumptions. Don't assume that strong assertions are fact. Do your own research. The more facts you have, the better your chances are of making an adult, informed decision. Don't deny your instincts. Don't let anyone else make the decision for you. However tempting it is to let your agent or your best friend or even this book's authors tell you what to do, do not yield. It is your career and your decision. You are the one who has to live with the results.

How will you know if your choice was right? You won't. It is impossible to predict what might have been. Why waste your time?

Who do you blame if your choice was wrong? You have already worked out the answer to that one, haven't you? That's right: you have no one to blame but yourself. That is why being an adult is such a drag. But why blame anyone? Once you have made your decision regrets and recriminations simply get in the way of doing the job. Play the hand you're dealt.

Marketing

Actors sell a product. Not pets or vinyl tiles or packaged holidays — they sell themselves. You are selling the way you look, the way you sound, the way you move. To do so effectively, you need a hide tough enough to bear constant rejection and the sensitivity and vulnerability to do the job you have been trained to do. The reality is if you don't have the first, you won't need the second.

From *Marketing for the Not-For-Profit*: "Marketing is like going on a diet. It is good for you. It takes discipline. It requires a balanced approach. Meaningful results are not immediate."

Richard Nelson Bolles writes in *What Color Is Your Parachute?*, "The person who gets hired is not necessarily the one who can do the job best but the one who knows the most about getting hired."

Like any business, you have to know what you're selling and who is buying. You learn about your market by reading plays, watching movies and television, going to the theatre, talking to other actors, attending workshops, and reading trade journals. Your market is any possible engager in theatre or the media. Search for information about:

- Theatre — musical, regional, dinner, children's, summer, commercial, alternative, fringe, lunchtime, cruise ships, industrial, specialist (audible/visible minorities, handicapped)
- Film — feature, documentary, in-house (training, industrial), student, independent
- Television — soap opera, sitcom, action, educational, made-for-TV movie, animation/voicing
- Commercials — on-camera, voice-over, radio
- Radio — drama, storytelling, docudrama

So, those are the markets. Now, what is your product? Your product is yourself: what you are and what you can do. It is not easy to know how you come across to the rest of the world. Inside, you may feel like a delicate flower, but if you weigh 350 pounds, have a five o'clock shadow by noon, and turn the air blue with four-letter words, you are unlikely to get cast as Ariel; go for Caliban. This is not to say typecasting is inevitable, but it is getting more and more likely, in theatre as well as in film and television. Carole MacDonald, EMI marketing director: "Image doesn't have to be a completely calculated thing. It's like anybody dressing for a night out, or even going to the office; we all think about how we feel, who we think we are, what we want to project."

Finding out what you project is never easy. When we look in the mirror we exaggerate some things and minimize others according to how we feel about ourselves. Talk to your friends and teachers; they can give you an idea. Ask what they see you cast as; that's sometimes easier for them to answer. Your agent, when you have one, has less reason to give you a polite lie, and more knowledge on which to base professional advice.

You do not have to look or sound like the popular actors of the day. Discover what makes you unique. Bill Cosby, as quoted by Arsenio Hall: "I don't know the key to being successful. But the secret to failure is trying to be like everyone else."

Once you know the market and know your product, you have to be able to put the two together. Self-promotion is tedious and time-consuming. It is also essential.

Self-Discipline

"Acting is a full-time job looking for part-time work." There is not much excitement in keeping files up to date, few laughs in writing engagers and agents, and no joy in being put on hold by endless receptionists. Logging phone conversations and looking up casting directors are not right up there with curtain calls and great reviews, but they are far more frequent. Thriller writer Dick Francis had this to say about jockeys: "The grind, the frustration, the constant failures, the long hours and the poor pay aren't obstacles in the way of the job. They are the job. The applause, the big fee, the award, the triumph — all these are simply occasional bonuses to be enjoyed when they happen." Just like acting.

There's No Business Like Show Business

Very true. In other businesses you start at or near the bottom and work your way up. You may not reach the top, but you move steadily towards it. In the business of acting you can start at any point on the ladder and spend your whole career climbing up and down. That is a puzzling not to say foreign concept for most people. You may be lucky enough to leave drama school and go straight into a leading role in a feature film or at a prestigious theatre (don't hold your breath). Or your first job will come after several months and you will earn $500 as a day player in a series. And so it goes on throughout your career. Success does not breed success.

Success does, however, breed self-confidence. So does knowledge. Having a clear understanding of what you have to do in the job market, and the tools you need to do it with, will give you that confidence. The courage you will need to get through the next chapter you'll have to find for yourself. Read on.

CHAPTER TWO

Gloomy Reality

"Fie upon this quiet life! I want work."
Shakespeare

Caution: The career of acting contains insecurity, unemployment, and rejection and is hazardous to your health.

Unfortunately, acting addicts, like cigarette addicts, ignore the warnings and insist on continuing the habit. So we will not try to put you off with gloomy admonitions; we will simply present the facts. Here are the professional realities you will encounter. At the end of the chapter, if you haven't given up in despair, you will have a better idea of the hurdles you face. The rest of the book shows you how to clear them.

When you decided to become an actor, you didn't worry that statistics say you are likely to fail. We all believe that we are going to be the successful ones, the ones who will beat the odds. Here's what those odds are.

Money

Unfortunately, figures showing actors' earnings always lag behind current activity, but it is interesting to note that the figures in the latest Statistics Canada survey have barely changed from those of ten years earlier. The latest survey, *A Statistical Profile of Artists in Canada*, by Hill Strategies Research Inc., September 2004, gives the following figures:

- The actor's average annual income is $21,597 from all sources. But the average includes a few actors with enormous incomes.
- The actor's median income (earned by the typical actor) is $12,652 from all sources — one-half the median income in the overall labour force.

Although no one publishes the figures for acting income only, we can assume that it is a great deal lower.

Statistics Canada rates the low-income cutoff for a single person in a community of 500,000 as $18,400. CUPE gives the 2004 figure for large cities as $20,101.

There is no question that people do not become actors because of the money. Just as well. The same survey shows that the number of actors more than doubled over the previous ten years, but their average overall income went up by less than 10 percent.

There are performers, even in Canada, who earn over $150,000 a year, but they form a minute proportion of the acting population. If you are planning to go into the acting business for the big bucks, think again. You will be doing unusually well if you support yourself solely by your acting.

Greg Ellwand is a Dora-award-winning stage actor with lead and guest star roles in major series and features, but he has worked part-time for years as a meat cutter to support his family.

Unemployment

All actors experience the see-saw of periods of intense work followed by aching gaps of unemployment. Even if you have a secondary job, you still feel unemployed. Even if you are busy training, promoting yourself, and preparing, you still miss the actual acting. When you work you have a structure and a meaning to your day imposed upon you by your engager. It is difficult to structure your unemployed time.

You will have a flurry of activity where you are going to auditions every day, followed by long silences where you keep checking your phone for the dial tone.

Those periods of work were gratifying to your artistic ego; they also paid your rent. It is easy to fool yourself into thinking that the $200 or $450 or $1,500 you get per week or per day is going to continue forever. It never does. It lasts as long as the job. In Canada, the Canadian Actors' Equity Association (Equity or CAEA) and the Alliance of Canadian Cinema Television and Radio Artists (ACTRA) surveyed their members. Look at the unions' figures for work in the areas they cover:

- Equity membership averages twelve weeks' work a year.
- A quarter of ACTRA Toronto's members did no work in 2004.

And remember, acting work doesn't qualify for unemployment benefits in Canada.

Migrations

If you think you have a better chance in the United States, think again. Lehman Engel, in *Getting Started in Theatre*, advises that a person of average weight and height, with good vocal or dance technique and some ability in the other regular skills, with something special to offer that few others have, will find it normal to attend classes regularly, go to sixteen Broadway and thirty off-Broadway auditions in one season plus all the summer theatre auditions, send pictures and résumés to stage managers of all the shows (for replacement casting) — and get no work. Certainly, there are more jobs with very high fees in the States, but the competition for any work at all is intense.

There is a lot of film work in Los Angeles and a lot of television and film out of New York, but both cities have a whole lot of actors. And both cities have film and theatre that people do for the exposure, not the money. Some warnings:

Bob Fraser: "In L.A., workshops, Equity waiver theatre, experimental films … can quickly become a way of life. In New York, one can be in a tiny 99-seat theatre and still have the pleasure of watching Eli Wallach or Brian Cox."

Katherine Bedoian: "We have managed to pay actors for rehearsal time … in many small L.A. theatres actors have to pay the producer to be in the company."

Sex

No, we haven't finally got to the good stuff. Women get a bad deal in most careers — less pay for the same work, less access to senior jobs — and things aren't changing quickly, regardless of the lip service being given to equality. Our profession should be free of this unfairness, but read on and weep.

Women make up 52 percent of Canada's adult population, but feature in media and stage casting much less, and typically as secondary, supporting characters that are defined by their relationship with a male character. It is still unusual for women to be offered pivotal roles and to be cast in parts where gender is irrelevant.

It is surprising to see that in the *Statistical Profile of Artists in Canada*, women earn 92 percent of men's income (71 percent in the overall labour force).

From a Screen Actors Guild (SAG) news release, November 2005: "Role distribution by gender in 2004 continues the well-established patterns of the prior four years, whereby males garnered the lion's share of roles; however, the total percentage of roles for female actors increased marginally." Without a Canadian survey, but given the nature of the industry, we can safely assume the Canadian industry moves in lockstep.

One piece of entirely good news: Rina Fraticelli surveyed the Playwrights Canada catalogue in 1981 and found only 36 percent of the plays had casts where the women outnumbered or were equal to the men. Our survey of the casts in the considerably larger 2003–2005 catalogue showed 45 percent female roles. Looking at the plays identified as new to the 2003–2005 catalogue, we found 47 percent of the total roles were female. Clearly, playwrights are writing and selling plays with more balanced casting; however, the majority of theatres are still working mainly from an older canon, weighted towards men.

As long as the proportion of artistic directors in Equity theatres remains overwhelmingly male (74 percent in 2005), the plays chosen will tend to have a male bias. We assume that classical theatre companies will have to engage considerably more men than women; however, even within the restrictions set by traditional classical casting, the artistic director's gender makes a difference. Among the three Ontario classical theatre companies — Stratford Festival, Shaw Festival, and Soulpepper Theatre Company — the two companies with male artistic directors, Stratford and Soulpepper, engaged 35 percent and 36 percent female actors respectively in their 2005 seasons. On the other hand, Shaw Festival, with a female artistic director, engaged 42 percent female actors in the same season.

Minorities

There are no universally accepted terms for people who aren't obviously white bread or who have physical disabilities. We use "visible minorities" and "disabled" for lack of better alternatives.

There is still a far smaller proportion of visible minorities on stage and screen than in society. We know that younger actors are a more diverse group than older actors, and we know that casting breakdowns regularly say "all ethnic groups," but we see that visible minorities are still cast like women — less often, rarely in pivotal roles, and rarely where the character is not specifically written as "ethnic."

There is no one group to blame. Agents may not give their visible minority clients equal opportunity to be seen. Brian Levy, casting director, said he gets a poor response from agents to an open casting call; Doug Love, of Young and Rubicam, put out an open call for construction workers and received one non-white submission.

Engagers still default to a safe, white option. Most producers and casting directors at least pay lip service to increasing casting opportunities, but perhaps not much more. Wrigley's is reported to have run two commercials in test markets, identical except that one featured a mixed-race family and the other a white-bread version. The mixed-race commercial increased sales by 5 percent, but the white-bread version was finally chosen. Clearly, a visible minority actor still finds it difficult to be cast in a role that might be Hispanic or Asian, for example, but doesn't have to be.

Stage casting has the same problems. From the latest census figures, Toronto's visible minority population is 53 percent, but in a February 2005 interview, Philip Akin, artistic producer of Obsidian Theatre, reported that visible minority actors make up only 12 to 13 percent of the population on Toronto stages.

Theatres are trying to address inequalities in two quite different ways: some are specializing in particular groups, while others are attempting to become more inclusive in their casting. Fu-GEN Asian-Canadian Theatre, Saskatchewan Native Theatre, Obsidian Theatre, and Native Earth Performing Arts Inc. are targeting specific acting, directing, writing, and audience communities. On the other hand, Richmond Gateway Theatre, Volcano, and Factory Theatre are attempting to engage the best actor, regardless of ethnicity, and to maintain casting practices that realistically reflect society. Theatres like Cahoots Theatre Projects and Firehall Arts Centre positively search out minority performers as part of their mandate.

Across Canada, theatres for young audiences have the best record for inclusive casting, probably because those audiences have not yet formed rigid expectations and have less trouble accepting what they see without preconceptions.

Buddies in Bad Times Theatre in Toronto, which has been producing gay-lesbian theatre for over twenty years, is the only theatre company in Canada (and we think the only one in North America) serving this particular community. Workshop West has its Loud 'n' Queer Festival, but only Buddies has gay-lesbian theatre as its full mandate.

People who are wheelchair-bound or are otherwise restricted physically are rarely pictured in film and television or seen on stage unless a point is being made of their physical restrictions. There is a continuous spectrum of physical ability in the real world, from Olympic athletes to quadriplegics. Six percent of Canada's working population is registered as handicapped. How many characters have you seen who aren't able-bodied? In our business, as elsewhere, the wheelchair-bound are thought incapable of expressing themselves physically. Doug Love of Young and Rubicam admitted that it is difficult for potential engagers to ask handicapped performers about their physical abilities. (Although they routinely ask the question of other performers.) Even specifically handicapped casting is not reserved for suitably handicapped actors — a recent scene featuring all wheelchair-borne characters was cast without one naturally wheelchair-borne actor (with luck, seeing the power on screen of the real wheelchair athletes in *Murder Ball* might encourage producers to lose this prejudice).

After considerable lobbying, ACTRA's casting directory, Face to Face Online, now makes it possible for an open call search to include qualified performers from minorities while cloaking their differences. The new philosophy is: if they don't ask, don't tell them. Let them see an executive assistant in a wheelchair; let them meet a friendly local black police officer.

It is illegal to specify gender, age, or physical or racial type unless the part demands it. But there is bone-deep prejudice, and nothing will change unless we push for it. We must show our contempt for personal prejudice, and our determination to change the system's prejudice. New lobbying and publicity campaigns are being planned, and ACTRA will continue to play an important role, but it's worth remarking that ACTRA Toronto meetings are set up so that people in wheelchairs have access to the theatre but can't get to the audience microphones to speak.

Location

You don't need to live in Ontario to be a performer, but 40 percent of Canada's performers do, with 23 percent each in British Columbia and Quebec (including francophone actors). Ontario's actors also have the highest average income, followed closely by Quebec and B.C. Although incomes are lower elsewhere, so is the cost of living. In Toronto, Montreal, and Vancouver artists' incomes are the closest to other workers' incomes, suggesting that artists do relatively well in these communities compared to other locations in Canada.

The type of work is different, though. Small independent, co-op, and guest artist contracts, mostly poorly paid, make up 35 percent of theatre work in British Columbia but only 9 percent of the work in Ontario and 13 percent in Quebec. On the other hand, film and television work in Vancouver more than rivals that in Toronto, with an even larger amount — mainly francophone — in Quebec.

Typically, small centres have fewer engagers but proportionally fewer actors. If you live there, you may work just as much as you would in a larger centre. Halifax, Saskatoon, Edmonton, and Winnipeg have a range of theatres and fringe festivals, far more than one would imagine, given their size. Fredericton has the only truly regional theatre in the country. Atlantic Canada has some of the most exciting indigenous theatre in North America. Winnipeg, Edmonton, Calgary, and the Maritimes are growing their own production centres as the provinces compete for media work by offering tax breaks. Halifax is leading, with its new sound stage. Success in Montreal depends on functioning in French-language theatre and media work.

Vancouver, Edmonton, Calgary, Toronto, and Montreal have enough work and enough actors to support a number of agencies of different sorts. In some cities, engagers go through agents but also deal directly with actors. Small communities know about their agents, and, if you decide to have one, your choice may well be who you like best as a person.

Almost without exception, in any city except Toronto and Vancouver, the majority of your work will be in your home base, and where you base yourself will determine your professional life. In the larger centres, there's plenty of work, but more than plenty of competition. In the smaller centres, performers are more involved with becoming part of the in-group at the few local organizations that hire regularly. This has the major danger that only a handful of engagers know your work first-hand, and when two or three move out, as will happen eventually, you will be an unknown has-been. Wherever you live, it pays to spread your publicity net wide.

Luck

Even statisticians recognize luck as an aspect of the actor's career. Statistics Canada: "Full-time involvement in the acting profession … can be the product of many factors besides the individual's skill. Not the least of these is luck. Where one actor may find his working schedule filling with engagements which neatly and rapidly succeed each other, another actor, equally regarded, will spend substantial periods out of work." We lose out on jobs because the dates overlap by a week, or the director wouldn't give us a day off rehearsals to shoot a commercial. Knowing that luck has so much to do with employment is not a comfort. It is a danger. It tempts us to give up actively working for our careers. Luck is what gets you hired, but grunt work on research and publicity is what will get you considered.

Rejection

In the course of a year, you may be turned down for literally scores of jobs. You will get work from about one audition in ten. And your agent will tell you that you were submitted for many more parts where you didn't make it into the audition.

Actors are not usually turned down because they aren't good enough. You are turned down because you aren't tall enough or young enough or fat enough. You are turned down because you remind the director of his ex-wife. You are rarely told why you weren't cast, and after each rejection you have to go through the process all over again.

Willy Loman got depressed when he couldn't sell his products, but your product is yourself. Your head knows that you simply didn't fit the casting slot in some way, but your gut doesn't buy that.

All these pressures take their toll on the human psyche. Actors fall into the all-too-easy trap of negativity and anger. They don't use the empty hours to go to workshops and classes, work out, read plays, go to the theatre, get involved in union activities, create new projects for themselves. They find it easier to sleep late, watch television, drink, and complain to anyone who will listen that if there were any justice, they would be down in L.A. working in films.

Sorry, we seem to have started preaching. Okay ... here is Dr. M. Plant, in the British journal *Alcohol and Alcoholism*: "People in artistic and literary occupations are peculiarly susceptible to alcoholism and by extension to other forms of overindulgence in mood-changing drugs. Five major studies from England, Scandinavia and America show entertainers are at high risk." Out of nine high-risk factors in one of the studies, six are applicable to actors. Occupations with maximum risk of heart disease are those with low power to control the job and high psychological strain. Sound familiar?

The Future

TECHNO-ACTORS

In the last few years it has become more common for productions to digitize performers and work with the files to produce the performances. ACTRA routinely sees film contracts being used for video games, hockey stars have been digitized in action, and computer enhancement is so widespread that stunt performers have to find ways to persuade audiences that they are watching real people doing real things.

Long-dead movie stars now sell cars and Coke. Nelvana's Patrick Loudest says, "In recent years ... the lines between live action and animation are blurring." Andy Sevleis, the actor behind the digital Gollum in *Lord of the Rings*, received an Academy Award nomination. Even the techno-leaders admit you need an actor somewhere in the mix. Jim Morris of Lucas Digital says, "You get a lot out of your money for an actor." However, as the technology continues to get cheaper, we shall certainly see more generic characters and Extras being added in post-production.

TECHNO-CASTING

Searchable computer databases were praised as offering equal access casting to all, but they still seem to favour those in large centres, with agents. Online Casting and UBCP Talent Online continue to be a basic part of the casting process in Toronto and Vancouver; ACTRA's Face to Face Online is still a poor third.

Mega-Musicals

For years, the mega-musical was the mainstay of young triple-threat performers coming out of drama schools specializing in musical theatre training, but now those young performers are looking in other directions. Cruise ships engage scores of singers and dancers, summer stock theatres are doing musicals on a regular basis, and Stratford and Shaw have added more musicals to their seasons. Large regional theatres continue to produce one big musical a season, often jointly with other theatres, sharing costs and thus enabling a bigger, splashier, larger-cast production.

The crash of Mirvish Productions' *Lord of the Rings* spelled the end of Toronto's 2005 hopes for a new generation of mega-musicals; new Canadian musicals are more modest. Those emerging companies committed to developing and producing new Canadian musicals are starting small. Even ScriptLab, which is looking not only to develop new scripts but also to develop and expand previously produced scripts originally cut for cost, does not have plans for anything like the size of the former mega-musicals.

Funding

"The proposed budget reductions in letters, sciences and the arts ... are insignificant from a financial standpoint and harmful from every other point of view." Victor Hugo to the French Assembly in 1848. Plus ça change ...

Cultural spending is only 1.5 percent of the federal budget (down from a princely 2.5 percent in 1990); performing arts gets less than a twentieth of that, and it's dropping year by year. Established theatres are being hit by a shift from maintenance to short-term, new-project grants, and the Canada Council plans to involve business leaders in grant decisions. In 2006, England's Royal Shakespeare Company got 56 percent of its income from government grants. In the same year, our Stratford Festival's income from government was 4 percent.

Clearly, we shall see sponsors exercising more corporate control over seasons at established theatres, more need for artistic directors to be hired for their business skills, and less artistic risk-taking and arrogance in large and small operations.

We could go on, but you've probably got the message by now. All right, you know what the odds are. Let's get to work on shortening them.

CHAPTER THREE

You're Selling Yourself — What Shape Are You In?

"Perfection is such a nuisance that I often regret having cured myself of using tobacco."

Emile Zola

A good carpenter wouldn't dream of working with dull or rusty tools. A successful realtor won't show a dirty house. An actor worthy of the name, working or not, must have a supple, finely honed instrument responding to its owner's needs. That instrument is the most complex mechanism known to man: the human body and mind.

Personal Fitness

HEALTH

All the exercise classes in the world can't do anything for a body that is being abused internally. Get enough sleep, don't smoke, don't drink to excess, and, for God's sake, stay away from drugs. We know we sound like your mother, but she's right again. One of the few advantages of an acting career is that there is no mandatory retirement. As long as there is breath in your body, strength in your limbs, and a neuron or two in your brain you can continue. But once your wind has gone, your limbs are wracked, and your brain is fried, you're finished.

Start as you mean to go on. Be sensible about your body. We've all heard about college football stars who limp along through their adult lives after toughing out knee injuries. An actor can't afford that. If you have a sore throat, do something about it right away. Unless you plan to become a mime, you can't get away with wrecked vocal equipment.

If you have over-indulged in drinks, smokes, or M&M's, back off for a while. No one is expecting you to wrap up in cotton wool or live the life of a monk, but be aware that your body is only so resilient. And gets less so.

You should also be aware that a reputation for being unreliable through heavy drinking or drug taking is easy to establish and difficult to shake. David Cronenberg, film director: "You want stability. It's very common for directors and producers to check with others on whether an actor is an alcoholic or a druggie or is neurotic. Life is too short to use a wonderful actor who will hurt other aspects of your film. You weigh all those things."

Speaking of weight, don't ignore diet in your never-ending search for the healthy life. Touring, living in digs without cooking facilities, working on films with fabulous catering, working weird hours — all these are great excuses (and sometimes reasons) for wolfing down everything that's smaller than your head. Find ways to get healthy, balanced meals on a regular basis.

Working among strangers and living alone far from home means you have to be responsible for your own health. We can't advise you to become an actor if you have physical problems like diabetes, epilepsy, or major allergies, although there are successful actors with these conditions and more (one of your authors is a diabetic). Come to that, we wouldn't advise you to become an actor even if you were as fit as a fiddle.

You should know your body and its problems. Carry enough necessary medication, wherever you are. Inform someone in authority about your condition if it might affect the work. Lin Joyce: "The perfect actor comes clean about anything that would scare stage management half to death if they don't know about it ahead of time."

Try to get back to the same health professionals for preventive maintenance. See your dentist regularly: actors need their teeth in the worst way. We know it's expensive, but try to find the $200 for regular check-ups so that you're not hit with a $2,000 bill for dental work down the line.

Please don't become a full-time hypochondriac. That's the worst sort of dressing room bore.

FITNESS

Assuming your insides are squeaky clean and functioning as they should, how do you best maintain your outsides? Almost any kind of exercise is good for you as long as you do it consistently and don't become an Exercise Bore. Actually, being an Exercise Bore isn't as bad for you as it is for your poor friends, who have to listen to how many reps you did, or how many laps you swam, or how high your pulse rate was in step class. (We know about this. One of the authors was an Exercise Bore until the other author threatened to cite the Y in a divorce suit.)

Exercise that uses the whole body in an aerobic activity — swimming, rowing — is probably the best, but only if you do it all the time. It is better to walk briskly every day than to do a more demanding exercise at irregular intervals.

Exercise makes your body flexible and toned. It gets oxygen-rich blood moving, lowers blood pressure, and is great for the complexion. It also eases tension. The high you get from a good workout is real and physiological. Even if it weren't, who cares? Physical activity makes you feel good. Things don't look so black when you have just set a personal best in your bench presses or finally managed to do a whole length of the pool without needing CPR.

Working out also helps give a structure to your day when you are not acting. As Tallulah Bankhead once said, "Exercise is good for the heart, the lungs and the unemployed."

Workshops and Classes

Mohammed Ali: "The fight is won or lost far away from witnesses, behind the lines, in the gym and out there on the road, long before I dance under those lights."

Exercising the body is good; exercising the body and the mind together is better. Many actors continue to take classes throughout their careers. In Canada this is less routine than in New York and Los Angeles, where classes are the major outlet for many actors' skill and passion.

In any large centre there are voice classes, singing lessons, audition workshops, improv classes, scene study, Shakespeare classes, acting for the camera — all these and more, at all levels of experience. At a basic level, if you lack a skill completely, look for Continuing Education classes in community colleges, outreach programs run by local theatres, and professionals brought in by city parks and recreation departments. Be cautious about private teachers and private schools. Look for their membership in a local association and affiliation with a reputable organization, but mainly listen to what other people say and audit some classes. A class should be a place where you can fail and not worry. A good class is one where you are encouraged to take chances. You are there to experiment, to learn, to grow.

Classes ready you for performing. If you've been temping or teaching or waiting tables, it is easy to be ground down. We can all improve our skills, and we all need to keep the rust off. Gail Singer: "People who keep their juices flowing seem to have the work more easily accessible to them when it's required."

Beware of using casting director workshops as a means of being brought in to read for a role. This is what Bonnie Gillespie, herself a casting director, has to say: "I think there are many better uses of an actor's money, in terms of career investment. I've often likened signing up for a casting director workshop to buying a lottery ticket … it's no different than going to Vegas for the weekend. You're down the money, but you took a chance. And you knew the odds going in."

If people say there is value in the actual class — clues about cold readings, demystifying the audition process — then go for it. Otherwise, use the money to edit your demo reel or pay your rent. Or find another class.

Classes and workshops not only exercise your body and mind, they also keep you in touch with the acting community, even when you are out of work. Moving among fellow actors keeps the networks growing; you will not only learn skills at classes, you will plug into opportunities to use the skills. And remember, the cost of any professional class is tax-deductible.

Other People's Work

Exercise for the mind: learning through watching. Get over the jealousy we all feel seeing someone else playing the part we should have got. (How many actors does it take to change a light bulb? Ten. One to screw in the new bulb and nine to say, "I could do that.") Watching great performances can be an inspiration. Watching them analytically can be an education. The ordinary audience member enjoys the excellent performance; the professional studies the techniques and original choices that make the performance excellent.

CHAPTER FOUR

Working to Get Work

> "*Nothing is more common than unsuccessful men of talent.*"
> Calvin Coolidge

Actors spend more time looking for work than they do working. They spend about 45 percent of their expenses after food and rent on self-promotion. It is boring, depressing, and difficult, but it has to be done. *People* magazine: "As an actor, your real job is job hunting." However good you are, however well-toned your body and well-honed your craft, if nobody knows who you are or what you do, you won't get hired. Actors who don't believe in the necessity of promotion may find themselves overtaken by less talented actors who do.

Be practical, businesslike, and efficient in your search for work. Keep files with names, addresses, and phone numbers of anybody and everybody who is a possible link to a job. You don't need a computer program for this, although they do exist. A three-ring binder is sophisticated enough, provided you keep it up to date. Put in details of interviews and information you get from radio, television, or newspaper items. Make a note of phone conversations. Write down when you wrote and what you said. Write it down straight away. Keep in mind the Persian proverb, "Fortune is infatuated with the efficient."

Don't decide too soon to concentrate on one area. Actors need every source of work they can get. Scott Hylands: "The boldness and breadth of a stage performance enlivens the work you do on film and television. The subtleties of film and television acting give detail and texture to your work on stage. One format informs the other." By focusing on only one area of the business, you are cutting off opportunities to expand both your career and your bank balance.

Spread your net wide. Keep in touch with people across the country. You may not change your home base, but other people change theirs. Artistic directors constantly move from one city to another. You never know who is going to pop up where and in what hat. Bob Baker went from the Phoenix Theatre in Edmonton to Canadian Stage in Toronto, and then went back to Edmonton to the Citadel Theatre. Jackie Maxwell was artistic director of Toronto's Factory Theatre, dramaturge/director at Charlottetown Festival, and is now the artistic director of the Shaw Festival. James Roy was an artistic director in Blyth, Victoria, and Winnipeg before becoming executive producer of "Stereo Drama" in Toronto. Naturally, you will concentrate on the likeliest and the closest engagers, but try not to cut anyone off completely. You never know when a contact is going to pay off.

The best time to look for work is when you don't have to: when you are still working. Pick up the bits of information that float around back-stage or on a set. Chatting to make-up and wardrobe people can generate all sorts of useful news. You will be able to invite people to attend your show or watch your film. When you go to an audition when you have work, you give off a confidence and ease that is hard to fake and attractive to see.

Initial Investment

You've got to spend money to make money, but you don't need to buy new, full-price items. Look through bargain-hunter newspapers, scan notice boards in laundromats, seek out garage sales, or be truly coura-geous and brave the Boxing Week sales.

The most important piece of equipment for an actor is a telephone. Without a phone, you are unreachable. And if they can't reach you, they can't hire you. The phone must be manned every minute of the day, which means you need an answering machine (for about $50) or voice mail (around $5 a month).

Another option is a cell phone, which is convenient, but even the cheapest plan is expensive to use. The cheapest pagers simply give you the number that called, fancier ones take a message, but in either case, you have to find a phone to call back.

You'll need to use a computer to lay out your letters and résumés. A really old model for as little as $100 will do the job. Add another $100 for a new printer and you're in business. This might be too much for your budget right now, but there are alternatives. Many large photo-copying stores rent computer time, and public libraries have computers and printers available.

Invest in a small cassette recorder. Recording your lines, listening to accent tapes and taping your own, learning lines, and rehearsing audition speeches are activities best done in private. A machine of your own with an earphone can avoid household rows and allow you to be independent of flatmates or parents.

Every actor needs a television set. If you are going to be doing any television work, you have to learn about the market. You have to keep abreast of the new programs, directors, and other actors. Find out what is popular, what sells. Keep in touch with trends. If the casting director describes the program as a *Corner Gas*–type show, you should know what that means. If you are told it's a regular beer commercial, that should mean something to you. A VCR or DVD player is useful for taping important programs that you are unable to watch and for viewing films you have missed.

If you are a member of ACTRA, be sure you're in Face to Face Online and be sure your entry is up to date. Your local ACTRA office (see Addresses at the end of the book) may also put out a smaller scale directory. Being listed with these is worth the cost. They are well respected and distributed free to engagers in film, television, radio, commercials, and theatre.

Computer Casting

We know of only four successful casting projects based on computer databases. Back in 1993, the CBC's Talent Resource Centre was ahead of its time, with computer records running alongside its hard-copy performer files. CBC will search their database for actors matching any description, and their service is available to independent producers. You can be listed by calling in with your photo and résumé or by writing for their application form. It's open to anyone, and it's free.

Online Casting's Casting Workbook and UBCP's Talent Online are databases accessible to casting directors, but their main power is that they are part of the production/casting director/agent machinery. Casting directors post casting breakdowns accessible to agents, agents post their actor submissions, casting directors look at the details on the database and post the audition calls for the agents. The majority of casting in Toronto and Vancouver uses these services. Online Casting charges actors around $55 a year for listing photograph and résumé with some free updates; it charges more for adding video clips. UBCP Talent Online, which lists its members as part of The Link, an American service, doesn't charge.

Also free, ACTRA's Face to Face Online has never been as successful. Independent producers willing to work with ACTRA members can search the database for their character descriptions and choose from the actors that fit, but the information may not be accurate and the actors' availability is unknown. The extra work of searching and then verifying each actor may be worthwhile for small independent producers, but mainstream productions can't spare the time.

All four systems allow performers to register without having an agent, but Casting Workbook and The Link favour performers in the larger centres, with agents.

Public access Internet sites promise that your listing will be seen by top international casting directors. That may be true, but let's face it: your chances of being hired by a production in Venezuela have to be fairly slim. More local sites list the casting needed for mainly non-union and student productions and allow subscribers to submit themselves.

People who want on-set experience, but who don't have agents, have praised the best of these sites.

Actors' personal websites are becoming more popular. Many ISPs offer the space free, some with basic web design programs. It's easy and cheap to put a basic few pages together — your résumé, a few publicity shots, "what I did in the summer" — but for most people, giving your URL is only a smarty-pants way of sending someone a photo and résumé.

All right, you have all your equipment. Now, what do you do with it? How do you actually go about looking for work? How do you get to meet engagers and casting directors? How do you find out about auditions? What do you do after you have found out?

Background Research

Before you start writing letters, phoning, or pounding the pavement, find out as much as you can about the people you want to meet and the places where you want to work. Engagers are looking for solutions to their problems. You have to find out what their current problems are.

Established theatres first: What's the show? What's not cast? You cannot write an effective letter or show yourself off well at an interview if you are whistling in the dark. Brian Levy, casting director: "Know what's going on — read the trades, know who's who. Have up-to-date lists of directors, and theatres with their seasons. Make notes on people you've seen and written to." You have dozens of sources of information. All organizations mentioned below are listed in the Addresses section. The Professional Association of Canadian Theatres (PACT) publishes a directory of Canadian professional theatres, with addresses and other information.

Go to the theatre itself. What sort of plays do they produce? Phone the box office for the new season's plays. Pick up a brochure. Attend some plays. Read the artistic director's notes in the program. If the theatre is out of town, write for a brochure. Most theatres have websites with season information. Does their studio space/second stage have a separate director you should write to?

There are information notice boards at the Equity offices in Vancouver and Toronto. The Equity newsletter, which goes to Equity members, some libraries, and drama schools, is also available online. It contains new appointments and general information about the theatre scene across the country.

Canadian Theatre Review (*CTR*) is the only national magazine about Canadian theatre work. Get it from a theatre bookstore or by subscription — but look for new trade publications and support them.

Check out your local Fringe organizer for their information and local theatre notice boards for the names of independent theatres you can find out more about.

Industrial shows and cruise ships cast mainly through agents (see Chapter 7).

Learning about film and television is easy. Watch them. Find out what the market is. Buy the trade magazines. *Playback*, published every two weeks, is a national magazine with reviews and information about upcoming film and television productions, including their casting directors. Most major centres have their own media periodicals and directories, which you can find in local libraries and in your local ACTRA office. The ACTRA offices have lists of local media engagers and casting people, plus productions planned and in progress.

For all casting, newspapers, both local and national, are good sources of information. In Toronto, TheatreBooks's *The Actor's Organizer* is a handy-dandy directory as well as a datebook. Look for your local equivalent.

Agents, engagers, and casting directors like to know that you care enough about them to do some research. You are paying them a compliment if you know about the proposed production and their previous work. Don't try to use all you know at the interview, but let it give you an air of competence. It will help you keep control, you won't waste time, and the interviewer will know you are serious and professional.

Up-To-Date Research

Equity has e-drive for its members and apprentices. It's a computer mailing list with audition notices. It is updated as soon as new information comes in and covers auditions nationwide. Internet sites such as canadianactor.com have audition postings for film, television, and theatres.

Theatre service organizations such as Theatre Ontario, the Quebec Drama Federation, Theatre BC, and Theatre Alberta have audition notices, as do many local ACTRA offices. Edmonton's Citadel Theatre, the Centre for the Performing Arts in Calgary, and Winnipeg's Manitoba Theatre Centre post information from other local theatres.

Some non-union engagers — film, television, and theatre — post their casting needs on websites. Subscribers can get all the information from the various casting bulletin boards in town, and more. Ask around. See what is offered, and at what cost.

Commercial theatres advertise their open calls, and smaller theatres and indie films regularly have casting notices in newspapers and local alternative papers (such as *NOW*, *Eye*, and *Georgia Straight)*.

Networking

Networking goes on in every business and in every part of life. It involves casual and not-so-casual personal contacts. It means meeting people, talking, trading information. Nicholas Rice, actor, in the *Globe and Mail*: "When I saw unemployment looming, I sent chatty cards to everyone — to agents, directors, producers — telling them I would soon be free.… But it all takes time.… I had not always been able to network.… So, persevere. Continue to make at least one phone call a day. Send out at least one letter. Keep your ear to the ground, and ask as many people as you can, 'What's happening?'"

Some actors frequent actors' pubs. Some acting communities have local newsletters and regular get-togethers. Fitness clubs, workshops, seminars, and classes are used, not just for the professional skills that you gain, but for the conversations that can lead to information about auditions, new productions, who is leaving what management and going where. Taking part in student films and indie productions not only helps you gain experience and build your résumé, it also plugs you into a network of professionals who may be a source of information or even of future casting.

But networking is a two-way street. There is no advantage to be gained by hoarding news about a change of artistic directors or an audition for a new film. Giving that information out won't hurt your chances of getting a job. Be as generous with your information as you would like others to be with theirs and it will come back to you a thousandfold.

Be sensitive in your networking. No director wants to be hounded about work at a party. Make sure that you are behaving in an appropriate manner for the situation. (We don't expect you to turn to a fellow pallbearer and whisper, "So, doing any casting?" but we have heard stories that are nearly that bad.)

Some people find this kind of promotion a strain and a bore. If kibitzing in a bar is what you love to do, go for it, but don't let it be the only string to your bow. If you hate face-to-face chat, try to do some, but concentrate on writing letters and phoning friends.

Letters

Canada Post gets in where the actor can't. Letters are the most practical way of introducing yourself. An email is not a letter. Agents and casting people routinely filter out email from people they don't know. And sending your photo and résumé as attachments just doesn't cut it.

General Rules:
- The letter should look professional. Plain white bond paper with the text typed clearly in black, with adequate margins, centred on the page.
- Make sure the letter has your full name, return address, and phone number on it.
- "Dear Sir or Madam" is death. We know people who see that and chuck the letter unread. Use the person's name. And spell it right.
- Edit, edit, edit.
- Better still, edit. The fewer words you send, the more chance of having every word read. Besides, if you say it all in the letter, what are you going to talk about in the interview?
- Be direct and natural. Your letter should be businesslike, without

being stiff and formal. Write the way you would talk at an interview — use contractions, avoid business clichés.

- Stress the positive; omit the negative.
- Avoid being aggressive, familiar, or cutesy. You are writing to a stranger about something that is important to both of you. Even if you are writing to someone you know very well, keep the tone professional. There are some engagers and casting directors who don't mind slightly off-the-wall correspondence, but unless you know who they are, it isn't worth running the risk.
- Don't concentrate on how wonderful an opportunity this would be for you. Engagers are more interested in how hiring you will help them.
- "Be professional but not too cool. This isn't a business letter — it's a small commercial about your talent." David Switzer, Sears and Switzer acting studio.
- Don't say how good you are; give information that shows how good you are.

Margaret Mooney is much missed after thirty years with the Citadel Theatre, Edmonton. She loved and respected actors, but she used to say, "Tell me the specific role you're interested in. Be sure you're right. Read the play! Drop me a postcard. Tell me your availability. Don't ask me for advice about your career; I'm not your agent. Don't badger me; if you ask and I put your name forward and the director won't see you — tough."

Stuart Aikins, casting director: "I like getting pertinent information in letters from actors: career developments, performances in town, media work. I won't go to see you in a show, but the topic may come up in a conversation with someone. Actors do disappear if they don't keep in touch. They slip through the cracks. Don't give your own opinion of your work. What actor is going to say he's bad? But including other people's opinions in reviews is a good way to let me know."

A Toronto casting director: "By all means send notes. They are no intrusion. But be specific! There's no point in saying, 'I have just been working in Halifax and have done some commercials and would like to do more.' What were you doing in Halifax? What commercials have you done? What sort of commercials are you best suited for? Give me something to go on."

INTRODUCTION

This letter accompanies your résumé and photograph. Like all the letters you write, it should be short and direct. The letter should give a feeling of enthusiasm without hysteria, confidence without arrogance, and modesty without diffidence. Easy, eh? Your first sentence should be a grabber. Don't assume the letter will be read right through. Think of it as a tabloid newspaper: your headline should encourage people to read on.

Find a selling point. Why should this busy casting director see you? What do you have that makes you especially useful? That is what promotion is all about. How can you solve the engager's problems?

Find a hook to hang the letter on. If you are in a show, extend an invitation. Most casting directors keep abreast of films and plays. One casting director told us that the only films he misses are sci-fi and teenage romps: "I go to the theatre a minimum of two nights a week. First, because I enjoy it; second, to see the talent. I want to stay current." Brian Levy: "During the season, I probably see three plays a week. I watch as much TV and go to as many films as possible." If you know that the engager was recently at one of your school productions, mention that and the role you played. If you have a mutual acquaintance with some clout, ask if you can say, "So-and-so suggested that I write to you." If nothing else, suggest that a meeting will be useful to transform you from a picture and résumé into a flesh-and-blood human being.

End with a specific next step. "I look forward to hearing from you" is vague and useless. They won't write and they're unlikely to call. "I'll call your office next Monday to see if we can set up a convenient time to meet" is positive and gives you a second chance of being in touch. (Many directors will not see actors if there is no specific reason, such as casting a show or general auditions. The only way to find out is to try.)

Specific Casting

In a way, this letter is easier to write. It's still a tabloid — you can't assume it will get a careful reading — but at least you have a clear purpose. You want something particular — a role — and the letter is to say why you should be considered. Don't concentrate on what you will gain from the experience but on what you can offer. Be specific. If you are responding to an audition notice, wait for their reply, if any. Otherwise, set a date when you will call them.

Keeping in Touch

You should be doing this every few months, just to let people know what you have been doing, what you are doing now, or what you are going to be doing. Its basic purpose is to get your name on the desk and into active consideration. A great way to keep in touch is to send a postcard with a production shot of your latest show, or even with just your headshot. (In February, just before they hold auditions, you might send one to all the summer theatres with news of your winter.) Tina Gerussi, Toronto casting director: "It's always a good thing to drop off a note to casting directors to let them know what you've been doing and if you're going to be in a show. Your agent won't necessarily do it."

Phone Calls

Before you know someone well, a cold call is a dangerous thing. You can't know how busy the office is when you phone, and you are likely to get the polite runaround from a secretary. From one casting director: "I dislike direct phone contact. If I have three lines busy — a client, an agent, and an actor — guess which one I'm not going to get to?" Write first, saying you will call and giving an idea why it might be worth their while taking the call.

Before you lift the receiver, write down all the points you will want to cover — not a script but every single important fact and name. Treat the call as an audition — the Confident Professional. Rehearse it out loud, with a friend if you like.

Once on the phone, introduce yourself and ask to speak to the engager or casting director. If the receptionist or secretary asks you why, don't stumble, mumble, or ramble. Have a capsule reason why the engager should take your call: "It concerns the upcoming *Hamlet* casting" or "It's to arrange an interview. I wrote to Ms. Blank saying that I would phone today." If the person is busy, ask when would be a good time to call back. If the secretary says that the engager will return your call, simply leave your name and number — no long message. If you are not successful the first time, get the secretary's name so that next time your call can be more personal. Getting the secretary on your side can make all the difference.

Once you have reached the correct person, make sure you introduce yourself even if you have already done so to the secretary. Do not assume your name will ring any bells; refer to the contents of your letter. State clearly and confidently what you want. It shouldn't be difficult. You've got your notes right in front of you. Tick things off as you cover them. Do not prolong the call. Once the business is over — you've been given an appointment, you're to call back next week — reconfirm the information and finish.

If the engager or casting director does not return your call, call back. You will have to use your own judgment about how soon to do this. And how often.

Unless you are asked to, never phone a casting director or an agent at home. Ever.

Personal Visits

There was a time — you'll read about it in all the books — when actors expected to go from casting director to agent to theatre, looking for work. "Doing the rounds" is in the past, and you'll get short shrift if you turn up anywhere without an appointment.

But if you can get that appointment, a ten-minute visit is worth ten thousand written words. Make the most of it; you are not likely to get any longer. There is at least one casting director who says that if he does have the time to see actors, he sees them for five (count 'em, five) minutes. He will give them 100 percent of his complete and undivided attention, but five minutes is all they get. In most cases, you will get more time but be interrupted by phone calls. Keep your cool — you are not the centre of this person's life. The phone calls represent current work, and you are, at best, an investment in the future.

You have only a limited time: use it effectively. Why are you there? What do you want to say about yourself? What do you want to gain? If this is just an introductory interview, be prepared to talk about anything. Make life easy for the interviewer. Have answers for the questions your résumé might suggest. Reply fully and show your interest.

Don't be afraid to disagree; there is nothing wrong with having an opposing opinion. A director is more likely to remember a lively debate than a bland acceptance. But be careful how you express yourself; angry confrontation is not attractive.

Don't be afraid to admit ignorance. No one is going to expect you to know everything. Besides, people enjoy explaining things to others.

This is your time to show what sort of person you are. If you've been given ten minutes, use them. On the other hand, don't monopolize the conversation. It's far more interesting if both parties take an active role in the interview. Apart from "Can you ride?", the questions you're asked are only to give you a chance to speak. Tell stories that will help the interviewer decide on you. That's the important information, not whether you had a good summer, or what is was like working with SpongeBob SquarePants. Learn to read body language; keep your antennae working. When it's time to leave, leave with a smile and a thank you. You won't gain anything by trying to prolong an interview that has come to a natural end.

After the interview, drop the interviewer a quick note of thanks. It is polite and it puts your name on the desk once more in a legitimate fashion.

Make a note in your files of what you discussed, so that the next time you meet you will be able to pick up the conversation and build on it.

Persistence

Promoting yourself through letters, visits, phone calls, and social contacts is not a one-shot deal. Self-publicity is an ongoing activity. Engagers and casting directors hear from actors and their agents daily. Ensure that you don't get lost in the shuffle — not through constant badgering, but through a relaxed, professional, individual approach.

Strut Your Stuff

Let people know when you are working. It is the best way of introducing yourself to an engager or casting director. Casting directors agree: "Actors should be involved in showcase productions. It's a great way to remind us that you've around. No matter where you are in the hierarchy, do something constructive and visible. Recognize the power and importance of visibility and take advantage of it." Many directors will attend community theatre productions if the quality of the work is known to be good. In Toronto, Equity Showcase productions use both union and non-union actors and are seen by media and casting people. If you have some time, money, and friends in a similar situation, mount your own production. It may be expensive, but you are making an investment in your professional future. Fringe festivals now flourish across the country from Victoria to Halifax, making it easier to mount your own showcase.

It's hard to showcase your film and television work until you are actually working. Tapes of your class work won't cut it. Independent and student films may give you the tape as well as the experience you're looking for. Fortunately, the route to mainstream work is via casting directors, who know the problem and appreciate theatre skills.

Directors and casting people are intensely interested in new talent, but however good you are, if no one knows about your talent, you won't work. They won't beat a path to your door if they don't know where you live.

CHAPTER FIVE

Show and Tell

"God has given you one face and you make yourself another."
Shakespeare

Your promotion is only as effective as the materials you use. The two most important weapons in your publicity arsenal are your résumé and your photograph. Your publicity package must include a letter, but people look at your photograph and résumé first. They encapsulate just what it is you are selling. The résumé shows at a glance where you trained and who trained you; your height, weight, and colouring; your union status; your stage and media experience; and your special skills. Your photograph gives an idea of your age range, your image, and your personality.

Directors, producers, casting people, and agents are bombarded with photographs and résumés from hopeful actors. These packages arrive in the mail; they are shoved under doors; they accompany actors to auditions. How can you ensure that your little publicity package will be remembered? You can't. What you can do is ensure that it won't be tossed out without a glance. However exciting and frequent your work has been, a wrinkled résumé, badly printed and poorly photocopied, won't even be looked at. However physically right you are for the role, a family snapshot won't get you seen. In this business, the form is as important as the content.

NANCY PATEL

Represented by Marc Matthews, BCA (604) 674-9000

17 Real Street #2   Height: 5'5"
Vancouver   B.C.   Weight: 118lbs
V9Z 1H8   Eyes: Brown
(604) 555-7856   Hair: Dark Brown
npatel@email.com

SELECTED THEATRE

Humble Boy	Rosie Pye	Nesbitt Hall	Susan Carr
The Pajama Game	Poopsie	Webb Theatre	Ray Davey
Chimera	Claire McGuire	U of Vancouver	Lloyd Snow
The Crucible	Ann Putnam	U of Vancouver	Elise Jacobs
The Oxford Roofclimbers' Rebellion	Nancy Nicholson	Carpet Theatre	Joe Lowe

SELECTED MEDIA

Bear Faced	Body Double	Ursa Films	Mary Lofts
Extension Courses	Principal	U of V Studios	Michael Goldman
Banxx Rock Videos	Principal	Skeezit Prodns	Joanie Nolan
Tomb Threat	Principal	Sony Playstation	Dan Zaley

TRAINING

BFA: University of Vancouver
Voice: Nana Jory, David Greenberg
Singing: Vittorio Silver
Movement & Dance: Clarence Duthie, Peter Epp
Stage Combat: Robert Bienfait

SPECIAL SKILLS

Performance Combat: FDC Certified Actor Combatant, broadsword, etc.
Gymnastics: U of V team
Horse riding: Western and English
Singing: Rap, rock, classical mezzo
Driving: Standard shift

Resumes

You aren't likely to be cast on your résumé, but you won't attract the interest of a theatre or a casting director without one.

There are several books on the market that discuss what makes an effective résumé, and there are résumé services that will create a résumé for you. Although the books have some interesting and useful ideas, and most of the résumé services are reliable, they use a standard format that fits most clients' needs. A standard résumé tries to indicate the applicant's personality as well as goals, ambitions, and attitude towards the job; an actor's résumé deals solely with work done, training, and saleable skills. The two résumés are quite different in content and form.

Content

Your name is the most important piece of information on the résumé. It has pride of place at the top of the page. If you have an agent, you may be using agency stationery. This is a potential problem. Understandably, the agency wants its name to be displayed properly, but you are advertising yourself, not your agency. Perhaps you could agree to have two résumé formats: one for the agency to send out and one for your own use (see Chapter 9).

Do not head the page with "Résumé." What else could it be? A bowl of borscht? Don't waste the line. Everything in your résumé should earn its space.

Give your contact details. A potential engager must know where to reach you. All media casting and most theatre casting is done by phone. If you are using your agent's letterhead, the agency phone number and address is your contact, although you may want to add your own phone number. If you are using your own stationery, then your phone number is vital. You can include your email address as well, but most people will contact you by phone. In the early stages of your career, you may be moving frequently. If you have a cell phone or pager, wherever you go your phone number follows. (Nowadays, some actors — mainly women but some men as well — are reluctant to reveal any personal contact information, from a legitimate fear of stalking and/or harassment. If this is a concern, use your agent's number or an answering service. Thank goodness it's not a common problem, and happens mainly to highly visible stars.)

Your vital statistics come next: height, weight, hair colour, eye colour. Some casting people suggest that you have your age, or at least your age range, as part of your physical description. We think this limits your casting potential. The moment you say how old you are, that is how old you will look. It is a self-fulfilling prophecy. If you let them make the decision on the basis of your photograph, without being influenced by seeing a number on a résumé, your casting opportunities will increase. So no date of birth, no age, and no age range or playing age. As for the rest, do not lie. Or at least don't use a lie you can't get away with. If you plan to add a couple of inches to your height, you had better wear heels or lifts to all your auditions. If you insist on taking ten pounds off your weight (so much easier on a résumé than in real life) make sure your clothes reflect a slim image. Better still, go on a diet.

Performers' union membership must be put in. If you are not a member, it is not necessary to say "non-union." People will assume that if there is no information, there is no membership. Social Insurance Number, citizenship, and marital status should not be included, but it's worth mentioning foreign working papers.

The main information on your résumé is your experience — professional, drama school, community theatre, student film. Engagers want to see what you have performed to get an idea of your style and who you have worked with. Unless you won some sort of prize at a nationally known festival, avoid including any high school productions. When you compose your first résumé, this section may look a little skimpy. Later in the chapter we will suggest how to show off what little you have to the best advantage.

Don't be tempted to lie about your credits. You will be found out — this is a small world — and any potential benefit is severely outweighed by the real humiliation and shame of being caught out in the lie.

Training next — not just college courses but also workshops and classes. Include classes in any performance skill, not just acting but dance, stage combat, singing, musical instruments, juggling, etc. There is no need, unless the résumé is very thin, to mention every teacher who has given you instruction. You will get most benefit from the names of those who are currently active in the business. At the beginning of your career, your résumé will be heavy on training and light on experience. Don't unbalance it more than you have to.

The last section is special skills. These are any abilities that increase your casting potential. Any sport at which you are proficient, any musical instrument you can play, any vehicle you can drive, any language you can speak, any accent you can use — this is the place to put it down. Give details that show your level of expertise: awards, qualifications, years of experience. Do not put in hobbies unless they are professionally useful. Most engagers aren't all that interested in how well-rounded a human being you are: you aren't going to be around long enough for that to matter. We have seen résumés listing reading as a hobby. We assume that you read. Don't waste space that could be better used to list windsurfing or guitar-playing.

"Commercials on request" is an effective catchphrase that demonstrates on-camera or on-air experience. Don't list your commercials: no one outside the advertising field is interested.

As your résumé fills up with professional and then union work experience, you will drop your college and non-professional credits. Next to go is the institutional part of your professional training. Cut your drama school training but leave in the Singing Master Class with Ben Heppner or the Television Presenter Workshop with Daniel Richler. However, all that is in the future. For now, it is more a question of finding things to put in a résumé rather than deciding what to take out.

FORM

Your résumé must be only one page. Trust us: more than one page will not be read. To be honest, even one page often isn't read. A recent survey of Canadian executives showed that one-third spent less than two minutes on each job résumé. When you have a huge number of credits, you should be selecting and distilling to keep it all on one page. Two pages is not twice as impressive as one — it is twice as much bother to read.

Any word processing program has all the features you need to lay out an effective résumé. Back up the final version and keep it up to date.

You don't have to own a computer to use one. There are places, even in the smallest centres, that supply computer time: computer rental outfits, large photocopy shops, libraries. Work out in advance, in as much detail as possible, the form and shape of the résumé so you don't waste computer rental/borrowing time. Store your finished résumé on a floppy disk or CD-RW, take the disk away with you, and return whenever it needs changing, updating, or printing.

Don't be tempted to use coloured paper for your résumé on the theory that it will stand out from all the white ones. Our advice is to aim for classy and professional.

When you have collected all the information for your résumé, decide what is going in. You are probably thinking that, at this stage in your career, everything should go in, if only to fill up the space. Not so. Empty space is better than second-rate credits. An over-filled résumé looks like a big grey blob; the proper margins and space between sections turns it into manageable mouthfuls.

The sections of a résumé are: personal information (name, contact address, and telephone number, vital statistics, union affiliations), work experience, training, and special skills (usually in that order).

Your name, at the top, should be in larger and bolder type than anything else on the page. Play with the arrangement of the rest of your personal information until it looks tidy and is easy to read.

Work experience is usually broken into stage and media work, under headings like Theatre Highlights, Selected Stage, Some Film Roles, Television.

Few people will bother to read the whole résumé; they skim from section to section. So start each section with its most important credit first. What makes it most important is up to you. It could be the lead role, or a famous director, or a prestigious theatre, or a prize-winning film, or just the first part where you had more than eight lines. Professional credits, no matter how small, come before community theatre, student films, and college credits, no matter how large.

If you decide to list your work chronologically, don't include dates in your work experience. By doing without them, you have removed any evidence of unemployment. Everyone knows that actors have periods when they are not working, but why call attention to them?

Another possibility is to order your credits geographically. It can be useful for a director to know where you have worked, particularly if you can show that you have been to places more than once. (It is always reassuring for a director to see that you have actually been asked back somewhere.)

Accentuate the positive. Don't panic because your work experience consists solely of school scene-study and final-year productions. Call the section Workshops and list the scene work you have done. This is not cheating. You are making it clear that you were not taking part in finished productions, and you are giving the potential engager a picture of the kinds of roles you are familiar with and have worked on. If you have done one radio show, one television show, and one film, having three separate sections is going to look rather bare. Amalgamate the three under Selected Media Work and present a more positive picture.

The training section may be arranged chronologically, and if you want to put in graduating dates, that's fine. It can be useful to know how long you have been out in the real world and to see how much you have done in that time. Obviously, you will not include the dates if you graduated two years ago and have done two days on a film since. The rule is: If it makes you look good, put it in. If it doesn't, leave it out.

In Special Skills, it is easier to get a picture of your accomplishments if they are not all strung out on the same line. For example, you can have a line for sports, another for dancing and singing, one for any musical instruments you can play, a line for accents or languages, and one for any vehicles you can drive. Special Skills is also the place to put in your singing range and style, unless you are primarily a singer, in which case they go in your vital statistics.

Most Canadian actors' résumés have their credits arranged in columns. This presents the information in the most accessible way. Remember, people only glance at résumés: your selling points have to leap off the page. Your layout need not follow our example as long as it is simple, neat, and easy to read. Set adequate margins, keep the spaces between topics equal, and make sure all the columns line up. Accentuate section headings in some way (upper case, bold, underline). Be consistent. If you decide to use both underlining and colons for the topic headings, make sure you use them for them all.

Do not abbreviate anything unless you are sure the short form is common enough for everyone to recognize. The University of British Columbia is generally known as UBC, but it is unlikely that anyone other than alumni would recognize GBC as George Brown College. If the full title is threatening to ruin your beautiful layout, rethink the layout.

Accentuate the names of the productions (under Selected Theatre and Selected Media) perhaps in bold or upper case letters. In the second column, avoid saying "various parts." Use either the biggest role or, if they are all of a size, the two most successful (Dotty/Liz) or the most interesting combination (Priest/Madman).

If it was a school production done outside the school, in a proper theatre, put the name of the theatre. Use the series title for television credits (*Degrassi*). Use the program title only for one-time specials or movies-of-the-week (*Above and Beyond*). The third column will be the production company (Alliance) or the network (YTV), whichever is more recognizable. Giving a bunch of student filmmakers a name, like Skeezix Productions, say, is all right, providing you don't lie about them in the interview.

Use "Actor" or "Principal" (see Chapter 6) rather than the name of the role in media credits. No one knows how good a part Serena was in episode 117 of *Stargate*.

Finished

Not quite. Make sure you have the correct title of each play or film. This is particularly important with films, where titles can change between shooting and distribution. (One of the authors paid for a hundred copies of a résumé with the film *Twins* as one of the media credits. Three days later, the title was changed to *Dead Ringers*.)

Proofread! Believe us, there is nothing more frustrating than sending out 137 beautiful résumés and then noticing that you played Ratty in *Toad of Toad Hell*. Find out how people spell their names. Don't trust your program's spell-checking feature. Go through each section word by word; go through each word letter by letter. Yes, it is tedious. Yes, it is time-consuming. But yes, it is worth it.

Now you have your master résumé. Even if you have an excellent printer, photocopying may be cheaper if you're making lots of copies. How many copies you make depends on the number of people you plan to send it to right now and how often you expect to update it.

Never send a résumé out on its own, or with just a photograph. You always need a covering letter.

Photographs

Lloy Coutts, freelance director: "Your photograph should look like you now, and should show what sort of person you are." Don't waste money on fancy framing, tricksy shots, or composites showing you in various poses. There is only one publicity photograph actors need — the glossy, the headshot, the eight-by-ten. Black and white, eight inches wide and ten inches high, stapled to the back of your résumé. Sounds easy? Wrong!

According to Suzanne McLaren, freelance photographer: "Most people find black and white more flattering; however, colour photographs can highlight features lost in black and white: red hair, green eyes, beautiful white teeth."

No one in the world is totally satisfied with the face that peers out of the mirror. We know how tempting it is to choose the most flattering or the most glamorous shot, but it is a temptation you must resist. Your photograph should look like you on a good day, but look like you it must. It is a waste of your money and the engager's time to send out pictures that make you look like Keira Knightley or Leonardo DiCaprio if, when you walk into the office, you look like Olive Oyl or Hagar the Horrible. Sell what you are, not what you want to be.

With that warning in mind, be careful with your make-up. That goes for males as well as females. You do not want to look any more made up in your photo than you will in the audition. Making up for a photo session can be difficult. Many photographers work with make-up artists, who know how make-up translates onto a photograph. If you plan to do your own make-up, take the photographer's advice.

Don't allow the photographer to touch up the eight-by-ten unless the offending blemish is temporary. The mole on the cheek stays; the pimple on the end of the nose goes.

You may need more than one style of picture to send out. A moody, sullen shot, very effective for a specific role, might not be the ideal photograph to send to a theatre, which needs to see the closest thing to the "real" you. Photographs for commercials tend to show high energy and lots of teeth. Whatever photographs you decide to use, make sure they have a good, strong image. There is little point in sending out pleasant-looking, bland pictures of you showing no personality. You might as well use your high school graduation picture.

Publicity photographs are called headshots, but you will see three-quarter and full-length shots, the theory being that a fuller shot gives a better feel for the whole person than does a close-up of the face. John Raitt, CBC casting director, then agent, now photographer, says that if your face is critical, why use a full-length shot in a five-by-seven image surrounded by an inch-and-a-half border? Our advice would be that if you are selling long hair or an unusual body shape, go with the fuller shot. Otherwise, go with a tighter shot.

Your photographer will ask you to bring changes of clothing. Even in close-up shots, some of your clothing will show in the photograph. Suzanne McLaren: "Choosing clothing to contrast your skin tone will help draw the viewer's eye to the face."

Most people take off their glasses for photographs. That's fine, as long as you do not wear them for interviews or work. It might be worth getting the photographer to shoot a couple of you with glasses on: you don't have to choose them but they may turn out to be surprisingly useful. In commercials, Paul Brown, an actor who lives in Toronto, made a name for himself with his elfin face and big horn-rimmed glasses. He was as instantly recognizable as the products he promoted.

The simpler the picture, the better. Beware of outdoor shots with a busy background. There is nothing wrong with having pictures taken outside — the light can be excellent — but foliage, brick walls, or mountains can pull the attention away from that all-important subject. You. Again, please, nothing tricksy. A shot with your pet monkey might

Avoiding Text Anxiety

Some anxiety about taking tests is normal, but when the anxiety affects how you perform on the test, it is time to build your confidence. Review your skills either by yourself or with another person, preferably a counselor at your institution. Learn how to study and manage your time. Organize your material that is to be studied. Be aware of outside influences that affect performance. Learn from your test anxiety mistakes.

When you are ready to take a test, approach it with confidence. Tell yourself you will do well. Prepare yourself by studying. Pick a good place to take the test. Make sure that distractions will not affect you. Give yourself time for the tests. Stay relaxed. Don't talk with students who are not prepared. Eat something before you go into the test.

As you are taking the test, make sure your read the directions and answer the questions asked. Watch your time. Skip over difficult areas and go back to them. Move around in your chair, but don't fidget. Don't worry about other students finishing first. If you go blank on an essay or short answer test, start writing something on another sheet of paper. It may trigger your mind.

While taking the test, stay relaxed. Don't tense up. Take deep breaths. Expect to be a little anxious, but don't let it control you. Think positive thoughts and tell yourself that you can take the test.

When you have finished the test, think back over what you did and what did or did not work on the test. Congratulate yourself on a job well done.

- **Interest**-- The brain prioritizes by meaning, value and relevance. To have meaning, you must understand what you are learning. In order to remember something thoroughly, you must be interested in it and think that it has value and relevance in your life.

- **Intent to Remember**-- Your attitude has much to do with whether you remember something or not. A key factor to remembering is having a positive attitude that you get it right the first time. Attention is not the same as learning, but little learning takes place without attention.

- **Basic Background**-- Your understanding of new materials depends on what you already know that you can connect it to. The more you increase your basic knowledge, the easier it is to build new knowledge on this background.

- **Selectivity**-You must determine what is most important and select those parts to begin the process of studying and learning.

- **Meaningful Organization**-- You can learn and remember better if you can group ideas into some sort of meaningful categories or groups.

- **Recitation**-- Saying ideas aloud in your own words strengthens synaptic connections and gives you immediate feedback. The more feedback you get, the faster and more accurate your learning.

- **Visualization**-- The brain's quickest and probably the longest-lasting response is to images. By making a mental picture, you use an entirely different part of the brain than you did by reading or listening.

- **Association**-- Memory is increased when facts to be learned are consciously associated with something familiar to you. Memory is essentially formed by making neural connections. Begin by asking, "What is this like that I already know and understand?".

- **Consolidation**-- Your brain must have time for new information to establish and solidify a neuronal pathway. When you make a list or review your notes right after class, you are using the principle of consolidation.

- **Distributed Practice**-- A series of shorter study sessions distributed over several days is preferable to fewer but longer study sessions.

be momentarily diverting, but think how embarrassing it would be if the monkey got the part.

Your focus in a photograph is vital. By that, we mean where you are apparently focusing your attention, not how fuzzy the picture is. The more you seem to be looking at the person who is holding your photograph, the better. A clear, direct look is engaging and compelling; a sideways or off-centre glance is not.

Deciding which photographs to use is not easy. The photographer will supply you with small prints or contact sheets containing copies of each shot taken during the session. You will want a magnifying glass of some sort, a good strong light, and a couple of L-shaped pieces of paper so you can see how a picture looks properly cropped.

You have two areas of decision: technical and professional. The technical side is easier to deal with. Is the photograph in focus? Is it too light? Too dark? Is your head cropped? You don't have to be an expert to make choices on the basis of these questions. Some problems — centring and overall exposure, for instance — can easily be corrected for the full-size print. Where the technical problems are incurable — poor focus or dirty negatives — any decent photographer should agree to reshoot, free.

Professional suitability is a more subjective area. You have to decide which photograph is going to sell you best. You need to think about image and energy and style; which picture show the "real" you; which shot is useful for film and which is better for stage; what personality the picture projects. If there are no useful shots, the photographer may agree to reshoot for the cost of materials. He is arguably obliged to do so by law, but it may come down to a battle of wills.

Get as many outside opinions as you can stand. Certainly, you should ask the person who took the shots, although those recommendations may be very good photography that doesn't show you off well. Agents see hundreds of photographs and usually have a keen eye for what sells. They know their clients, how they come across in the flesh, and which headshot best projects those qualities. When push comes to shove, accept your agent's advice. What she sees in the shot she likes will be what she thinks she can sell. If you are still in drama school, ask your teachers. (Be aware, though, that they may not have had any dealings with the professional side of the business for some years and may be out of touch.) Ask your spouse-equivalent and your friends in the business, but remember, they may know you too well to be objective.

Whatever you do, don't ask your mother. She'll pick the one with the neatest hair.

PHOTOGRAPHERS

Choosing a photographer who is right for you isn't easy. Ask your agent, if you have one (but see our warning about in-house photographers in Chapter 9). Look at friends' glossies. Performer notice boards always have photographers' advertisements.

When you have a short list of candidates, call them and ask some questions:

- What is your session fee?
- How long is a session?
- How many shots do you take?
- How many eight-by-tens do you supply? Do you have a make-up artist?
- How long before the prints are ready? When is the first available appointment?

Compare the responses and ask for an appointment with your first choice just for a chat. Discuss your image, clothes, and make-up. Ask to see examples of actors' headshots. You will see the photographer's style running throughout, but each actor should look quite different.

How do you feel about the photographer as a person? Do you seem to have good rapport? Is this the sort of person you want to open yourself up to? Having your picture taken can be a tense and trying experience. If you do not feel comfortable with the photographer, chances are the session will not be successful.

Discuss the method of payment. Any reasonable photographer should agree to part of the money in advance and the rest when you have satisfactory prints. This gives you some leverage if you are not satisfied with the results. Discuss copyright. Will you be allowed to use your image online and otherwise? Will you be able to choose who does your repros? Until the Copyright Act is amended, you own all these rights, but your photographer may not agree.

REPROS

Over the course of a career, you will send out thousands of photographs. This would be prohibitively expensive if each one were an original print from the photographer or from a photofinisher. Luckily, you can get cheap mass-reproduced prints in most cities, either from a photographer with the equipment or from a specialist photo repro house. Most people have their name added to the repros. This is worth doing — if your headshot gets separated from your résumé it will have to be tossed if it doesn't have your name on it. If your photographer can't do repros and there isn't a repro house in your centre, Galbraith Photo Digital in Toronto and Rocket Repro in Vancouver accept mail orders and send reproductions across Canada (see Addresses).

Photo litho or good photocopies of your eight-by-ten are acceptable in some cities. They are cheap, but find out what the custom is in your area. Check with the local ACTRA office; you don't have to be a member. If you are sending your photograph outside your immediate area, only a first-rate photo reproduction, difficult to tell from an original, is acceptable.

Don't order too many repros. In Vancouver and Toronto, agents get photographs returned from casting directors, and computer casting means fewer photographs are sent out. As well, if you have dramatically changed your hair, gained ten pounds, developed wrinkles, or made any other noticeable change to the way you look, you will need new photographs taken. As we said right at the beginning, your picture must look like you — the way you are now.

Demo Tapes

There is a third weapon to add to your promotional armoury: the demo (demonstration) tape. It comes in two flavours: video and voice.

Video

Confusingly, the demo tape is often called a "reel," from the days before TV when your demo would be on film to be projected. Nowadays, the demo tape may be on VHS, but it is more and more likely to be on DVD or in a file for your website. Demo files and DVDs are still called tapes or reels, though, just as the end of a show is still called the curtain, even in a studio theatre with no stage curtains.

A video demo will show a selection of your professional media work. The contents are useful to introduce yourself to agents and casting directors who are unfamiliar with your work or who know you in only a limited context. If an agent hasn't seen you in action, she might ask you to audition, but the demo tape is a way for her to see you actually working. She doesn't have to go to the theatre or the cinema, she doesn't have to remember to tune in the television to catch your scene. Whenever she has a minute, there's your work waiting to be viewed.

Getting tape of work you have done from the various production companies is not always easy, and it can be expensive. Having the best bits edited into a professional-quality demo is fairly easy in a large enough centre, but it is very expensive — some hundreds of dollars.

When the authors of this book asked a selection of casting directors how important they thought a demo tape was, the answer was a unanimous "very." But they did not agree on where that importance lay. Tina Gerussi: "It's a tool and it's very useful for my own purposes, when there's someone I'm not sure about and I want to reinforce him in my mind. But demo tapes don't really tell me what a person can do. They are simply an extension of showing your résumé, not necessarily showing me how good you are." On the other hand, Stuart Aikins: "The director uses the demo tapes to find out three things: (1) Can you act? (2) Are you directable? (3) Are you right for the role?"

Most of the casting directors feel that demo tapes are useful for audition purposes, if you have a decent track record. Stuart Aikins: "I can't tell you how many times established actors lose stuff just because there's nothing to show a director if they are not available for the audition. Actors who are available for the shoot but can't make the audition should have a demo tape." But for inexperienced actors, Tina Gerussi:

"For actors just starting out, using a demo tape instead of attending an audition (if you can't make it) is not all that great. The audition is all-important. Also, it depends what it's for. For episodic television, we don't look at a lot of tapes. There is a new show every ten days, casting sessions every few days. There are enough people around to choose from. If it's a big feature, you might just want to remind a director who a person is. But it depends on the material on the tape. If you've done a lot of work and have some juicy scenes to put on, then it's worth it. It won't get you a part, but you'll get to meet the director. We don't show tapes unless there's something substantial to show."

Producers have their own take on demo tapes. Gail Harvey, creative producer, *Terry*: "Edit your scenes down to focus on you. I don't like opening montages." Jennifer Jonas (*Childstar*, *The Perfect Son*): "Show your range. Don't choose by the prestige of the person you're on screen with."

The quality of the tape is something casting directors don't agree on. Brian Levy: "It has to be of excellent quality. Even if it's a good piece of work, if the production values are bad, don't use it." Other casting directors concur: "Don't put one together unless it is fabulous!" "Poor production values are the same as a lousy eight-by-ten — reshoot it. If it is cheap and shoddy, people won't buy it." However, Stuart Aikins disagrees: "As long as the material is visible and audible, that's all that's important. I will even look at peer-group tapes [actors recording their own scenes]. They can be useful, although I'd never show them to a director." Tina Gerussi makes a good point: "If you can get your demo professionally edited, do.... Having the second ear and eye, that of the editor, helps to get rid of extra stuff you don't need or shouldn't have. It's an investment."

Your demo tape should be short. Brian Levy: "Actors make the mistake of having too much on a demo tape. Nine minutes is absolutely tops." Stuart Atkins: "Four minutes is best." Tina Gerussi: "Five to eight minutes. They won't get looked at more than that. Casting directors look at the tapes longer than engagers. Producers and directors look at a tape for about two and a half minutes. If something hasn't caught them by then, it's finished."

Most casting directors agreed that if you are featured in a film, you could put a longer section on the tape after the short segments, for engagers who are interested in looking at more of your work.

Slating your tape is important. You must identify it at the beginning with your name and your face. For one thing, tapes can be put in the wrong boxes, and for another, if there are three young men in a scene, how is the director going to know which one is you? Tina Gerussi: "The worst thing is looking through a demo, not knowing who you're looking for." You can identify yourself in a variety of ways. First comes your name and your agency. Then a short (ten-second) montage of close-ups. If that isn't possible, a ten-second viewing of your eight-by-ten, or a montage of eight-by-tens, just to let them know what you look like.

Brian Levy: "Try to make the content of the tape as varied as possible. But remember, the people who watch it are likely to switch off after a couple of minutes. Start with something really effective." Stuart Akins: "Segments should show a range — period, comedy, drama, action." All casting directors agree that you should put your strongest scene first, although some casting directors will cue up to what they think is your most useful scene before they let a director see the tape.

Having commercials on a tape is fine, as long as they don't overbalance the content. One casting director described a demo tape done as a television show: scene-commercial-scene-commercial, all done in about five minutes and very effective. Actors who do mainly commercials may want a tape showing only commercials, but for most actors there should be a proper balance of commercials and drama.

All casting directors said they vetted (and occasionally vetoed) the tapes before letting a producer or director see them.

Although many agents go to the theatre regularly, they are often interested in seeing demo tapes. Actors do not always come across the same way in media work as on the stage. Actors who can't reach out to a live audience may have the ability to bring an audience in to them on screen. Only a demo tape will reveal that.

If you decide that a video demo is worth its substantial cost, make more than one copy of the tape and never, never let the master out of your possession.

Voice Tapes

Voice tapes can be ordinary cassette tapes, but more and more they are CDs or MP3 files for the Internet. They are still called tapes, or sometimes reels, from the 1970s reel-to-reel recorders. Voice tapes are the audio equivalent of a photograph and résumé. You can put together your own voice tape of commercials and narrations, but you should go to an expert if possible. Many voice studios run classes and make demo tapes. Some agencies doing a lot of voice work use recordable CDs to put their clients' work in the hands of producers. If you are with an agency that does a lot of voice-over work, great. If not, you will probably find that area of the business closed to you, unless you live in a small centre and can talk directly to stores needing announcements or companies needing recorded messages. Elsewhere, it is not something you can do without an agent, who will have the facilities and the casting information you cannot get.

All right, you have all the equipment you need. Let's put it to work. Let's go to an audition.

CHAPTER SIX

The Art of Auditioning

"Behave like a duck — keep calm and unruffled on the surface but paddle like the devil underneath."
Jacob Braude

Actors treat auditions as if their lives were on the line. Yes, you should treat them seriously and professionally, but keep your perspective. Marion Paige, New York casting director, quoted in *How to Act and Eat at the Same Time*: "What's the worst thing that can happen? You don't get the job. You didn't have it when you came in, so what's the loss?" Tom Hanks says, "It's another chance to act." Treat the audition as an opportunity to meet potential engagers and to sharpen your auditioning technique. If you come out of the room satisfied that you gave the best showing of yourself that you could, then the audition was a success. Getting the part is a bonus.

With your photograph and résumé clutched in your trembling hand, you head for your audition. Whether it is your first audition or your fiftieth, some things never change: the desire, the nervousness, and that photograph and résumé clutched in your trembling hand. It does not matter how many times you have walked into the same casting director's office or how many times you have auditioned for the same director, you must take a photograph and résumé to every audition. Stuart Aikins, casting director: "I hate actors who don't bring photos and résumés. It is self-centred and unprofessional." Tina Gerussi: casting director: "I know a producer who won't hire actors, however wonderful the audition, if they haven't brought their photograph and résumé. The producer needs the reference. He's seen thirty people; how is he going to remember who's who? Keep a set in your car, in your briefcase. Make sure they're stapled together. And no excuses. 'I thought my agent sent it' is just dumb. We've heard every excuse in the book."

As long as you are taking one photograph and résumé, take two. You never know who else might be at the audition. If it is an audition for a musical, you can give the musical director the second set. If there is an associate director present, it would be polite (and unusual) to give your second set to him. An associate director today could be an artistic director tomorrow, and will remember kindly those who remembered him.

Know where you're going; get the address; know the name of the show or product and the casting director. Often there are two auditions going on at the same time.

Be on time — the first rule of any job interview. In this business, being on time means being early. Give yourself a chance to calm down, brush your hair, and reapply your make-up, if any. Find out if any new information on the theatre is available. Look for brochures with the confirmed season. In media auditions, give yourself a chance to look at what you're going to have to read. Tina Gerussi: "For episodic television, the script gets in only just in time. Give yourself fifteen or twenty minutes with the sides."

Sometimes you will be late; catastrophes do happen. Don't rush in breathlessly, tossing apologies to all and sundry. Apologize briefly to whoever had to juggle the schedules, then shut up. No one is interested in your traffic jam or stolen wallet. Don't apologize when you get into the auditioning room. The director may have no idea who is next in line until the actor appears. Why draw attention to your tardiness?

You never get a second chance to make a first impression. The audition starts the moment you walk into the room. How you greet the director and present yourself to the producer are as important as your prepared speech or reading. Tina Gerussi: "The first impression is so important: how you walk into the room, how you present your photo and résumé. The handshake is vital. We know you're nervous, but cold, sweaty hands are not a good thing. Try to dry them off and warm them up!"

In fact, the audition really starts in the waiting room. There is often an engager's representative outside the auditioning room who comments on you before you ever get through the door. Be polite to everybody. The "receptionist" may be an associate director who popped out to use the phone. Ask which washroom you may use and if you are allowed to use the phone. Don't knock the product before a commercial audition; don't make jokes about the theatre's personalities or political leanings. You are the guest in this situation, not the host.

Dress appropriately. You want to feel comfortable and look attractive. You must be able to move the way the character you will play does. Don't wear anything that distracts from what they want to see in you. Michael Shamata, freelance director: "Don't mask your shape with heavy sweaters or outsize jackets." Dress as you would for any other job interview. Actors' working clothes may be casual, even sloppy, but until you're got the job, dress so that your mother would be proud of you.

If you are auditioning for a specific role, you may dress with that in mind, but don't go in costume. You insult the intelligence and imagination of the engager. Deirdre Bowen, casting director: "Give the impression. If it's a cop, wear a crisp shirt. [But] if the character is a slob, don't be such a slob that they are looking at your clothes." The one exception to this rule is in auditions for commercials, where the client may even ask to see the actors in costume. We have seen actors turned away from auditions for commercials because they did not comply with the costume requirements.

Be prepared. As a general preparation, ask your agent to show you sides for different styles of commercials. You should be watching television to find out what the market is. Deirdre Bowen: "The biggest mistake in an audition is lack of preparation." Stuart Aikins: "You should look at the material in advance so that you can make choices ahead of time." Tina Gerussi: "On episodic television, you rarely get told much about the story or character. You should watch the show before you go, so you know the style, know what they're looking for. Nothing is worse on a regular series than an actor saying, 'What's the show about?'"

Although you may be informed in the morning that you have an audition that afternoon, there are still ways to prepare. Get your agent to send you the story synopsis to give you the best idea of the character. Tina Gerussi: "For a feature film, try to find out about the director, if possible. Maybe something about his past work." Get the sides as soon as possible. Stuart Aikins: "I always give out sides the day before. Actors have no excuse not to be prepared." At the audition, read the copy again, make sure it's the piece you've been looking at, look for key words, and be sure you've read the whole scene through. It's easy to miss that extra speech right at the end — we've done it. For a commercial audition, make sure you're pronouncing the product name right. The casting director will let you know.

Preparation is important for theatre auditions, too. Andy McKim, associate artistic director, Tarragon Theatre, Toronto: "Eighty or ninety percent of an audition is determined even before [you] enter the room." Richard Ouzounian, *Toronto Star* theatre critic and former artistic director: "You should do your homework; you should know the season and the previous repertoire." Even if you are auditioning for a theatre specializing in new work, you should have some knowledge of the theatre itself and the sort of work they do.

The more information you have, the more confident you will feel. Confidence plus genuine interest and enthusiasm are almost irresistible.

The director is not the enemy. He would like nothing better than for you to succeed. God knows you would make his job an awful lot easier if you were perfect for the role.

Don't try to second-guess the director. If he knows exactly what he wants, and you fit the bill, wonderful. If you don't, tough luck. Much of the time, the director doesn't know exactly what he wants. If he doesn't, how can you? Andy McKim: "I am looking for actors who have something specific to offer me. When they show it to me, then I try to figure out how to use that strength." Jerry Ciccoritti, independent filmmaker: "If an actor comes in and they bring something that I find absolutely extraordinary then I would always rather rewrite the part to get that actor on screen." On the other hand, from Anne Wheeler, filmmaker: "You have to be able to just throw away what you've prepared and go for it from another direction.

Be yourself: that's the hardest piece of advice to follow. Every engager and every casting director we spoke to said the same thing: they don't want to see a routine. Tina Gerussi: "Present yourself as honestly and directly as you can." Michael Shamata: "All you have to offer is yourself." Jackie Maxwell: "Show me who you are before you pretend to be someone else."

Although being yourself should be a snap (after all, you've been doing it most of your life), it's the toughest acting job you'll ever have to do. The situation is tense and unnatural. If you were really being yourself you would plead for the job or babble on about how nervous you are, or embarrass yourself in a dozen other socially unacceptable ways. The auditioners understand your terrors and take them into consideration. Jackie Maxwell, Shaw Festival artistic director: "I try to make the chat as non-threatening as possible."

Saying "be yourself" is the same as saying your photograph should look like you. You should be presenting the best you there is. In *The Color of Money*, Eddie (Paul Newman) says of Vincent (Tom Cruise): "He's got to learn to be himself — but on purpose." You should project a confidence and an ease. Respond to the other person, listen, contribute. Being yourself, or rather presenting yourself, is a job you can learn to do. When a solo improvisational comic bombed in Montreal's Just For Laughs Festival, the critic at *La Presse* said, "I think he has learned that he has to be more prepared in order to improvise."

Karen Hazzard, casting director: "There are three performing disciplines: dance, singing and acting. All dancers exercise. All singers vocalize. Actors wait for the phone to ring." While you're waiting, pick up a newspaper or magazine and read a paragraph out loud — no preparation. Practise reading out loud every day, then when you're thrown a cold reading, it won't throw you.

Try to make the audition easy for the auditioner; he's working hard too. Look at your résumé, work out the likely questions ("What have you been doing lately?" "What children's theatre have you done?" "Did you enjoy touring New Brunswick?"), and have some answers ready (preferably something other than "Nothing," "None," and "No"). The audition is an opportunity to tell the engager how you think, react, and feel. Jackie Maxwell: "The director is looking for someone she wants to work with, not just someone who is good."

Don't lie. Although you want to paint as good a picture of yourself as you can, you've got to be able to come up with the goods. One of the authors of this book got a part in a mini-series where everybody had to ride. Never having seen a horse outside of the movies, he responded modestly, "Well, of course, I'm not an expert," when asked about his riding abilities. However, he knew there were six weeks between the audition and the first shooting date, which gave him time for hours of expensive lessons to learn which end of the beast was the front. Unfortunately, it's the exceptions you'll hear about; they make better stories. If you do lie about a skill, make sure you have turned that lie into the truth by the time you have to use it. Your failures will stick in the mind much longer than any successes.

You may be offered advice in an audition about your photo, résumé, appearance, or acting. Don't argue or justify yourself. It may not be what you want to hear, but it was offered as a gift. Accept it graciously. You don't, of course, have to follow it.

Know when to leave. Trying to extend the interview beyond its natural length won't do you any good. Learn to read body language. Judge when the interviewer is preparing to say goodbye and get your parting ready. But don't shortchange yourself: Robert Rooney, freelance theatre director: "Concentrate on yourself. This is your time. Don't rush to help them get back on schedule." Millie Tom, casting director: "Be prepared. Commit to your choices. Own the audition."

Theatre

GENERAL AUDITIONS

Artistic directors use general auditions either to meet actors for the first time or to see actors they haven't seen in a few years. You will normally do one or two prepared, memorized speeches in a rehearsal room or an office, rarely in an actual theatre. All the auditioner can find out is if you can walk and talk at the same time. With luck, you'll get onto a list of possibles and get cast from a second audition two or three years down the line. Edward Gilbert, freelance director: "I want some basic knowledge of the human being. And I mean very basic: height, weight, age, vocal quality. A general audition is only the first step in the process and quite a small one. I want you to pique my curiosity, encourage me to explore further."

General auditions usually have two parts: the interview and the audition speech, familiarly known as your "party piece." Some directors don't bother with the interview as such. You walk into the room, do your speech, and walk out. Some directors feel the interview is as important as the speech and spend as much time on it as watching you act. Be ready to go with whatever the director has decided.

The Interview

The director is giving you an opportunity to show what you are like. Be prepared to talk about anything that might come up. Most directors use your résumé as a jumping-off point for a discussion, so think what questions you might be asked. Remember, this isn't an exam; they don't need the answers. It's like a talk show: their questions give you a chance to sell yourself. What do you want them to know about you? How can you attach that to the names and places on your résumé?

Don't bad-mouth anybody. A common question is, "How did you like working with So-and-so?" What do you say? What do they want to hear? Are they So-and-so's lover? If your relationship with So-and-so was like Lizzie Borden's with her father, how do you turn it into a positive experience? Remember, this isn't a test. It's just an easy way (so they think) to get you talking. Try to go from the personal to the professional. "It was the first time I'd ever worked with So-and-so and I learned a lot." From there you can segue into something you're comfortable talking about. However honest and open directors say they want you to be, listening to you knife one of their fellow directors in the back will make them itch between the shoulder blades.

The Speech

Choose a part that's in your casting range. Auditions are not the time to stretch. Show your strengths. Go with what you can do, where you feel comfortable. Jackie Maxwell: "What's the point in showing me a forty-year-old Brit? I'll never cast you as one." Andy McKim: "Selection of audition pieces is critical in displaying one's strengths. These can change over time, so it's good to reassess … regularly."

These days, many directors want to see pieces that show you. Find something that speaks to you personally, that you can talk about with knowledge and understanding.

Choose a speech you enjoy doing. Nothing is more attractive and entertaining than seeing someone having a good time doing a piece.

Choose a speech that shows you in a way the company can use. Why do something from *Titus Andronicus* if you are auditioning for the Singalong Musical Dinner Theatre?

Look for a Canadian audition speech. Many theatre companies have Canadian plays in their mandate. Some theatres do nothing but, and require one or two audition speeches from Canadian plays.

Choose material that shows an emotional, physical, and vocal range. Brian Paisley, founder of the Edmonton Fringe: "For me, an audition is a time for the actor to show everything he can do, including movement and musical skills."

Look for a speech that is happening now, not a memory speech. Plays take place in the present. You want a speech that allows you an immediacy in your emotions and desires.

Keep it short! Directors don't need time to make up their minds. Jackie Maxwell: "You can have a sense of someone very quickly." Two minutes is quite long enough for any speech, and no one will be upset if it's shorter. Never go over your allotted time. Audition schedules are tight, and ignoring the time strictures will endear you to no one.

The speech should stand on its own. You need to set up the situation, but that's it. If you are prefacing a two-minute speech with a twenty-second introduction, something is wrong.

Most directors appreciate hearing new or unusual speeches. Don't choose something second-rate just because no one knows it, but if you can find something good and different, use it. Some speeches in collections, in print and online, were written to be used for auditions but have no context for discussion. We suggest you give them a miss. Robert Rooney: "Why does no one ever do one of Shakespeare's minor characters? They've got some great speeches."

Don't risk embarrassing the director. For instance, overtly sexual speeches may work well in the play, but on their own they are an assault on the sensibilities of the auditioners. For any general audition, avoid extreme choices. A wild, emotional speech may work in the play, but this is 11:15 a.m. in a church hall. Or, as Jackie Maxwell so succinctly put it, "I don't like obscenities yelled at me."

Make 'em laugh! The auditioners will be spending most of the day watching pain and angst. Anything light and witty will come as welcome relief.

Contrasting speeches do not necessarily mean one classical and one modern. Speeches can be contrasting in mood, emotion, vocal range, character, point of view, physicality, place. Two plays written five hundred years apart aren't necessarily different in anything other than their language.

Keep your audition material ready to use. Lloy Coutts, freelance director: "Read a play a week, at a sitting. Wait for a speech to offer itself. Don't force it. You should have six speeches and a song." With this size of repertoire, you will be ready to audition at the drop of a hat.

As well as the memory speeches we've mentioned, you should avoid speeches from the previous season, speeches from the coming season, the great classical speeches, characters playing other people, and presentational speeches such as prologues.

Read the whole play. You cannot possibly develop a three-dimensional character without that knowledge, nor can you carry on a discussion if the director uses the play to hang the interview on.

The introduction of the speech is as important as the rest of the audition. It should be clear, concise, simple, and direct. Tell the director only what he must know to understand the context and get on with it. Assume the director knows the stories of the classical plays.

Some directors advise actors to take their time to prepare before starting a piece, others suggest leaping in. We think that actors often dissipate their energy by doing a whole preparation routine. Do that outside and use the introduction as your springboard into the speech.

Don't stick yourself in a chair or stand motionless for the whole speech. Moments of stillness are effective, but only when seen in contrast to movement. Why not walk out of the acting area and start your speech with a definite entrance? That way you present the speech with an extra energy.

Start with a grabber. Katinka Matson in *The Working Actor* recalls being stopped mid-speech: "When they stopped me, all I could think was, 'But I haven't got to the good part yet!' You have to get to the good part right away." Put your better speech first. Of course, you do them both brilliantly, but chances are you are more comfortable with one. An audition is not the place to get the worst over with first. You may not be allowed to do the second.

Use the space you have available. Do the speech far enough away to be seen full-length. On a stage, be sure you are in light. Use the voice that fills the space.

Avoid using props. Generally you're better off without them, but occasionally a single prop can make a clear, dramatic statement.

Don't rely on furniture. Rehearse your piece with a simple, hard chair, which you will find in almost any audition space, or with nothing at all. Never fiddle with furniture or use it to hide behind; you're just avoiding commitment to the speech.

Actors often fix the auditioner with a steely glare and address their pieces to him, as if he were another character in the play. Don't. At best, it's unlikely to do you any good, and it's a risk better avoided. If you really think it's necessary, every director we spoke to wanted to be asked beforehand.

Move from the first speech to the second without dropping your energy. Rehearse the two as a unit. You are more likely to be stopped after the first speech if your body language is saying, "This is an ending."

The auditioner may re-direct you. Respond as openly as you can; jump in with both feet, regardless of how dumb you think it is. The director simply wants to see how you take direction, what you will be like to work with.

Don't be afraid to stop your speech if you got started on the wrong foot. Don't be like one of the authors, who got a terrible attack of nerves at the beginning of a speech from *The Beaux' Stratagem*. Her mouth dried, her upper lip caught on her teeth, and she played the entire speech like a Restoration Bugs Bunny. Michael Shamata: "If you screw up early enough, start over." Mind you, you can only stop once — and your second attempt should be noticeably better than your first.

Don't start by apologizing. If you have a fever of 102° and a nose plugged up from here to Cleveland, ignore it. If you apologize in advance, you are setting the stage for a sub-standard performance, whatever you give them. If you can't manage to be "on" for fifteen minutes at the most, stay home. Phone to cancel the audition, and drink plenty of fluids.

It's going to happen to you, we promise. One of these days you are going to forget your lines right in the middle of your speech. What do you do? If you have read the whole play and are firmly grounded in the character, you can probably paraphrase your way out of the situation. Even if the director realizes what you're doing, he could well be impressed with your quickness of mind and ability to carry on. If the worst happens and your brain has truly ceased to function, just stop. Don't look at the director or try to explain. Take your time to recover your concentration; then, after a brief apology, finish the speech with renewed energy and attack.

When you have finished, shut up. Don't make a face, don't apologize, don't explain. The ball is in the director's court. If you have really screwed up, leave the "Oh, God, I want to die" routine until you get home.

Very occasionally, you will be asked to read something from one of the plays in the season, cold, without preparation. Having read all of the season's plays will help. They're not expecting your best performance, so dive in and have some fun with it.

The general theatre audition is the only one you may crash. Theatres accept that actors who couldn't get official appointments will just show up, in the hope that someone will cancel at the last minute or simply not appear. Often this is a way for non-Equity people to be seen. If you do crash an audition, be extra polite. You are there hoping for the generosity of the theatre company. When you arrive, give your name, résumé, and photograph to whoever is organizing the audition. Crashing is usually done on a first-come, first-served basis. And if you are lucky enough to get seen, make extra sure you write a thank-you note the moment you get home.

A postscript to crashing: The reason crashing is successful is that people with official appointments don't turn up. If you are ill or discover you have a conflict and cancel in good time, that's fine. If you just don't bother going, that is appalling. You are messing up the theatre's schedule, for which they will not remember you kindly, and you are also preventing another actor from being seen.

Auditioning for a Part

Auditions for specific roles are done with a prepared reading of a scene or two. You may not know in advance which scene they'll choose. Directors rarely use readings to meet new actors. These auditions are for people the director knows in some way. They've been recommended, he's worked with them before, or he has seen them in a general audition or in performance.

In readings, the interview will be minimal. You may have a bit of a chat about the play, in which case you should be able to contribute your own ideas, but you're just as likely to have to plunge right into the reading.

Leap in at the deep end, with a definite character and a definite point of view. The tentative reading, which tries to play it safe, is simply boring.

When you study the scene, find a powerful, effective move. It will free you, energize the scene, and show how you might tackle the physical side of the character. Don't just amble about.

Don't rush! If you give in to all that adrenalin, you will find yourself out the door before drawing a second breath. Take the time to make every moment count.

Generally, the theatre will have someone to read the other lines. You are the star in this scene. Don't upstage your reader, don't trample all over her lines; you are working together. But you are the star. If you don't get the reading you expect or need, try to use whatever you are given as honestly as possible. The director isn't stupid. He will see that you are reacting to what you are getting from the other reader. Hold on to your character, but don't try to force your version of the scene through like an armoured car.

Be familiar with the scene but don't work at memorizing it. Even if you do know the scene by heart, hold your script. Without it, the director will expect a more developed performance than is possible at this stage.

Do the accent, if the role requires it. But in a cold reading, where the director suddenly decides to hear you as another character or even in another play, don't waste energy on the accent unless you can do it in your sleep.

Musicals

Not everyone can be a singing-dancing-acting triple threat, but anyone can make the most out of what they've got.

SINGING

"I'm not a singer, I'm an actor who sings." That's code for, "I can't sing." But you're probably good enough for plays with songs, where the musical director will work with your two notes and make you look good.

"I'm not a singer, but I could manage chorus work." No, you couldn't. Chorus singers get no individual time, they deal with constant changes to accommodate everyone else, and they dance.

Even if you consider singing an activity to be done naked, wet, and alone, you can use this section to broaden your opportunities for casting. For those of you who are trained to sing clothed, dry, and in public, the following will increase your chances of doing it.

Preparation

There's that word again. Can't we just go in and wing it? Of course we can. And here's the reaction when we do. Bill Skolnik, composer and musical director: "Nothing makes me angrier than an unprepared actor or singer. I want nothing to do with them, no matter how good they've been. It shows a lack of discipline. If someone says to me, 'I just found out about the audition this morning,' that cuts no ice with me. A professional is prepared."

Ongoing singing lessons are expensive, but they're a must if you are serious about auditioning for musicals. Doug Kier, actor, musician, and musical director: "Get a music teacher versed in musical theatre, not opera. Find a teacher you're comfortable with." Music teachers advertise online and on Equity and ACTRA notice boards. Talk to friends who take lessons. Shop around. Most non-singers need to build up their self-confidence as much as their vocal chords, and the right teacher can make a big difference.

Your teacher will help you prepare material that suits your voice and range. Bill Skolnik: "You should have a stable of songs at the ready and keep that stable maintained. You should have about four or five songs of different styles and moods, so that on a moment's notice you can just walk in. Have a patter song, a ballad, a comic song, a semi-classical piece (for those Shakespeare plays)." Doug Kier: "Look through all the musicals; learn the different styles." Tape yourself.

Our tame experts don't always agree about specifics. Doug Kier: "If you can, find out the specific range of the role (top and bottom notes)." Bill Skolnik: "It doesn't matter if you don't know what the exact range of the part is." We suggest that you find out the general range (lyric tenor, baritone with high extension) and prepare material of the same sort that makes you sound good. Our experts do agree on one thing. Doug Kier: "If a director wants you, they'll be willing to transpose up or down a note or two." Bill Skolnik: "If you don't have the top two notes, it won't stop you from being hired."

If the audition notice requires a specific range, they won't transpose for you. If you haven't got the high A, don't audition.

New musicals are a problem. Doug Kier: "Find out the style of the musical, and suit the song to the style of the show. I don't mind actors phoning to find out what they can. Be as prepared as possible. It's better than wasting my time in the audition."

Nerves are particularly dangerous in musical auditions. It's pretty hard to hide the quaver of fear in a sustained note. Bill Skolnik: "Everyone is nervous. I try to make people as comfortable as possible. If it's too bad, stop in the first five seconds. Then do it right — you've got to show that it's just an aberration. Deep breathing helps, so does chewing gum. Bring something to keep you warm. Maintaining a good body temperature helps. Wear something that makes you feel comfortable and good."

According to Doug Kier, dairy products produce phlegm and should be avoided before a singing audition. According to the doctors we asked, all foods produce that coated feeling for some time after eating.

Approach your song the way you would a straight audition piece. Doug Kier: "To begin with, forget the music. Look at the lyrics in the context of the show. Find out as much as you can about the character and how he grows, in the song and in the play. Even if you are only doing part of the song, be as familiar as you can with the full piece."

Choice of Material

Bill Skolnik: "Find something that shows off diction and range — especially diction. You have to show that you can take something musical and still be understood. That is the sort of thing an actor can do as well as a singer, if not better." Doug Kier: "Singing is sustained talking."

Try to find a song that has not been done to death. Doug Kier: "There are songs from very famous shows that are not famous themselves. Also, avoid songs that are identified with a particular singer; they invite comparisons." Bill Skolnik: "It is possible to do a song they've never heard of, but that may focus too much attention on, 'Who wrote that?'"

If one of the audition requirements is to do a song from the show, you do it. If they don't ask for anything, you must decide if you want to sing something from the show or do something that demonstrates you can handle the style, the range, and the energy of the character. Bill Skolnik thinks you should do something from the show; Doug Kier doesn't, although he suggests that you have something from the show up your sleeve, so you could do it if asked. You pays your money and you takes your choice.

Our resident panel disagrees on one more thing. Doug Kier: "It's better to stick to the repertoire. If it's not from a show, it's not musical theatre style." Bill Skolnik: "I can be knocked out by a piece of music, even if it's not from a show. I want to be entertained." (Don't ask us.)

Pick a song you know you can do well. Gary Wedon, conductor and chorus master: "I love to hear people sing easy things. I don't want to see how hard the singer is working. I want triumph, not sweat."

Keep it short. Sound familiar? Unless you are specifically asked to do a long, dramatic piece, less is more. In fact, you are often told the number of bars to sing; in that case, that's what you sing. But be prepared to sing more, just in case.

Presentation

Present the song the same way you would present a speech. You are trying to show the same things, character and emotion, through voice and movement. Doug Kier: "A song's progress is one of action and character. It is not just a beautiful sound; you have to act the words, keep the character." Bill Skolnik: "You have to know your space. Don't sell the song to two thousand people; sell to the four or five people who are there. Don't play to just the casting people. Play to the stage manager, the assistant stage manager, everybody. There's sure no point in playing just to the MD. I've never met a musical director in my life that's got to cast a show. All they get to do is veto."

Selling the number is vital. Fred Silver, author of *Auditioning for the Musical Theatre,* says, "What makes a song a theatrical experience, as opposed to primarily a musical one, is the acting of it." Read his book; he talks a lot of sense.

Accompanist

Bring your own accompanist if you can afford it and if auditioners allow it (check first). You will feel more comfortable with someone you know and have worked with. If you are auditioning for something huge, like *Lord of the Rings,* you will probably have to use their accompanist and lump it. But with most shows, your own accompanist will be fine. Bill Skolnik: "The MD often accompanies, and that's lousy. I can't hear and I'm concentrating on reading the music. That's why it's better to bring your own accompanist." Doug Kier: "Auditions can be ruined by a so-called sight-reader who (a) is nothing of the kind and (b) doesn't know what the word 'follow' means."

Don't be afraid to sing the song in any key that suits you. In the original production, the key wasn't set until late in rehearsals, when the orchestrations were done. If you are cast, you will have to perform in a set key, but you audition in the key that shows your voice at its best.

Make the accompanist's life easier. Bill Skolnik: "Don't bring music where the accompanist has to muck around, flipping pages back and forth. At the very least, you should come in with a legitimate piece of music that shows you can sing and that can be played without a great deal of strain by anyone who sits down at the piano and calls himself an accompanist." Doug Kier: "If the material is in the wrong key, get someone to transpose it for you. Don't expect the accompanist to do it on the spot."

However well you sing, you're judged before you open your mouth. Dixie Neill, McGill University voice coach: "One talented singer was rejected ... because her skirt hem was down. [The artistic director] reasoned that if the singer wasn't conscientious about her skirt, she wouldn't be meticulous about her singing."

After the audition, if you make the cut, you may be asked to stay to read — or dance. Our advice would be to go for it. They know you're not primarily a dancer, but they want to see what you can do.

Dancing

For those of you who are not trained dancers, there is no way on earth you can succeed at a dance audition by faking it.

For those of you who are trained dancers, you know far more about dance auditions than we do. But we asked Beth Russell, talent agent and former casting director for LiveEnt, Anne Wootten, director and choreographer, and Stephanie Gorin, casting director for *Lord of the Rings* for their advice.

Preparation

Anne Wootten: "Besides the obvious prep of showing up in advance and warming up, the best preparation for a dance audition is, if at all possible, to take a class with the choreographer. You'll become familiar with his style, and he will know you and your work."

You can't buy the choreography written out like sheet music, so see the show.

Stephanie Gorin: "It's good to research, to know what the choreographer has done, to find out the style of the show. You've got to be in top physical shape. Don't assume there will be a place to warm up at the audition. Warm up well before you get there, just in case. Make sure you bring water and a snack. I've seen people faint."

Beth Russell: "Be prepared to spend the whole day at the audition. For an open call, we expect three hundred to five hundred people; they will be seen in groups of thirty to fifty and taught one combination. Those who make the first cut will be asked to stay on, broken into smaller groups, and taught further combinations."

Stephanie Gorin: "If you're non-union, be prepared to wait. Equity members are seen first at all open calls."

Clothing Code

There is a definite clothing code for dance auditions. Auditioning for a Fosse production requires quite different gear than auditioning for a Stratford musical.

Beth Russell: "The clothing code will be spelled out in the casting breakdown — different choreographers, for different shows, will want different wear. If you're called for specific casting, you'll be told by the casting office precisely how to dress, and will be given a detailed description of the characters you're auditioning for."

Anne Wootten: "Pay special attention to the footwear requirements of the audition. When the audition notice says 'no heels' it means *no heels*. Since you have to lug a heavy dance bag with you anyway, most dancers throw in tap shoes, pointe shoes, sneakers, soft shoes — everything. You never know when the choreographer will decide to change his mind and add something else to the audition."

Stephanie Gorin: "Don't cover up your body."

Since your dance bag already weighs a ton, a couple of pages of sheet music aren't going to make that much difference. Take them along. Even when singing auditions are happening on a separate day, it is not uncommon for dancers who make the first cut to be held back to sing. Stephanie Gorin: "If they like you as a dancer, they're going to ask you to sing."

Television and Film

There are no general auditions for film and television, no reciting of prepared party pieces. You can sometimes get on a director's list of possibles with a great audition even if you're not cast in that role. Anne Wheeler: "If someone does a great audition for me, I will make sure that I work with that actor sometime."

For the most part, a film or television audition is similar to, but shorter than, an audition for a theatre role. A major difference is that most media auditions are taped — so don't wear black and white. Even with modern cameras, medium shades photograph best.

Your agent should give you the character description, the story outline, and the sides. Read the sides, think about the character, and make strong choices — right or wrong. There are different views about learning the lines (in L.A., we hear, it's often frowned upon). Most people agree that you should carry the sides into the audition, as a safety net, but be absolutely familiar with the script so that your face will be on camera, not the top of your head.

There may be no one present with casting authority, and the gofer-in-a-suit will send the tapes to whoever is casting. Even if the director or producer is actually there, the casting choices will be made largely or entirely on what is seen when the tape is reviewed. Peter Lauterman (producer on *Zack Files* and *North of 60*) says that he uses audition tapes as a filter, but needs to see the person and smell the character before major casting. Gail Harvey (creative producer of *Terry*) adds that producers often fast-forward through tapes if the first seconds don't grab them. Every second on tape should show the energized, focused you. Don't try to second-guess the director. Peter Lauterman: "Trust yourself, make the choices, don't give your impression of what they want to see." You will start the reading by slating yourself, which is media talk for naming yourself and your agent. Give the camera a straightforward, "David Desperate, Ronald Rip-off Agency." Then take a second (no more) to get yourself together and go for it. As with introducing your piece in a theatre audition, use slating yourself as your preparation.

Because one thing is certain: you don't have much time. The authors have been in and out of an audition room in less time than it took you to read this sentence. Well, that is probably an exaggeration, but auditions lasting less than thirty seconds are not unknown. You go in, smile, present your résumé and photograph, read a short scene, smile, say, "Thank you," and you're out. Now, if the director is seeing that fifty times a day, or choosing between twenty pieces of tape before a power breakfast, exactly how do you impress him enough to choose you?

Don't even try. All you can do is present an interested, vigorous you. Offer a strong, honest character choice, and make it as real as you can. After all, what do directors want to see? David Cronenberg, film director: "The audition is often the first time I've ever heard the dialogue spoken. So I'm looking for readings that will make it come to life. Someone who does a wonderful reading, quite different from anything you've expected, can convince you that is a better way to go. That's always very exciting. I try to be completely neutral in my expectations." Gail Singer, film director: "I look for a concentration, an ability to focus on the moment. Even if you are not the right person for this role, you might be for something else."

Concentrate on the reading. David Cronenberg: "What I'm not looking for is a whole routine. I'm not looking for someone to establish a personal relationship with me. I've seen all the tricks and I don't want them. Of course you have a little chat, you say a few words, but you're seeing forty people in a day. You just want to get on with it. I know how vulnerable an actor is in an audition. His response to that pressure lets you know how he might react under the pressure of filming. The more stable you can appear, the better."

Don't be afraid to ask questions. Gail Singer: "An actor should ask for everything she needs." David Cronenberg: "Any questions to do with the actual reading are fine." Listen to what you are told about the character and build that into your reading. And get the pronunciations right.

Often the part is just a couple of lines. How do you make a "strong, honest character choice" with "The doctor will see you now?" Stuart Aikin: "Sometimes characters are just generic — the Doctor, the Lawyer. They are functionaries who are used as suppliers of information, or they get the actor from one place to another. The only thing you can play is 'I want to do my job,' and make a choice as to how you do the job. When you're faced with that kind of character, sometimes a physicality will give it life, create something a little fuller."

If you feel that there are a couple of ways to approach the scene, how do you choose? Go with your first instinctive choice. You can't second-guess the director, so you might as well give him your natural response. "But," says Tina Gerussi, "you have to leave yourself open. If the director gives you a totally different tack, you have to be prepared to let go of your preconceptions and go for something else. Be flexible." If you really aren't sure which would be the most effective reading, ask. David Cronenberg, the actor's director as always: "It would be fine if you could articulate that there are two ways of doing this scene, A and B, and ask which is closer to what the director wants. If the director says 'I'd like to see both,' do both. If he says, 'No, A would kill the scene,' do B. Of course, if you're going to do a reading more than one way, you've got to be sure you do two discernibly different readings."

You may be asked to do something totally out of left field. The director doesn't necessarily think that's the way the part should be played; he just wants to see how you take direction. Jennifer Jonas (producer on *Childstar, The Perfect Son*): "Can you adapt? Are you listening?"

A film or television audition is a close-up shot. The other person in the scene will be out of shot behind the camera, feeding you lines, and you'll be open to the camera. Stuart Aikins: "You don't 'present' to the director. Relate strongly to the other person reading, create a moment of intimacy. Make the director come to you. It's what the camera does." This does not mean that your audition should lack energy. Tina Gerussi: "The hard thing is to try to stay contained in your performance but give it energy at the same time."

As always, effective movement would energize your reading, but on camera, you may not have that choice. Tina Gerussi: "If you are being put on tape, you don't have a lot of space to move around. It's a good thing to learn how to be physical, but at the same time staying stationary!" (Yeah, sure.)

Don't outstay your welcome. They'll let you know if they want you to stay past the reading.

Don't ask the casting director how you did. She may not know. She may not remember. A busy casting director may have organized a hundred auditions for minor characters since yours. Bonnie Gillespie, casting director: "Ask your agent to get [feedback] for you. I can usually have a much quicker conversation with your rep."

With hundreds of submissions from agents, just being auditioned is a great compliment — Gail Harvey says, "If you are in the room, you've succeeded."

Demo tapes may be used late in the casting process for a major role, to resolve a disagreement. Don Carmody (thirty years as a producer, including *Chicago*) says don't send your tape directly to the producer unless you have a reputation and the necessary credentials. Jennifer Jonas: "It's a long shot, but everything is a long shot."

Most directors feel that the casting process is where most of their work gets done. Brigitte Berman, film director: "Finding the right person for the part: that to me is the most terrifying part. You've got to get the right ingredients for the story, the right ingredients so the actors are good together, the right ingredients so that you can work with the person and that person can work with you."

On the other hand, Norman Jewison says the most important thing for a director to have is good shoes.

Commercials

The content of commercials auditions can be very strange; find out what details you can when you get the audition call. The routine is pretty standard. You check in with the casting director and fill in two forms (bring your own pen). The ACTRA form (for everyone, not just members) asks for your name and audition time and when you finally left. Remember this; it may bring you a fee for a callback or a long audition wait. On the second form, fill in your name, height, weight, clothes sizes, agent's name and phone number, your ACTRA number (if any), if you are available on the planned shooting dates, and — most important — any on-air or upcoming commercials. Clients are paranoid about a possible conflict. If you have done a commercial for Dominion lately, the Loblaws people won't want you doing one for them. Put down everything: your idea of a conflict and the client's idea may not be the same.

If you are already booked for one of the possible shooting dates, say so. You may lose the job to someone else no better than you because you aren't completely free, but that's better than being cast and having to turn the job down. Casting directors don't like being let down. And they have long, long memories.

Give the second form to the casting assistant, who will then take your picture. Even though you should have brought your photograph and résumé, they will generally only use their snapshot, which they attach to the form. They will ask you to smile, but give them a look as close to the character as you can.

Arrive in plenty of time to look at the copy. Look for the things that identify your character instantly for the camera. Then look for the quirky details that will make you different. Sometimes you are paired with another actor in the waiting room. If so, get together and work on the copy. If you can develop a strong character relationship, you are both ahead of the game.

ACTRA requires that the lines be visible in the audition room, but you should be familiar enough with the script so that you make contact with the other actor. Learn your first words so that the interaction can be seen. Memorize the last line so that you can "give eyes" at the end of the scene. You should cheat strongly toward the camera. But not down its throat.

ACTRA has finally followed the Screen Actors Guild by charging for improvisation in auditions for commercials. Stay loose, though, and be ready to play the script however they suggest.

Stay open to the other characters, as well. Don't let them drive you, but your character must react to what they give you.

The camera is your auditioner. When you slate yourself, do it with energy and a smile. Give your name and your agent's name, and keep up your energy and focus into the camera until it passes on to the next actor. You will be judged on what the camera sees.

Casting a commercial is a serious process. Director Eugene Beck: "The audition is harder than the day of shooting. What happens on the floor is the least of what directing is. I am matching a person with a given set of ideas. Can you bring life to the part and make it believable? Most parts are unbelievable."

You may be asked to do almost anything, from a major improvisation to simply showing the camera your forearms. You may find this degrading, and you may be right. Part of the problem is input from the advertising agency and their client, who don't understand acting. They'll know what they want when they see it. It's your job to show them. You may be asked to do some awfully silly things. Be prepared to be embarrassed. If you are going to go to commercials auditions, you have to be serious, committed, and positive. (It may help to think of the big cheque.)

Think about commercials not only as good money but also as media work in a concentrated form. Tina Gerussi: "Commercials train actors to get the message across very quickly. I watch for that. When you're casting small parts in films, people don't get a lot of screen time to give out those two lines. Commercials are valuable to do and valuable to see. That's what casting directors do when watching television, concentrate on the commercials!"

Voice Work

If you've got the special skills (a big if), the audition is straightforward. You tape the copy at your agent's or the casting director's or the studio. You don't even have to change your clothes.

Don't get wedded to what you were told when you got the audition call. The director may give you a totally different take on the script, so go with it. In fact, you're pretty much guaranteed some direction and a second take.

Radio

The main body of radio drama (between 60 and 70 percent) comes out of CBC Toronto. Linda Grearson, their casting director, sees actors for a chat and a reading on Mondays. Call her for an appointment. Also, Linda says: "I try to see as many plays as possible. If you're in a play, it's worthwhile sending me a notice in advance; I'll do my best to attend."

CBC Radio Drama in Vancouver is busy, with new producers who are eager to expand its pool of actors.

CBC producers across the country cast their own shows and like getting voice tapes. Beth Russell, former casting director of CBC Toronto: "Your voice tape is the general audition. The cassette tape can be prepared in your own home, whatever costs the least amount of money. Put together a tape of no more than four minutes in total, with an opening monologue that is contemporary, speaking in your own voice — very naturalistic. Then you can do one or two other monologues, whatever you wish. Do a piece with an accent, if you feel you can handle the accent very well. Don't worry about performance quality as long as you slate the tape at the top, identify the speeches one by one, and record them at a level loud enough to be heard when it's played back. It doesn't have to have everything you are capable of doing; just an indication of acting ability and general vocal quality."

People who cast for radio want to match a face to a voice. Always include a photograph with your résumé and tape.

Callbacks

You've made it over the hurdle of the first audition. Now they want to see you again. Why?

- Not everyone with a vote was at the first casting session. The first session's tapes have been thinned out and now you get to see the director. You have seen the director but not the producer. You have auditioned for the artistic director of the theatre but not for the person who is actually going to direct the play.
- They have seen twenty-two Hero's Best Friend and have narrowed their choices down to three. They want to compare you more closely with your competition.
- The engager wants to make sure that there is a good balance between all the characters. You look fine by yourself but may look too old to be the lead's younger sister when you're standing next to her.

Do not try to impress them with a whole new approach. They asked you back because they liked what you did in the first place. If the part has an accent, your grasp of it should be much firmer at a callback. Otherwise, give them the same energy, commitment, and enjoyment you gave them before.

Also, give them a chance to see you in the same clothes. Wearing basically the same outfit will help to identify you.

There will be a great deal more tension the second (or third, or fourth) time around. The stakes are higher; everyone has more to lose. Try to accept it, then ignore it. Directors appreciate any actor who minimizes the stress.

Sex

Unfortunately, sexual harassment and the casting couch are alive and well. Equity and ACTRA, who frown on nudity and semi-nudity in auditions, have strictly enforced rules. Read them in the Agreements, and read about harassment of all sorts in our Chapter 9. If the audition is for a non-union production, you have only self-preservation and your common sense to protect you. The union Agreements will provide you with a useful guideline. Occasionally, directors arrive from out of town and hold auditions in their hotel suites. Nine times out of ten, the auditions are as straightforward as those held in church basements (no vicar-and-choirboy jokes, please). Just watch out for the tenth. If you feel you are being harassed, you probably are. The best thing to do is remove yourself from the situation quickly and calmly, making your lack of interest very clear. You will not be blacklisted; you will not lose work; you will not make your agent angry. If you're a member, inform Equity or ACTRA right away. Don't wait; this is an emergency. Don't bottle it up. Warn your friends. Blow the whistle, loud and clear.

Rejection

You could tell they liked you, you felt good about what you did. Why didn't you get the part? David Cronenberg: "You can't second-guess why you didn't get the part. There are so many things that don't have anything to do with you or your performance. It's just the chemistry of the movie or the style of acting I'm looking for. I know that someone is wrong to play opposite an actor I've already cast. I can know that the minute they walk into the room. No matter how good they might be, it just isn't going to work." It could be your appearance. One of the authors was once told that she was too short to be a mother. Bonnie Gillespie: "Actors don't want feedback. Actors want to know why they didn't get cast. [You] didn't misread the room; the folks beyond the room just had other ideas." Don't take rejection personally. Eve Brandstein in *The Actor*: "Detach your identity from rejection … You are a salesman selling your acting services and that's all there is to it." Don't let rejections affect your enthusiasm or drive. Easy to say, hard to do. Being rejected is a major part of most actors' lives, but you never get to like it. Marsha Chesley, casting director: "We have very few slots to bring people in. I wouldn't waste the director's time … bringing someone I didn't think could do the part."

Nobody likes doing the rejecting, either. David Cronenberg: "I think about the other side, about rejection. I say to the casting director, 'Please let that person know that I thought he was really good, that I like his style, but he's just wrong for this role.'" Not many directors go to that much trouble, but nobody enjoys turning you down.

You will never stop auditioning, however powerful or successful you become — or how old. Eighty-seven-year-old Gloria Stuart won a Golden Globe nomination for her role in *Titanic*, and she had to read for the part. Auditions become less formal, and eventually you may be offered jobs without reading for them first, but the audition process never really ends, it just gets more complicated. Deal with each opportunity as a single step, another try, and one day soon you will be dealing with the hassles in the following chapter.

CHAPTER SEVEN

Get Ready ... Get Set ...

> *"Keep strong if possible. In any case, keep cool."*
> B.H. Liddell-Hart

Your troubles are over. The audition was great and the phone is ringing with a job offer. Sorry, my friend, your troubles are just beginning. You are about to enter the big, bad world of negotiation. Let's freeze that phone in mid-ring and take some time out.

First, you have to decide whether you want to do the job at all. In the early stages of a career, almost any job in the business is better than no job. Any job will give you new contacts. Any job will add to the professional credits on your résumé. But what if the part calls for a nude scene? What if the product you are being asked to promote offends your political or social views? What if the film, in which you are to play a perfectly ordinary bank teller, is actually a soft porn flick? Decisions you make early in your career about the kind of work you are willing to do may affect you years down the line.

Hold on, there's something else before you pick up the phone. Make sure it is an offer, not an availability check. If you are asked whether you are free on Tuesday, April 9, or whether you have any commitments for the months of October and November, those are not job offers. Someone is simply asking whether you are available for work on those days. An availability check may include talk of the program or play, the role, and the money, in general terms, but there is no commitment on either side. Many an actor has had a drink on the strength of an availability check only to wake up the next morning to deal with the double whammy of a hangover and continuing unemployment. A real offer says, "We want you" and lays out what you're doing, where and when you're doing it, and for how much.

Don't touch that receiver! Assuming it is an offer, how do you know the money is reasonable?

Fee Structure

With some leeway for individual negotiation, your fee will be determined in union media work by the size and importance of your role, and in union stage work by the size of the theatre. In non-union work fees are less structured and often lower, but these union minimum fees give you a ballpark figure.

TELEVISION AND FILM CATEGORIES

These are rough-and-ready definitions that change slightly from Agreement to Agreement, and the daily minimum fees are approximate, but for our purposes:

- Principal: a performer who speaks more than ten lines of dialogue or who has a major role with little or no dialogue. Minimum fee: $570, plus residuals.
- Actor: a performer who speaks ten lines or less of dialogue or whose part has individual characterization regardless of the absence of dialogue. Minimum fee: $385, plus residuals.
- Background: a performer whose dialogue is not distinguishable and who has no individual characterization and who performs, either solely or in a group, activities that the ordinary person could do. Minimum fee: $165, with no residuals.

Residuals vary according to the use of the recorded production: the larger the viewing audience, the larger your residual. The fee may be paid for each use, but often the television producer will buy five years free television use for another 105 percent of the original fee, paid with the session fee.

COMMERCIALS CATEGORIES

Television

- Principal: a performer with a speaking role. Session minimum fee: $625, plus residuals.
- SOC: A performer who is Silent on Camera, but has individual characterization. Session minimum fee: $625, plus residuals.
- Background: basically just a warm body to help set the scene. Session fee: $380.

Usually, there is more money to be made per day in commercials than in film or television work. The daily rate is higher, and residuals (or use fees) can amount to as much as twice the original fee every thirteen weeks. In commercials, although the session fee is the same for Principal and SOC performers, Principals get almost twice the residual fees. Background Performers, or Extras, are paid only a session fee, no use fee.

Radio

- Performer: Session minimum fee: around $245, including first use.

RADIO DRAMA CATEGORIES

- Principal: an actor engaged to perform a major role.
- Actor: a performer who says ninety-nine words or fewer.

Principals get paid more than Actors, making radio drama the only occasion on which you may legitimately count your words. The fee structure is based on the length of the program and whether it is going to be aired locally, regionally, or nationally. Half a day in the studio brings in about $315, which includes the first use.

Theatre Categories

Under most Agreements, Equity calculates each theatre's minimum fee from the size of its potential weekly box-office revenue. The richer the theatre, the higher the minimum fee. It doesn't matter if you're Hamlet or his understudy, the minimum is the same. Of course, you can negotiate a fee above the theatre's minimum — at least, you can try. At the time of writing, the minimum fee at a small theatre is less than $550 a week, and for a commercial long-running production in a large theatre as much as $1,075 a week. On tour, you get about $110 a day to cover hotel and meals.

Equity is constantly developing new arrangements to make it possible to stage artist-driven, low-budget, and experimental work. Currently, the SSTA (Small Scale Theatre Addendum) and the "Indie" (Independent Artists Projects Agreement) offer lower fees and more flexible conditions than for full-scale productions.

Co-ops are artist-driven projects where the members of the co-op share the profits — or losses — of the venture.

The Guest Artist policy enables semi-professional companies to engage Equity members from about $535 to $750 a week.

We are talking here about union actors. If you're non-Equity, it's anybody's game, even if the rest of the cast are making union rates.

We know you're getting antsy, but the phone is still frozen and this is a major point.

Negotiation

Negotiation is an expression of the balance of needs between artist and engager. You have something they want; they have something you want. Negotiation is the process by which the two sides come to an agreement on what each will give to and take from the other.

We have all had the feeling of wanting to pay someone for the privilege of letting us work. We have to remember that we have something they want, that they are getting as much from you as you are from them. They are not offering you the job out of the goodness of their hearts.

They want you! If you enter into a negotiation knowing it is a two-way street, you are more likely to get what you need.

If you're hired as a media Background Performer, you don't negotiate, you get the union's minimum fee for whatever you're doing. For other media work, the producer and the casting director decide which roles will be over-scale and allow a little extra for contingencies. Not until you are playing major roles or are much more experienced will you be auditioning for over-scale roles: two-thirds of ACTRA members work for minimum. The expected fee will be part of the casting breakdown, and only a good agent with an excellent case to argue will get you more than the first offer. Therefore, the following section relates mainly to theatre and non-union media work.

Whether or not you have an agent, in theatre the original offer is likely to come to you. So pick up the phone.

Rule #1: Never say yes immediately. (An actor character in a deodorant ad says, "Three rules of Hollywood: never answer the phone on the first ring, never say 'I'll be right over,' never let them see you sweat.") Your job is to get as much information as you can during the first call (role, dates, money, etc.), thank them for their interest, express your interest, and say you will get back to them. In most cases, you will not be given all the time in the world to make your decision. Engagers are eager to get casting tied up as quickly as possible. You must be prepared to be pressured: engagers excel at this game of nerves. And you must be prepared to lose. It is possible for an engager to withdraw an offer at any time if you do not decide quickly enough. However, no engager should expect an immediate unconditional answer at this stage.

Rule #2: Put the phone down and yell and shriek with joy.

Rule #3: Once you are calm again, assess your situation. We are not suggesting that you delay making your mind up just to prove you are not desperate for work, but things are seldom as urgent as they are painted.

If you have an agent, now is the time to get in touch. Your agent will negotiate for you, but it is up to you to set the limits of the negotiation. After all, your agent works for you and should not be making decisions that are yours to make. Since you should know every step of a negotiation, let's assume you're handling things yourself.

Even if the offer comes from the theatre's director, you will be negotiating with the business manager. First, do your homework. Find out as much as you can about the company. Talk to actors who have worked for them. Find out the union minimum for the job. In the breathing space you have given yourself, work out what you would like and what you really need. Make up your mind in advance where you would draw the line and refuse to sign the contract. (We know that the last sounds unlikely, but it does happen.)

In theatre your fee is an important part of the production budget, but even in feature film and commercials, where it is negligible, managements may dig their heels in over an extra two bucks. Decide ahead of time whether you will settle for their first offer if you fail to get more money. If the money is non-negotiable, perhaps the theatre could help out with accommodation. Maybe they would agree to some form of billing. They might say yes to a full-price economy airfare, instead of the cheaper advance booking fare, which gives you less flexibility. Even a poor non-union film production company can guarantee to provide transport to the set or may promise you a free dub (a copy of your scenes) to use in a demo tape.

Rule #4: Practise. Make a list of Things to Talk About. Use a friend to role-play. Improvise phone calls. You may rather enjoy using the phone. It allows you to have all your points written down, and no one can tell that you are actually working from a script. You may find it easier dealing face to face, being able to study the other person's body language, but you must learn to deal over the phone, so polish your telephone skills.

Practise being devil's advocate. Making up arguments for the engager means there will be fewer surprises when it comes to the real thing.

Rule #5: You won't get everything you want. In the beginning, you might not get anything you want. Don't let that stop you trying. If you don't ask, you certainly won't get.

Rule #6: Get it in writing. Legally, a verbal agreement is binding if you have agreed on:

- Role
- Dates (beginning and end of contract)
- Location
- Money

But to avoid a dispute, cover a verbal agreement with a cheerful and excited, but businesslike, follow-up letter, giving the essential details agreed on and an invitation to correct any misapprehensions. The letter should contain:

- Your name
- Name of the production company
- Role
- Name of the production
- Date of first rehearsal and final performance
- Money
- City in which you will be rehearsing and performing
- The wording of any special details you want in a rider (see pages 106–108)

This letter is particularly important when dealing with a non-union company. If the engager has posted a bond with Canadian Actors' Equity, an Equity contract should be available. If the contract is delayed more than a couple of weeks, you should send the letter. But check with the Equity office first; there may be some problems you should know about.

This may seem like tedious and unnecessary drudgery, but it's a lot more fun than arriving at the first rehearsal to find someone else reading "your" part. Oh yes, it does happen.

Rule #7: Negotiation is serious, but it's not war. There is no need to treat management as the enemy. They want to get your services for the least amount of money, and you would like to work for them for as much money as possible. Within those boundaries, there is a variety of options to be explored and discussed. Whatever you do, avoid confrontation. Go into the negotiation feeling that you and the engager are working together to find a solution that is acceptable to both sides. That way, everybody wins.

After you have been in the business for a few years, you will become more demanding. Although you should have developed more confidence and an understanding of where you are in the bargaining hierarchy, don't be afraid occasionally to accept a lower-than-usual offer. Brian Levy, casting director: "Don't restrict your work possibilities by insisting on doing only principal roles. If you do well in an actor role, directors have long memories."

We can vouch for the truth of that. One of the authors was asked to audition for a tiny Actor role in a TV Movie of the Week. She hadn't worked in a while and decided to go for it. After auditioning for the three-word part, she was on her way out the door when the director called her back and asked her to read for another role. She got it. A two-hander — her and the star. (Don't you just love happy endings?)

Don't be too grand to work as an Extra. We know established Principal actors who work as Background Performers on commercials. The money is useful, the work is easy, and who knows, you might get upgraded.

Contracts

A contract is the written record of a verbal agreement. A union contract also relies on the negotiated Agreement between the union and the engagers. If you sign the contract, you are agreeing to all the provisions as written down. So, read it first. If your agent signs your contracts, you should arrange to be told ahead of time exactly what they say. If the contract doesn't appear until the day of the engagement, don't be pressured into signing before you have gone over it thoroughly, despite the sighs of impatience and toe tapping from whoever is handling the paperwork. Take the time to check every section: dates, part, money, and riders (if any).

The engager must sign the contract and initial all the changes and riders on all the copies before you sign and initial; otherwise you are committed without getting any commitment in return. Sign all the copies. Send the union's copy to them yourself. Always keep your copy safe.

A non-union contract needs careful reading. You should look at the ACTRA and Equity Agreements, which are available online, to see what's not covered in your contract. You could also have a lawyer look over the contract. Although seeing a lawyer can be expensive, it could save you future costlier problems. In Toronto, there is an excellent service: ALAS (Artists' Legal Advice Service) has lawyers who give free advice on arts-related problems. If you live anywhere in southern Ontario, it would be well worth the bus trip to take advantage of this organization (see

Addresses). Unfortunately, there is no similar service in the rest of Canada. Unless you have a tame lawyer in your family, or know someone just coming out of law school who might want to practise on you, your cheap choices are limited.

A theatre may ask you to sign an "as cast" contract. This means that the engager wants you but is unable (or unwilling) to tell you what your role is to be. It may be that the director is casting you for an entire season but hasn't finished the specific casting for each play. It could be that a play you are to do is still being written and no one, including the playwright, is sure what characters are going to remain in the script. Whatever the reason, you are being asked to sign a contract with no assurance of the role(s) you will eventually be playing. Your decision to accept or not will have to be based on the reputation of the theatre and director, and on your need for the paycheque. "As cast" contracts are not necessarily bad things, especially at the beginning of your career.

ACTRA engagers must provide free accommodation for out-of-town work. Equity engagers must provide an accommodation list with prices — but only if you request it — and who pays is negotiable. Find out what the accommodation includes and where it is in relation to the theatre and public transit. Both ACTRA and Equity Agreements specify who pays for getting you to the out-of-town location at the beginning of the job and back home at the end. In non-union work, accommodation and travel are both negotiable.

A signed contract before you start work is your only legal protection. Union engagers are obliged to have you sign before you start, and union actors are forbidden to start without having signed. Usually you will receive a theatre contract well in advance, giving you plenty of time to remedy any errors or omissions. ACTRA contracts often don't arrive until the first work-break. If you start work without signing, you are tacitly agreeing to all the provisions in the contract and are legally bound by them. The least you should do, when told the contract is not available, is say you should have it now and you must have it as soon as possible. After the shoot, tell your agent and ACTRA what happened.

On media jobs, at the end of the day, you should be asked to sign a time sheet, which is a record of your hours worked and breaks. You will sometimes be asked to sign a blank time sheet before the work has been started, not from any evil motive on the part of the management but simply because it makes the production assistant's life easier. CBC Radio Drama is notorious for doing this. All around you, actors older, more experienced, and theoretically wiser are signing blank sheets. The pressure for you to do the same and not to make waves is enormous. Try to resist; it's like asking you to sign a blank contract. Engagers don't often make mistakes and will pay out when overtime is due, but be aware that if anything goes wrong, you have signed away your power to fight. (The authors sign the time sheet and add in brackets "Signed blank" or enter the time it was signed.) If you are working as a Background Performer, you will be given an Extra voucher at the start of the day's work, but it will be filled in and signed when the work is done.

Riders

A rider is a special provision added to a standard contract. Until you get major casting, your union media contracts won't include riders, so this discussion is about theatre and non-union film and television. Riders must be agreed on before they are written into the contract; you should not be expected to sign a rider you have not discussed. More times than we care to remember we have received theatre contracts with great lists of riders added by management, none of which had been discussed ahead of time. Often they are harmless, unremarkable, and unnecessary, and all you can reasonably do is sigh inwardly and sign. But other riders are not so harmless, unremarkable, and unnecessary, and they must be dealt with before signing. The easiest way to avoid problems is to ask the business manager during negotiation if the theatre has any riders it wishes to add. (Something to add to your list of Things to Talk About.)

Anything can be added as a rider to the contract if both parties agree, and, in the case of a union contract, if the Agreement allows. If you want the theatre to provide babysitting services for your child and they agree, put it in the contract. If Smalltime Films agrees to drive you to the set, put it in the contract. If the engager is sincere about these extra provisions, it shouldn't mind adding them as a rider. If they assure you there is no need to put it in writing — beware! If these people don't want to put their signature where their mouth is, chances are they have no intention of doing what they promised.

A rider's wording is crucial. Compare: "The theatre agrees to provide babysitting services for the artist's baby while the artist is in rehearsal or performance" with "The theatre agrees to provide babysitting services acceptable to the artist for the artist's baby at all times that the artist is engaged in theatre business, which includes but is not limited to performance and rehearsal calls, wig fittings, wardrobe calls, publicity interviews, and photo calls." See the difference? The most crucial phrase in the second, improved version is "acceptable to the artist." This means that when you arrive at the theatre with your bundle of joy, you won't be greeted by the director's Aunt Lucy, ninety-three years old and whacko, who cheerfully admits that she loathes children but she's getting a free ticket to opening night for babysitting. Or, if you are so greeted, the theatre cannot say, "Well, you wanted a babysitter, there she is. We have fulfilled our contractual obligations." The clearer and more precise the wording of the rider is, the fewer chances there will be of misinterpretation or disappointment.

Negotiated billing is a fairly new development in non-commercial theatre, although Equity's negotiations with theatres have opened the question of promoting individual artists. R.H. Thomson once said, "There are no stars in Canada. To have a star system, you need the proper mechanics.... We have it in hockey, but practically nowhere else." Well, we're making a start.

At the beginning of your career the question of billing is likely to be academic — you aren't going to get it — but it becomes more important as the years go on. Even early on, it could be a bargaining point with a small, non-union production. The production may not be able to pay as much, so to sweeten the deal it agrees to give you some sort of billing. It costs the engager nothing and makes you feel good. The billing rider can go on and on. Does your name appear on the poster and in newspaper advertising? How large is it? Does it come first or last or somewhere in the middle? Above or below the title? Are you mentioned in publicity releases every time the production is mentioned?

Billing is a tangible sign of your worth to the production. (In many cases it is also a tangible sign of how tough your agent is.) Although most managements still shy away from it, we hope billing will become a standard part of contract negotiations.

The Golden Rule: You don't get what you deserve, you get what you negotiate.

Job Conflicts

It is a cliché in this business that either no one wants you or everyone does. Actors can go for months without a nibble, and then be presented with two jobs at once. And, life being what it is, the jobs will overlap.

What do you do? How do you decide which one to take? (Remember, no one can make these choices for you. Your agent and your friends in the business can advise and suggest, but only you can decide.) What are the factors you have to weigh? In no particular order they include money, role, prestige of the theatre or film/TV company, location, director, length of contract, and your gut reaction. You are rarely offered the perfect job, so decide what your priorities are in each case. The play is exciting but the money is dreadful. You want to work with a particular director but the part is not one you feel comfortable with. You don't care for the script but it means doing a scene with Johnny Depp. The pay is great but the show is touring northern Manitoba in February. One job is a brilliant showcase for you, the other job will get you out of debt. One show is a pilot for a possible series, the other show is a secure ten-week contract. Just to complicate matters further, there will come a time in your career when the type of role you play will determine your decision. If you have been offered your sixth pathological killer, do you accept, knowing you will be successful, or do you opt for something new and challenging at which you might fail? All these questions boil down to: "How will this job affect my career?"

All you can do is find out as much as you can about the offers, take a good, hard look at your present artistic, professional, and financial situation, and get advice and suggestions from people whose opinions you respect. And don't forget your gut. Sometimes an immediate, instinctive reaction is as good an indicator as anything.

You are going to make wrong decisions. It is inevitable. Comfort yourself with the knowledge that some of the greatest learning experiences come from bad choices, and besides, you get far more entertaining stories out of disasters than successes!

Research

There is not much you can do to prepare for most media jobs. Get people's names straight; be sure you know how to get to the set; iron your character's shirt, the one you used at the audition; solidify the accent you managed to get a shaky hold on. With one scene and three lines, this ain't *Hamlet*. Later on, or if you are a big fish in a co-op or small non-union production, your preparations will be more like those for theatre.

Once your theatre contract is signed and sent, you may think you have nothing to do until your first day of rehearsal. Wrong. Flesh out the research you did before you had the job and signed the contract. Find out more about your working conditions, the people, and the place. Talk to people who have worked with the director or at the theatre or in the city, if it's out of town. If you know other people in the cast, great. Chances are you won't know many. Again, see if you can discover something about them. This isn't crucial — after all, you will find out soon enough if you are going to love them or hate them — but it can be comforting just to have a basis for a conversation at the first coffee break. Very little of this will be possible for media jobs, but you might ask around about the director's way of working, or watch more of her work.

A theatre that's bringing in actors from out of town often provides an information pack about the city: restaurants, cinemas, laundromats, public library, main post office, bus routes, city maps, etc. It usually contains specific theatre information as well: theatre doctor, dentist, chiropractor, bank, and lots of company rules and regulations. All this information is vital, but you won't usually get it until your first day of rehearsal. If you get into town a day or two ahead of time, it would be comforting to know where to find your nearest supermarket, drugstore, liquor vendor, and other services necessary to life and ease. Before you leave home, go to your public library or go online and look at a street map of the relevant city, if only to get some idea of where the theatre is.

Going out of town demands planning ahead. We know what we do — a finely balanced routine based on running around in frenzied circles — but we thought the following might be useful. We are grateful for tips from a friend, Adale O'Brien, in her excellent book *See the U.S.A. with Your Résumé*, published by Samuel French.

Are you going to sublet your apartment? Make sure you've got notices up in laundromats, the union offices, your agent's office, and neighbourhood supermarkets, describing the place and the dates available. Tell your friends to keep their eyes and ears open. If you find someone (preferably through a mutual friend), put the sublet agreement in writing: beginning and end dates, who pays for what, instructions about pets and plants, no sub-subletting, fuse box details, phone bill arrangements. Get them to sign and date it.

Arrange for mail forwarding. Type up a stack of labels with the theatre address and buy some big manila envelopes. Get your flatmate or sublet (ask nicely and supply stamps) to shove your mail in an envelope every so often. It's cheaper and sometimes more reliable than Canada Post's mail-forwarding service. Stop the forwarding ten days before you're due back.

If you are planning to drive to your job and it's out of province, find out what the provincial laws are concerning registration. Some provinces assume that if you are living in their fair land for longer than thirty days, you have become a resident and must re-register your car. Check that your insurance covers you out of province.

Make sure your provincial health care insurance is aware that it is receiving bills from some nasty foreign province because you are temporarily resident there. Otherwise, they may decide after some time that you have changed your base, and they will stop your coverage. Ask your provincial health care department where you should write to assure them that your heart is true and faithful and you will be coming home. Otherwise, you could find yourself uninsured in both provinces.

If you are on any sort of medication, tell your doctor how long you will be away so that you can stock up on enough pills and potions. Take your optical prescription. Carry these (along with your script and any necessary theatre information) on the plane with you. Be safe — carry a change of clothes and a face cloth, too: luggage gets lost.

Find out ahead of time, if possible, how well equipped your accommodation will be. In any case, take the following items: sharp knife, can and bottle openers, corkscrew, rubber spatula, non-stick frying pan, saucepan, coffee/tea maker(s), salt and pepper, herbs and spices, and a couple of J-Cloths. You won't be able to take your entire kitchen and bathroom with you, so your first shopping trip will probably include paper towels, detergent, cleanser, toilet paper, Kleenex, soap, laundry detergent, and light bulbs, as well as your food staples.

You will also want an alarm clock, a radio or cassette player, an extension cord (the lights are never where you want them), a bath towel and washcloth, a hair dryer (for home or the theatre), vitamins, and Aspirin.

However busy you are going to be, don't lose contact with the outside world. Your "office" will need your address book, writing paper, envelopes and stamps, photographs and résumés, stapler and staples, calendar or diary, scratch pad, pencils, and pens. If you take your laptop, you'll need to find a secure place to leave it. Don't forget scissors (for office or kitchen), Scotch tape, and needles and thread.

Will you be ready for the weather? In this country, unless you are performing in Tuktoyaktuk, where the temperature is a pretty constant -40°, you should take at least two seasons' worth of clothes, a bathing suit (there's always the Y if the ice is still on the lake), rehearsal and workout gear, and at least one reasonably grown-up outfit for the first night.

The item you are most likely to forget? Your alarm clock. Don't ask us why.

And you thought you were going to have nothing to do. Most important, the time between signing the contract and starting work is the perfect time to research the play and the part, particularly if it is a period piece. Phillip Silver, designer: "As a designer, you spend a lot of time researching the way people look, the way they behave, the way in which they move. Often you find that the ... actor himself hasn't done the legwork. You design a lovely pile of costumes, put them on the actors and (a) the costumes don't look right and (b) the atmosphere of the world you're trying to create historically doesn't look right, because nobody's bothered to look at a John Singer Sargent painting to see how ladies held their hands in 1885. I would like to see actors spend more time on understanding the world out of which the plays they're working on come. Look at pictures, listen to music. Actors think that it's enough just to read the script, to be able to say the words, to breathe properly, and to do interesting movement. It's not. There is a whole world you are trying to create." Kate Greenway, former stage manager: "Think about what you can bring to a project. If it's a period piece, outside your own experience, do some research. I am amazed at the number of people who don't. It's important not only for your individual character but for the general ambience."

A warning: if you arrive and find the designer and director have made choices that fly in the face of your research, your information is wrong. Not really, of course, but they have made their choices to serve a larger purpose (the budget, say), or they may not have done any research at all. Don't make the mistake of setting yourself up as a bigger expert than those who hired you.

If there is a script available, get it ahead of time. Even with a classic piece, they may be working from an edition with subtle differences.

Once you have received the script from the theatre (try to get them to send it with the contract), you have the opportunity to read and reread without any pressure. Take advantage of it. You will soon be caught up in the rehearsal process, where unpressured time is more precious than rubies.

CHAPTER EIGHT

Get Set ... Go!

"A mystique has grown up around acting.... but [the stage] is where you do your job and find the satisfactions that come with doing well the job you like."
Claire Bloom

Theatre

The Nightmare: You arrive at the rehearsal hall for your first day of work. Who are all these people? The play has five people in it; there must be forty-five in the room. Where is the director? Someone shoves a cup of coffee in your hand, tells you she is Publicity and they need that hundred-word bio ASAP. (What?) Suddenly, the room is emptied of all but a few, and the director is giving a little speech about the play. You double-check your script. Yes, he seems to be talking about the same piece; why don't you recognize it? It is time to read the play. You listen desperately to the other actors, with one trembling finger holding the place in the script where you first appear. *They are all wonderful! They Are Getting Laughs! What am I doing here? ... Wait a minute, he's not so great. Why didn't I get that part? Oh, no! I'm next. Here goes ... Oh, God, that was terrible. I want to die!*

Enough! What seems to be a nightmare is actually a typical first day of rehearsal. It's overwhelming; it's challenging. It's terrifying; it's thrilling. You're at the top of the hill, ready to ski down. It's scary, but it's also as exhilarating as hell.

In order to introduce all facets of theatrical production, we have imagined a theatre that is relatively large and well-off. In reality, your play's budget and schedule may mean cutting down to the bone. Your rehearsal period may be a few snatched evenings, your play may still be in rewrites, and your theatre may be the back room of a pub.

But we all start from nowhere and end when the run ends.

First Day

Quite often, you will not be rehearsing in the theatre building. Stage management should inform you of this ahead of time, but it is just as well to check. Lauren Snell, production director and stage manager: "Make sure stage management can get hold of you. The stage manager has her own anxieties. If you are not going to be at the contact number the theatre has for you, make sure your agent knows where you are." When you speak to the stage manager or ASM (assistant stage manager), she should tell you how far the rehearsal hall is from your digs and how to get there. If she doesn't tell you, ask. If she doesn't know, she will get back to you. It's part of her job to see that you have that kind of information.

Many theatres get their whole work force — secretarial staff, technical crew, Publicity, Wardrobe, designers, actors — together for the first morning with a "Meet and Greet." Some of these people you will never see again in your five- to ten-week stay. Some you will see far too often. Usually, there are doughnuts and coffee, everyone is introduced, and the general manager or artistic director makes a little speech of welcome. You then mix and mingle and try not to look as terrified as you feel. Remember, you're not the only one suffering. Not only are the other actors nervous, however well they hide it, the stage manager is nervous, the director is nervous. They have responsibilities you have not even considered. Introduce yourself to as many people as you can. Try to meet the head of Wardrobe and the designer. If the stage manager is doing her job, she will make herself known to you. If not, find her.

Some directors encourage the support staff to stay through the designer's show and tell, the director's chat, and the read-through. Other directors clear the room immediately after coffee and doughnuts. Whatever the decision, the actors' preferences are not considered.

The designer(s) will run through their work: the set, scene changes, and costume designs. Evan Ayotte, designer: "The designer's main sources of information (like the actor's) are the script, which he has read over and over, and his discussions with the director." Before you shriek with horror at your costume design, read about the designer's budget and schedule realities in Chapter 9.

The director's little talk — and not all directors give them — can be about anything: what the play means, how he will approach it, how to act, the value of teamwork, the sanctity of his decisions. Don't worry if you find yourself disagreeing with his vision. Those concepts can change during the rehearsal process, as the director becomes influenced by what he is getting from the actors. Whatever he says, it will give you an insight into the person who, for the next few weeks, will affect your life more than anyone else.

Although many directors and designers are sensible, caring people wearing "Safe Sets" badges, there are just as many who demand, "I don't want it safe; I want it Tuesday." Watch out for yourself: you don't have to do or use anything you consider unsafe. That's not just common sense; that's the law. The problem is, we are often our own worst enemies, wanting to be seen to be keen, afraid of being labelled a poor sport or a troublemaker. But we're getting ahead of ourselves.

The read-through is full of stress. Remember; you already have the job; you don't have to impress anyone with how good you are. This is not a final performance, just a chance for everyone to hear how the whole play sounds before it is taken apart and worked on piece by piece. It is tempting to judge other actors' work by a first reading and to assume they are doing the same with you. Don't. It is a waste of energy. Just get on with reading the play as honestly as you can.

If this is an Equity cast, the Equity actors will elect a deputy. The deputy's job is to act as liaison between the theatre management and Equity. The deputy works with the stage manager to avoid potential problems, ensures that the theatre pays all overtime and travel expenses, and much more. Only union members may elect the deputy, and all non-union members, except apprentices, must leave the room while the election takes place.

The stage manager will hand out information packs to out-of-town actors. These will contain an assortment of goodies, such as maps of the area, lists of restaurants, drugstores, cinemas, banks, supermarkets, liquor stores, and interesting sights and activities. You will probably get scene breakdowns and a proposed rehearsal schedule as well as a performance schedule and other theatre information: theatre doctor, dentist, chiropractor, bank, and lots of company rules and regulations. Even if you don't ever read it, don't leave it behind! It's an insult to the SM, who has spent much time and effort compiling all the information. The SM will also discuss company business such as rehearsal times, meal breaks, the day off, and payday.

Usually the theatre has asked you, by letter or in the first phone call, to bring your publicity material. They may have asked you to send it as an email attachment, but if you don't have a digital photo, they will have to make do with your headshot. Lauren Snell: "With things like your bio and photo, please bring them if asked. Other people have severe deadlines." This is the "hundred-word bio ASAP" from the nightmare. Every theatre publicist has a program deadline in two days and needs a brief blurb to put by your name. They may offer to whip something up from your résumé. Don't let them. They'll only put things in you want left out and leave things out you want put in. Do it yourself. Try to see their program bio style first.

You may get your measurements taken later in the day. Often the theatre sends you a chart ahead of time, which asks you to measure everything you can reach and many things you can reach only with the aid of an intimate friend and a stepladder. Please do it. After you have filled it out and handed it over, you will find that Wardrobe wants to do it all over again. (Don't ask.)

When all the business is completed, you will finally get down to the real reason for the next few weeks — rehearsing the play.

Rehearsals

We are talking here about mainstream theatres, following the rules set out by Equity and theatre managements in negotiation. The rules are based on experience, so smaller, experimental, and non-union theatres tend to follow them, but the hours of work stretch and the breaks tend to be forgotten.

A rehearsal day is usually seven hours out of eight and a half (or eight, if you have a short lunch break). Rehearsals can be as short as ten days in summer theatres to four weeks in some of the larger provincial theatres. (The two large festival theatres, Stratford and Shaw, have quite a different set-up. You can rehearse for months, since several plays are rehearsed during the same period.)

Some directors begin by having the cast read the play several times, with discussions between read-throughs about character and relationships. Others begin by blocking the play, getting the actors up on their feet right away. Even the process of blocking may vary from one director to another. Some have very clear and specific ideas of where they want the actors to move; others know the broad shape of the action but let the actors feel their way around the acting area before deciding exactly where they should go. The stage manager writes down all the blocking as it develops. Lauren Snell: "Write down your own blocking, it's a help. It means the stage manager doesn't have to split concentration and coax an actor over to the right side of the room by waggling her head towards the general target area."

Although in theory the theatre may have you at rehearsal all day long, in practice you are usually called only for those hours the director will be working on the scenes you are in. Mind you, very few directors manage to keep to their schedules, however hard they try, so be prepared to do some waiting.

In the bigger budget shows, rehearsals will be broken up by costume fittings, wig fittings, and, possibly, publicity sessions. Evan Ayotte: "Ideally, you should have two costume fittings. The first is a silhouette fitting, just for shape and fit. The second is for the details and balancing elements. The actor should come to the fitting prepared to gesture and move in character. The actor should realize that a good designer is there to give the actor's ideas about the character a visual reference, as much as the director's ideas." Raise any concerns about costume safety now; changes will be more expensive or impossible later. You should have passed on your concerns as soon as you saw the problem, but the designer may not have thought about your bangles in the fight scene or known that the director had given you candles to light when you wear the shirt with the long, gauzy sleeves. Evan Ayotte: "The actor should consider the fitting and talk with the designer as a further extension of the rehearsal period."

With few exceptions, rehearsals are closed to anyone other than cast and stage management. This allows you to experiment, and if necessary make a fool of yourself, in private. Toward the end of rehearsals, you may have people dropping in. They are not there to watch you perform but are concerned with the technical aspects of the production — lighting, sound, quick changes of set and costume. Each new person who comes in raises the anxiety level by one notch.

By the end of each day's rehearsal, the director and stage manager will have worked out a schedule for the next day. It is up to the actor to get that information; it is not up to the SM to give it to the actor. Lauren Snell: "Any stage manager worth her salt will feel paranoid if she hasn't given the actor the call herself, but it's not always possible. The director might not give the call until 5:55 and you've been released at 3:00. It's a help if you call stage management. Even better, when you leave at 3:00, let the stage management know you'll be calling just after 6:00."

To begin with, you will be working with rehearsal props and furniture, with the scenery marked on the floor in tape. When you start rehearsing, you will probably not want to work with any props, since one hand will be holding the script and the other will be holding a pencil and turning the pages. As you learn the lines and start to come off book, good stage management will have rehearsal props for you to work with. Be aware that all the clever business you invented is going to disintegrate once you start using three-dimensional objects. It is amazing how difficult it is to set a table with real plates and cutlery — and how noisy. The next step can be even more painful. Having got used to the wooden rehearsal gun, going to a totally different performance gun is a nightmare. And another nightmare is the necessary distraction of learning the safety measures involved in using a firearm. Be patient with yourself. All these transitions are a natural part of the process. No one expects you to get it right the first time. Which is just as well.

As rehearsals go on, the physical moves become more important. This is the time when accidents happen, before the routines are set and while adrenalin is up. Fights and dances are obvious times when you are physically at risk, and part of the job of the choreographers and fight directors is to be aware of this. Peter G. Hurley, Fight Directors Canada: "No actor should be placed at risk to perform [action sequences]."

Daniel Levinson, president, Fight Directors Canada: "Stage combat is dangerous — safety rules should be non-negotiable. Fights should be rehearsed on an open surface that's clear of all debris with enough room to move both people and weapons safely. The space should be set up to be as close a replica as possible of the actual performance space. It's very important to have the tables, chairs, and, when available, the levels that the actor will be moving on and around. The fight rehearsal should have complete control of the space. Don't try to hang lights, paint flats, warm up, or run some other part of the show in the same space as the rehearsal."

Even in ordinary rehearsals, accidents often happen when new things are added. If you ask for a moment to think the new situation through, you'll get it. The law, and common sense, says that no one should do anything she considers dangerous. One of us fell headlong down a flight of stairs wearing costume shoes that didn't have dance rubber on the soles yet. Don't let enthusiasm make you careless.

Line learning is an individual process; there is no right way. A few actors come to a new play off book, having learned their lines beforehand. Some directors will pressure you to do so, despite rules saying in effect that the theatre can't tell you what to do until they are paying you. Line learning in advance can save rehearsal time (i.e. money), but decisions made in advance, in isolation, can shut off the discoveries to be made during rehearsal.

Many actors learn their lines in rehearsal, so that the lines and the blocking are absorbed as a unit. During the day, when people are not actually rehearsing, you will see groups of actors running lines. There are actors who hate doing that and find that being alone at home, with the script or a tape recorder or a spouse, is the best way to learn. A drawback of the tape recorder is the time it takes to record everyone else's speeches in the scenes you are in. However, it does mean that you are independent of the other actors when you wish to study. Be prepared to have forgotten every single line the first time you lay down your script. We wish we had a dollar for every time we're heard someone (ourselves included) say, "But I knew it on the bus!"

Be prepared for another shock when you run the whole play for the first time off book. This process is called, with good reason, a stumble-through. To say that it will be an unmitigated disaster is to be kind. Most of your energies will be taken up with "Which scene comes after this?" and "Is this the exit we changed yesterday?" and "God, this is going fast. Did we leave anything out?" Don't let the shambles upset you. It is part of the natural process, and within a week you will wonder what all the fuss was about. Work out a consistent routine for prompting with the SM. Let her know if you want her to call out the line or to let you struggle with it. Lauren Snell: "I sit there and see an actor with a wonderful strangulated look. Is he saying, 'Don't give it to me; I'm really trying to learn it' or, 'What's the matter with you? Why aren't you giving it to me?' Trouble is, it's the same look. Let me know ahead of time. And whatever you use — 'Line,' 'Please,' 'Yes' — be consistent."

Another transition to overcome is moving from the rehearsal room to the stage. Suddenly, you seem to have less space between pieces of furniture; there are stairs where there used to be a flat surface; the acoustics of the space are different. In the rehearsal room, there was eighteen inches between the end of the acting area and the wall; now you have hundreds of feet to the back of the auditorium. Everything is on a slightly different angle. The sightlines dictate your entering from ten feet farther back so that all the timing has changed. And on and on. Don't panic. This, too, will become familiar and easier to work with.

Tech Week

Simple shows have two light cues — on and off. In more ambitious productions, as opening night approaches, you may feel the actors are becoming less and less important to the production. They are. We are entering the world of the techie. Don't worry, the actors come into their own again, but these rehearsals serve the technicians. Remember, most of them have little or no idea about the play. Now they rehearse their work and learn the rhythms of the production. Now they discover how the set and costumes work, how well the designers foresaw the actors' problems when they made their drawings. Tech week (or production week) needs patience, patience, and more patience. It is the time to hang on to what you've discovered in rehearsal. The best thing you can do is keep out of the hair of the techies and the stage manager. Look what has to happen between the close of one show and the first tech of the next:

- The last show's set is struck and carted away to storage or to the dumpster.
- All the furniture, props, and set dressing are sorted and then returned to lenders, stored, or trashed.
- Costumes are dry-cleaned, mended, and sent back to the rental house or stored.
- Much of the lighting is struck; most of the colour gels are stored.
- The new set is assembled on stage and the basic lighting is hung and aimed.
- At least some of the furniture is put in place, supplemented with old friends from the rehearsal room.

About now, the actors arrive, all perky after a day off and eager to get on. The crew has been working with minimal breaks since curtain down on the last show, and look what they still have to do:

- Hang the rest of the lights, re-patch the board, focus and fit the gels. Put together the sound FX tapes and place the speakers.
- Finish painting the set.
- Hang the doors, build offstage stairs and platforms, carpet offstage walkways, set up masking flats and backdrops.
- Rig practical lamps, fireplace effects, rain, explosions.
- Fix doorknobs, locks and catches, light switches.
- Connect telephone, radio, stove, refrigerator, sink.

Even in this well-off theatre, tech week may in fact be as short as thirty-six hours, followed by a technical work-through, a dress rehearsal, and opening night. This is not the time for an actor to bring up any artistic problems. If it isn't solved by now, find a way to live with it. During this time, everyone is tired, overworked, nervous, and self-absorbed. Tempers are short. The best thing you can do is be available and keep out of the way — read a book, do a crossword, play cards, talk about how good you think everyone is, look at your script. What you do not do is complain about things outside your control.

These days run as long as twelve hours (much more if it is a non-Equity company). You may arrive at noon and not get near the stage until 4:00 p.m., although you have been on call all that time. When there is a break for coffee or lunch, take the opportunity to get out of the theatre. A change of air can freshen you up.

You often start technicals with a cue-to-cue (Q to Q) rehearsal. Instead of your going through the whole play, the SM will ask you to start a few lines before a technical cue — the hall light going on, the sound of an approaching car — and then carry on until the SM tells you to stop. (If you have a quick costume change, don't be afraid to ask for time to practise it before the Q to Q. Sometimes, because of time constraints, the Q to Q is the only technical rehearsal you have before the tech dress, where you will not be able to stop when things go wrong.) Q to Qs often turn into tech work-throughs, where you do the whole play but expect to be stopped when there is a technical problem.

The tech run-through is where the techies learn how long they have between cues, so don't stop unless the set falls down. Make a mental note of any problems; the moment you exit, write them down or you'll forget them until you reach the same point in the next run-through. Pass the information on to the stage manager at the note session after the run. Nine times out of ten the SM will have noticed it anyway, but there is always that tenth time.

The technical dress rehearsal, or tech dress, is the first time all the elements of the production come together. Although some directors don't mind if you do the tech dress without make-up, it can be useful to wear it, particularly if it is a heavy character make-up or if you are wearing a wig. Before the tech dress there is occasionally a formal costume parade, where you all troop out in costume to be seen by the director and designer. Often the director dispenses with a formal costume parade and uses the tech dress to observe and make notes on wigs, make-up, and costumes. He discusses these notes with the designer, who is making her own, far better and more detailed, notes, and then with the actor.

After the technical dress rehearsal comes the full dress. There may be an invited audience, but the real intention is to assure everyone that they can do it right at least once. If it's any comfort, a bad dress rehearsal traditionally means a good opening night.

PREVIEWS

Previews are designed to help the actors and director judge the audience response to a play. They are a particularly useful barometer for new plays and comedies. You will be able to find out more precisely where the laughs are in a show and where you will have to wait for audible reactions. (It is amazing how often cast and director can misjudge where a big laugh comes. Things that had everyone rolling about on the floor in rehearsal do not raise a titter in performance, and those lines you all felt should be cut bring the house down. The preview is the place to discover all this.)

Theoretically, everyone has less riding on a preview. It is made clear to the audience, by the fact that the tickets are cheaper, that they are not getting as finely tuned a production as they would see later in the run. Actors are assured, "It's just a preview. Use it." However, no matter how clearly we know on one level that a preview is just another chance to clean up and fine-tune and discover, we still treat previews as though they were "real" performances. Your first preview is, in effect, your First Night, without the cards and presents. There you are with lights, costumes, sets, props, and a real live audience. What actor could treat it like just another rehearsal? Your body certainly treats it like the real thing, with surges of adrenalin to help you fight this dragon of a play.

The director is likely to give notes after the previews, including what he has learned from the audience reaction to the work. Although there still may be some rehearsals until opening night and after, what you are performing during the previews is basically what you will be performing for the whole run. (There are some exceptions to this, particularly with new works, which can alter drastically from preview to performance, and even through the run, as audience responses reshape the work.)

Some theatres, because of time and budgetary restrictions, do not have previews. In that case you are thrown right from your final dress rehearsal into your ...

Opening Night

It's here! The night you have all been waiting for. Even if you have had a week of previews, there is still something special about openings. Maybe it's the knowledge that tonight the critics are in the house. Maybe it's the sight of the First Night cards and bottles of wine. Maybe it's the fact that you are throwing up in the toilet. Whatever it is and however it affects you, there is no denying that opening nights are unique. There is a buzz of excitement and energy that you feel at no other time. It is a remarkable natural high that can be as addictive as any controlled substance.

The Run

You've done it once. Now do it again. And again. And again. Keeping a performance fresh, clean, and alive is the mark of the professional. It is easy to give a sterling performance on opening, when the adrenalin is coursing through your veins. Try doing a similar performance three weeks later at a matinee, when the house is only a quarter full, three cast members have the flu — and you're one of them — two people aren't speaking to each other, and you have to do it again tonight. Try doing it three months into the tour, after riding in the van all day. Try doing it on a stage that won't quite hold all the set. It is your responsibility to perform, as closely you can manage, the play as rehearsed. We are not saying that the show shouldn't change. Of course it should — and will. But those changes should come out of delving more deeply into the text, discovering nuances in the playing, and exploring avenues there was only time to touch on in rehearsal. A production is able to absorb and incorporate such changes. What we are saying is that you have to sustain your performance, avoid tinkering, and bring to each show as much energy, enthusiasm, and concentration as you did originally.

The stage manager will see to it that you stay on the straight and narrow. Once the director leaves, it is the stage manager's responsibility to maintain the production. This may mean giving the actors notes. Lin Joyce, stage manager: "Actors don't consider the stage manager 'artistic' personnel and find technical notes easier to take than 'artistic' ones. They should trust that the rehearsal period is imprinted on the SM. She was there all the time and knows how you got what you got and why. Many actors have an automatic balk reaction to notes from a stage manager." Lauren Snell: "The stage manager is the person who has to keep a perspective on the whole thing. We are the ones who watch every night."

One final point: however many times you have done the show, the audience is seeing it for the first time. These people deserve as fresh and vital a show as the first audience. "Just a matinee" is a lousy attitude.

Industrials

Industrials are the live-performance equivalent of commercials. Here, the product is the star. You may be dancing and singing the joys of a Toyota Camry, or demonstrating good employer/employee relationships for a large corporation. You can rehearse as we have just discussed, or you can create a piece by improvising around a basis scenario. Performances are rarely more than forty-five minutes and can be as short as five or ten. You can do as many as ten performances a day, depending on their length.

If you have the skills necessary for this kind of work, it is worth pursuing; there are solid financial rewards for a small commitment of time. Actors are routinely treated as honoured guests, which makes a refreshing change.

Cruise Ships

Jay T. Schramek, performer: "Many ships have two lead singers and about six to eight backup dancers. Usually the backup dancers mouth vocal tracks, but the leads are live. Most do Vegas-style revue shows, some do Broadway stuff, some Disney, etc.

"Ship life is an entity unto itself. If you've ever lived in a small town, think about that with about twenty different cultures divided into jobs and status according to what nationality you are. I worked way too hard, was treated awfully, for little pay at best. Still, ships are a great way to see the world; a great way to make a lot of money, as you have no overhead. I paid off my student loan very quickly.

"It is the epitome of non-union work. There are no days off on a ship. You rarely, if ever, have any privacy. You are constantly 'on.' Passengers are both a terror and a delight; travelling Americans are beasts that make Medusa look pretty.

"My exposure to the world changed my life, and most importantly the ships offered me a chance to make some of the worst professional mistakes without affecting my work reputation here."

Thanks, Jay. We know a guy who came off cruise ships and bought a house — and another one who gambled on board and lost everything. Your choice.

There is other non-traditional work around: we discuss self-production, including co-ops and fringes, in Chapter 12.

Film and Television

The time frame in media work is tightly compressed. The whole process can take as little as a week from the time you audition to the end of your contract.

For a Background Performer, the time frame can be a matter of a day from start to finish. You get the call one day and you turn up at the set the next, wearing one costume and carrying changes of clothes. You sit with your Extra voucher tucked safely away. You are called, mill about on set, sign your voucher, and go home. Being an Extra is an exercise in patience, keeping cheerful and alert while being herded around like half-witted sheep. It's a real skill, and people make a good living at it, but generally it's a means to an end. You may never meet any of the talent (the Principal or Actor category performers), but you will be able to watch some of the work. It is a great way to learn to be comfortable on set.

By and large, Extras don't have to deal with wardrobe calls ahead of time, make-up, and the technicalities of screen acting, so the rest of this section is aimed mainly at Principal and Actor work. Read on anyway. The more you know about the whole picture, the better a Background Performer you'll be, and the more you'll learn on set if you mean to move on.

Wardrobe Call

Usually, before your first day of shooting, you will have a costume fitting. Even if your agent has already given them your measurements, someone from Wardrobe will phone you to find out what they are. At the same time, they will tell you the time of your wardrobe call. When you get there, you are likely to be presented with a couple of costumes. The first will be impossible to do up, the second will fit the star fullback of the Winnipeg Blue Bombers. So much for measurements. Evan Ayotte: "You are not always presented with, 'This is your costume.' You may just have a range of skirts or blouses to try on. They will be acceptable for the broad strokes of the character and Wardrobe will generate something out of it." The smaller the part, the broader the strokes.

Time is short, including the time you are in the costume. Evan Ayotte: "I can make use of pins, gaffer tape, or whatever for alterations. It doesn't matter. The actor will wear the costume for eight hours, not eight shows a week for four weeks. I haven't time to do proper alterations. I've driven Extras casting people crazy by saying, 'We can't use this actor, he doesn't fit the costume.' It's easier to change the actor than the period evening clothes."

Depending on what you are playing and the size of the role, you are likely to be asked to bring in some suitable clothes of your own. If you are doing a low-budget, non-union film, that request is a certainty.

In union work you will be paid for two hours at the contractual rate for a wardrobe call, even if Wardrobe has needed you for only fifteen minutes. The money for this call is over and above the fee agreed on for the job. If you are not offered a time sheet at the call, make sure the assistant director (AD) adds the call to your time sheet on the shooting day.

Script Changes

After the wardrobe call, you wait patiently for an AD to phone you with your call time. During this wait, especially with episodic television, you may be bombarded with different versions of the script, as rewrites come in. Each set of changed pages will be dated and each will be typed on different coloured paper. Check the changes. They may be small and technical and barely affect you, or they may cut out your favourite scene. Either way, there is nothing you can do about it. Sometimes you don't get these versions until the day you shoot, but in any case they make for interesting and colourful reading.

CALL TIMES

It is now the evening before the day you are supposed to be shooting and you haven't heard from anyone. Don't panic. Very often the director can't tell until the end of one day's shooting what the next day's schedule is going to be. Sometimes the shooting schedule is upset because of weather conditions. Just as often, there is a delay because of technical difficulties. (It is a rare television or film schedule that is delayed because of trouble with an actor.) Be prepared for your call time, or even the actual day of shooting, to be changed. On a union job you will be paid for a changed shooting day unless they tell you a day in advance, but the actual time they want you can be changed, without pay, at a moment's notice. If you're not available for an earlier call, you can tell them without having to give a reason.

Finally, you are phoned by the second or third AD. Important: get this person's name. Write it down. Write down your call time and the address of the set, or where the transport pickup will be. Resign yourself to the fact that you might be called as early as 5:30 a.m. and comfort yourself with the knowledge that one day's shooting pays as well as one week's work in the theatre.

Before you go to bed, get your stuff ready for the morning. Yes, we know, but your mother was right. You will need:

- Comfortable clothes that won't spoil if they're piled on a chair all day.
- Warm clothes to layer on if needed — you'll feel cold until you are fully awake, and television studios are notoriously cold.
- Any clothes or accessories you agreed to wear as the character. (Take off your rings or personal jewellery, unless you were asked to wear them in character.)

Take a shoulder bag or something easy to carry. In it:

- Emergency cash — not a lot because you don't know how good security is going to be.
- Script, character notes, any names of people you have found out, and the time and place of your call.
- Light reading, a crossword book, knitting, embroidery, letters — whatever will help you pass the time quietly and keep you relatively alert while waiting. We think it's reckless to take your laptop, but some people do.
- Lighter and cigarettes if you must.
- A toothbrush.
- A little treat in case things start to collapse around you.

You will be glad of this preparation when you are trying to kick-start your heart in the grey light of dawn.

Shooting Day

You may have a gofer pick you up, in which case your life is in his hands. If you are travelling under your own steam, arrive even earlier than the godawful hour you're supposed to. You will need the time to get yourself together. There is total chaos: dozens of people doing incomprehensible things, no one paying you the slightest bit of attention. If you were picked up, the gofer will know where you should go; if not, at least you have the second or third AD's name. You did write it down last night? You did bring it with you? Good. Find someone who doesn't seem to be handling anything vital and ask for your AD. That is your contact, the person you must see before anyone else. The AD will welcome you cheerily, point out where to change, and guide you to Make-up.

Make-up

This is the one call of the day you can rely on to be on time. Here is a quietly supportive group of experts who see it as part of their job to make you feel good about yourself. This is where you get yourself together and find out how the day is likely to turn out. This is Gossip Control. These people know how the scheduling is going to turn out in reality, who hates whom, and where you should be going next. Make friends with these people. They are sympathetic, helpful, and caring. Once you have been made up and combed, you will wait until you are called again.

WAITING

You'll get into costume either before or after your make-up and hair calls. Either way, you will be ready far too early. With luck, at this point you may be told to wait in a cubicle in the honey wagon (the dressing trailer). More likely, the wardrobe person or an AD will point out a communal lounge or three lawn chairs beside a Porta-Potty.

On any set, you will do more waiting than working. You will wait to get on the set; you will wait between shots; you will wait between scenes; and you will wait to be cleared at the end of the day. This is why you brought your book or your knitting. You can't spend all day talking shop to strangers, fascinating as that may be in small doses. Your job is to walk on the set when they want you, ready to give the performance they hired you for. Don't gear yourself up too early for your scene; by the time you get to it, you'll have no energy left. Don't compulsively read and reread the script. Once you have checked with the AD that you have the current version, leave it to your subconscious. Nadia Venesse, dialect coach: "Over-memorizing leads to inflexibility. You'll find it more difficult working with the dialect coach or director if your reading is totally set." If you want to stretch your legs, make sure an AD knows where you have gone. The worst sin on set is wasting other people's time. Don't make them come looking for you. In some organizations, and depending on the situation, you may be allowed to watch other scenes being shot. This is the best way to learn, without the tension of your work being recorded. Nadia Venesse: "Just make sure you stay out of the way. Extras and day players seem to gravitate towards doorways, the worst place you could possibly stand."

EATING

There will generally be coffee and doughnuts around somewhere all day, and meals every four or five hours. Try not to go overboard with food and drink. Most actors find it impossible to resist the lure of free food, and the food on film and television shoots is generally excellent. However, if after lunch you have a scene that needs energy, it would be as well to have the blood coursing through your veins rather than sitting in your gut, trying to digest the lasagna you have shovelled down.

ON SET

The call comes at last and you head for the set, not forgetting your costume pieces and props and your own shoulder bag. In small projects, you may be able to discuss with the director, before you get onto the set, what the scene is about, any questions you may have, and any specific route he wants you to take through the role. Don't expect this in mainstream media work: some directors do make a point of at least touching base with even the lowliest day player, but it's rare. Normally, you will be expected to work it out for yourself. According to director Gail Singer, "Lots of new directors don't know how to direct actors. They don't understand the acting process. In their own training they tend to use fellow directing students as actors. Also, some directors haven't worked on the text sufficiently to articulate to the actor what is needed." In studio work, the director may stay up in the control room and communicate through his floor manager (or first AD).

Down in the studio or out on the location set, you will be appalled by the chaos. Cables in all directions, lights on and lights off, lights humming and occasionally smoking, men and women looking confident and competent, with titles like gaffer, craft services, focus puller, clapper loader. Dire warning: don't touch the equipment. This is for your own protection. The equipment itself is rarely dangerous, but a glare from a union technician can kill at forty paces. Marc Green, sound recordist: "I can't stand it when someone blows into the mike! It puts pressure on the mike it's not built for and it puts moisture in it, which causes static. And it's a great way to destroy my ears."

It is likely they called you as they were finishing the previous shot, so that when you arrive they will be setting up the camera and lights for yours. They may have called you early and are still shooting. Obviously you won't walk into a studio when the "recording" light is on, but you won't get that warning on an outdoor set. Look for the cameras; catch an eye and ask where to wait. Wait there. Watch what's happening. Learn what you can — just a basic understanding some idea of what and why. The chaos will begin to have a shape, and you will see that the director has many threads to keep an eye on. You are only one.

ACTING AT LAST

You sometimes hear that a director has fought for a week of rehearsal with his major cast before shooting starts. This might happen once in a blue moon, and even then only the leads will be involved.

Reality is different for the rest of us. Deirdre Bowen, casting director: "The audition is your rehearsal. That's your one-on-one time with the director." Rehearsal amounts to a couple of run-throughs on set, to work out the blocking and set sound levels. You've got to bring your audition performance with you, and be prepared to change it to a different one if they suddenly don't like the one that got you cast. This is particularly true in episodic television.

In a feature film you may have more time. David Cronenberg: "What I like to do is block it just like theatre. At that point, I'm inviting the actor to participate as fully as he can in shaping the scene. Of course, I'm always keeping the visual elements in mind — what will work and what will not — but at that moment I'm completely open to actors' reactions and suggestions. I think it's odd to hire someone you think is good and then not invite them to participate in the movie." We should all be so lucky. But Mr. Cronenberg also understands how things usually work. "Actors must be aware of what the context is. If it's simply 'say the lines and don't bump into the furniture,' then do that." In many assembly-line productions, our work in smaller roles is just raw material. Clever editing will add the subtleties in post-production.

You will start with a master shot, which sets up a relatively simple framework showing all the action. Then the highlights are added:

two-shots showing detailed interaction, cutaways varying the camera's point of view, and individual close-ups. The whole is assembled in post-production, where the editor and the director establish the rhythm of the scene. The master shot establishes the general trend, and the later shots must fit in.

Close-ups are used in two ways: to give prominence to what you are saying and to show your reactions to what is being said to you. The most important information is in the tiny changes of expression, tone of voice, or focus. You'll need all your concentration, especially since you may be talking to part of the set to make your eyeline look right for the camera. If you are in a close-up, don't be afraid to ask the cameraman how much of you will be seen. There is not much point in doing something deeply significant if you are doing it out of frame. Don't be afraid to admit your ignorance and ask questions. No one is going to think any the worse of you because you don't know what a key light is (but see the Glossary). We all have to have a first time.

When you are told to stand in a particular place or move in a particular way, that is where you must stand and how you must move. If it is awkward or unnatural, too bad. You are rarely asked to do something without a good reason, usually technical, but you are rarely told what that reason is. If you can find a reason for your character to make this bizarre move, that is great. It will make you feel more comfortable and will probably read better on film. Just don't expect it to come from the director.

You do what you're told … up to a point. ACTRA and the major producers have elaborate safeguards against abuse, harassment, and actual physical danger, but even with those, you have to be ready to defend your rights. In union film and television, danger is the specialty of stunt performers. If you are asked to do something that is outside your experience and would normally be considered hazardous, you can simply refuse and say that it is a stunt performance, or you can agree to do a "risk performance," with an added fee. This extra pay acknowledges the danger, but it won't stop you breaking your neck. In non-union productions, you are certainly going to have to look out for yourself.

At the end of shooting a particular set-up, the sound recordist may want to lay down a minute of ambience. Every scene has a pattern of sound we don't consciously hear that will be needed for sound editing in post-production. If you cough during this minute, it starts again.

The biggest difference between the media and stage is the possibility of doing a section over until it is as good as possible. At any time during a shot, but generally at the end, you may be asked to do all or part of it over, to do a retake. Most retakes are either because of technical faults or because the director wants to have some editing choices. Remember that every time you do a take, it must be physically as close as possible to the previous take. Marc Green: "Try to keep the volume level the same for each take. It's OK to go from whispers to shouts, as long as you do it on the same word each time."

One of the most valuable people on a set is Continuity. She (for some reason they are almost always women) is responsible for ensuring that each take looks like the take before. If your sleeves were rolled down and you roll them up before the next take, it is Continuity who gets you to roll them down again. Quite often, she will take a Polaroid of you so that there is a record of how you looked at the end of the scene on Tuesday, because they are going to shoot the beginning of the sequence the following Monday. This is one reason to stay in position at the end of a shot until you are cleared.

Shooting out of sequence is one of the most difficult things to master. Unlike stage work, where the climax comes naturally out of what has gone before, in film or television, the end of a scene can be shot days, if not weeks, before the beginning. An argument in a scene may move from the kitchen to the garden and end in a summerhouse. The studio set for the summerhouse is ready now, the location for the garden is available next week, but we can't get access to the actual house until the end of the month. Get a clear idea of the whole sequence so that you can understand where each shot is in the context of the entire piece. The better you know your character's detailed story, the easier it is to pick up shooting at what is, for you, an arbitrary spot. Gail Singer: "You have to come to terms with the way film and television are shot. You simply can't experience development; you have to find what you can in the scene, the line, the moment. Any development — age, time of day, emotional state — can only be experienced in your script work." Brigitte Berman: "I've learned about the extraordinary vulnerability of actors.

They are relying on the director, when shooting out of sequence, to judge the strength, the emotional depth of a scene."

DAILIES

The dailies, or rushes, are all the shots that have been filmed that day, hastily developed, and "rushed" back to be viewed to make sure no unforeseen problems have shown up. In a feature film, you certainly won't be invited to watch the dailies unless you have a major role, and sometimes not even then. On smaller shoots, the rushes may be open to everyone. David Cronenberg is as remarkable as ever: "I always let actors see rushes, but I don't think that's very normal. The crew can be inhibited if actors are present. It's difficult for me to say to Make-up, 'I hate the way that actor looks' or for the DOP [director of photography] to comment, 'Do you see the way the light catches his bald spot?' if the actors are right there."

In television, and in film if they are running tape while filming, you can sometimes have a tape played back for you to look at immediately after a take. Even if you are not in a position to ask for that, you can certainly watch other people's scenes on a studio monitor and compare that with the live action. Doing this gives you a general idea of how action and emotions are translated onto screen.

The first few times you see yourself on film or tape, your overriding feeling will be one of deep depression coupled with hideous embarrassment. (Do I really look that awful? Why am I doing so much? Does my nose always twitch every time I start to speak?) Try to be as objective as possible. Learn as much as you can. How far is your idealized version of the scene from the actual image on the screen? Nothing teaches as well as actually seeing it in front of you.

COURAGE, MES BRAVES

Gail Singer: "I want an actor, even a small player, to want to be good. There could be something vital in a tiny performance that will give you something special on the screen." David Cronenberg: "It doesn't matter how small the actor's role, I'm happy to listen if it's honest discussion of the work."

But these brilliant, open-hearted directors live in the real world. David Cronenberg: "If it's one take, then do it. There's no point in trying to turn it into something it can't be." Gail Singer: "There are some who would rather talk than do. Better to make a decision, do it, and let the director say yes or no."

Student Films

From David Bronfman, actor: "I have had some amazing experiences working student films, as well as a bucketful of terrible times. Insist on reading the whole script before accepting the role. If for whatever reason this is refused, that's a great big flag saying you should get out now. Read your release form. Don't sign it unless you agree with it. The standard ACTRA student film release form gives actors a right to refuse the film being used for anything other than screenings, festivals, or advertising related to the school.

"Don't be afraid to ask for extra takes if you feel you can do a better job. Students try to conserve precious inches of film.

"Expect students to sometimes grow frustrated and vent anger at each other. This is a great time for you, the actor, to go on a coffee break.

"Expect to be called for pickup days and ADR. I've been on shoots where entire reels were out of focus or underexposed, and sound is possibly the most poorly produced aspect of student films.

"Don't expect to get a copy of the film without a fight. Email, phone, show up at their doorstep. It's amazing how quickly actors are forgotten. Contact the school if you do not get a copy after a reasonable amount of time.

"In the end, student films are a great way to gain on-camera experience; but they should always be done with the knowledge that everyone else on set is also trying to gain experience."

Commercials

In general, commercials for television are shot in the same way as an ordinary television program. A commercial is typically a fifteen- or thirty-second play to sell a product. The biggest difference is the importance of your timing: it is measured to within one-eighth of a second. One of the authors once did nineteen takes of an eight-second speech because she was consistently a quarter-second too slow. Eugene Beck, a commercials director, says, "You must be a good actor, with the same talent and skills as for any other job, plus the insensitivity for commercials! A problem is that commercials tend to be overwritten for the allotted time; advertisers attempt to put too much in. As a result, the actor is forced to speak too quickly and often has to group words together in a difficult or unnatural way."

Because commercials are so short, they deal even more than regular television in readily identifiable, recognizable types. Within these types, the clients are looking for ordinary-looking people. Gone are the days when only glamorous models were used for commercials, although they are still used for beauty-care products.

In all other ways, working on a commercial is like working on an ordinary television program. The same number of people milling round, the same long waits before you get onto the set. The technician is still king, but now the product is the star. The writing, however flawed, is Very Important. It has been thrashed through proposals and committees and focus groups and has now been Approved. The product, however grotesque, is Very Important Indeed.

Eugene Beck again: "The best actor is calm, interested, hard-working, and has a sense of humour. I try to keep the atmosphere on the set easy; there is a lot of tension and anxiety coming from the client and agency. They often continue to suggest 'improvements' even after everyone knows the job is done, so the director and cast do retakes with a shared smile, just to keep the suits happy. I am very aware that time is money and I must do the commercial in a businesslike manner. It is art for commerce's sake."

Time may be money, but less caring directors than Mr. Beck try to save time by risking lives. In a notorious case, ACTRA performers were asked to walk on an aircraft wing as much as thirty feet off a concrete floor. Two members called ACTRA, but by the time the steward arrived it was over. One member refused to walk; the others risked their lives for $400.

Some actors and teachers scorn commercials. Almost half the actors asked by *InterACTRA* about their work in commercials either declined to answer or asked that their names not be published. Why? Acting in commercials is a skill. The people involved in making them have talent and commitment. Eugene Beck: "It is far better to do three or four commercials a year than to wait on tables. It will give you enough money to get your act together and the freedom to keep auditioning." There are actors who make a handsome living from commercials and enjoy the work. It is a well-paying, legitimate way to practise your craft.

Voice Work

Envy the rare, lucky actor with a flexible voice, an excellent sense of time, and an agency with a reputation in the voice-over field. For there you have an actor who works all the time, doesn't have to leave town, and has a six-figure income.

Voice work is the single most lucrative area for an actor. Voice-overs are used in television and radio commercials, training and industrial films, and documentaries. Some actors have made entire careers from voicing animated productions. Some voice work is done outside the main centres, and you can get it through personal contacts with engagers. In the large centres you need an agency to get into the field. Even if you have the vocal dexterity and the range of off-the-shelf voices and accents they need, engagers concentrate mainly on a few hot agencies.

Voice work routine is simple. For a program of any length, you may get the script ahead of time so that you can familiarize yourself with its shape and content. For a commercial, you arrive at the studio, read over the copy, put on the headset, and do it. This may sound easy, but the skill involved is considerable. And the suits continue to make suggestions.

Don't fall for the "Be a Broadcast Star and Make Big Bucks" ads. There are very few on-air host and voice-over jobs, and they are done by a small number of specialists. For most of us, voice work is a profitable and enjoyable sideline at best.

Radio Drama

There is little radio drama work in Canada, compared to film and television, and the vast majority of it is done by the CBC. At present, up to 60 percent of drama programs originate in Toronto and 40 percent originate in "the regions" (a nasty Toronto word for anywhere that isn't Toronto). Regional stations also produce drama for the local markets. There are around five hours of network radio drama a week.

Most actors find radio the least pressured of all media work. There is rarely the same sense of urgency and racing with the clock that one feels so strongly on a film set. The process of getting the play onto tape is, from the actor's point of view, a straightforward operation. You arrive at the studio to see that, as on the first day in theatre, everyone except you knows at least one other person. You all sit round a large table with coffee and your scripts. The production assistant (PA) will pass around a blank time sheet, which all the actors will unthinkingly sign (see Chapter 6), you have a read-through, the director might say a few words, you get up, do a sound check for voice levels, rehearse each scene once on mike, and record it. Rarely will you do more than a couple of takes on a scene.

Radio is usually, though not always, recorded in sequence. Sometimes narration will be recorded separately, so that the action of the play isn't interrupted.

TECHNIQUE

The most important facility a radio actor must have is to lift the script off the page, which is another way of saying that it should sound as if you are talking, not reading. This is a technique that can be learned (practise with a tape recorder), but a simple trick is to keep your script up at face level, not bend your head to the script. Not only does holding your head up help give the impression that you are really talking, it means that the mike will catch what you are saying. If you are sitting at the mike, sit on the front edge of your chair to open up your diaphragm. Remove the staples from your script before approaching the mike. Nothing shows up a beginner more than script rustle. The microphone is a sensitive instrument that seems to have a knack of picking up all the wrong sounds, script noise being the worst. Removing the staples also makes it possible for you to carry only the pages you actually need for the scene, leaving the bulk of the script back on the table. Be careful of your breathing. Perfectly ordinary breathing in real life can, if you are placed close to the mike, make you sound as if you are in the final stages of emphysema. Listen to all your own faults — a simple popping "p" or whistling "s" can ruin an otherwise perfect take. A sympathetic studio engineer can cure almost all your faults, but most directors prefer to record over and over, and not rely on technology. It is terribly frustrating to have to do a big speech over again because of an avoidable technical fault.

If you do make a minor error in a speech, most directors like you to pause briefly and go back to a natural break in the speech to do your own retake. Other directors hate this. Wait for someone else to show you what the house rules are.

Now that you understand everything about the work process, let's discuss how to make that process as painless as possible.

CHAPTER NINE

Job Etiquette

"Life is too short to be small."
Benjamin Disraeli

Love thy neighbour as thyself. That's it, really. If you can remember that all the people you work with, from the lowliest apprentice to the highest-notched director, take pride in their work and have egos that need stroking (just like you), you will have no trouble getting along with everyone.

Actors inhabit a strange position in the business hierarchy. On one hand, we are at the mercy of all — from the producer and director who cast us, to the props, costume, lighting, and camera people who can make us look and feel as good or as bad as they want. On the other hand, we are the only really essential people in the business. You can record a scene on your cell phone. You can put on a play without sets or costumes or lighting. Try putting one on without actors. Lauren Snell, stage manager: "The audience is coming to see the play, not the set or the costumes. It's the actors and the words. Ultimately, the whole structure is there as a support so that you can get the best performance possible from that group of people."

The creative and technical staff have the power to free you from worry and allow you to commit yourself totally to the work. They also have the power to make your life a living hell. It's up to you.

Let's see how the "perfect actor" gets through the job …

Theatre

… Again, we're using as our example a fairly elaborate production in a formally organized theatre under Equity contracts. Your situation may be different: the designer and the wardrobe department and the dresser may all be the same person in your production. The basic advice is the same.

THE PHONE CALL

You will get a phone call from your stage manager or ASM in pre-production week. Lin Joyce, stage manager: "The perfect actor is always glad to hear from the SM. The actor asks questions about the first day of rehearsal — Where is the rehearsal? Is there parking? What's the rehearsal room phone number? She then pays attention when you give the answers. The perfect actor always comes clean about anything that might affect rehearsals. She doesn't assume the producer has passed on any pertinent information to the stage manager, so she tells the SM that it was agreed a day's rehearsal could be missed because of a film. She mentions allergies, epilepsy, diabetes, any medication. She says that her nursing the baby has been okayed. Whatever. If the call hasn't come by the middle of the week before the first day of rehearsal, the perfect actor calls the theatre."

FIRST DAY

Start as you mean to go on. Be on time. On time means early. If a rehearsal is called for 10:00 a.m., it means that at 10:00 a.m. you are working, not walking through the door, or hanging up your coat, or finishing your cup of coffee. There is never enough time to rehearse a play. Do not waste what little time you have. It can be frustrating to be ready on time and have to wait for the director. It is his prerogative to be late, not yours. He could be dealing with one of a thousand crises. His delay is unavoidable. Your missing the bus is not. Even on the first day, which will probably start out with a leisurely "Meet and Greet," don't be late. You're part of a team. However, try as you may, there will come a day when all of nature and technology conspire against you. Lin Joyce: "Call to say why you're late. The SM won't have to worry about what's happened to you, will explain the situation quickly, and the rehearsal carries on. They won't have to stop when you arrive. That way you waste the least amount of time." When you are late and the rehearsal is going on without you, don't make a lot of fuss. Apologize to the SM, unobtrusively if you can, as soon as you arrive. Apologize briefly to the director as soon as there is a natural break.

The first day of rehearsal includes finding out the ground rules. Lin Joyce: "The perfect actor comes to the first rehearsal wearing layers of clothing so that he can either strip off or add on, depending on the temperature of the room, which is never good for everyone!" Most smokers are aware that they are now in the unpopular minority, and they try to be discreet about their smoking. If you are a vehement non-smoker, you'll have to be tolerant.

Costume Problems

In the previous chapter, we discussed the designer's show and tell. The costume design will probably come as a surprise, and perhaps a shock. Before you say anything, remember there is no point in complaining about something you can't change. If you are playing First Burgher or Bar Room Floozy you'll have to learn to work with anything that isn't actually dangerous to wear.

Depending on the details of each situation, you'll have to decide if you're going to speak out, and who you should speak to. Phillip Silver, designer: "There is no set protocol for approaching a designer, as long as it is in keeping with the workings of the theatre. The main thing about these discussions is that they should not become confrontational. It is important that the actor listen to what the designer has to say as to why certain decisions were made." Evan Ayotte, designer: "Actors should never feel embarrassed about questioning something they've heard from the designer. A good designer will want to hear what an actor has to say."

In the best of all possible worlds, your comments and suggestions would be acted upon. Phillip Silver: "What inhibits a designer's ability to accommodate an actor is often stuff that is not in the designer's control. Some of it may be budget. We've bought the fabric already and we don't have any money to buy more. We've no money to buy the wig that you want, or we've bought the wig and I'm going to be in big trouble with the producer if we don't use it. A designer may be paid a flat fee for a certain number of designs. If you have problems and you are going to cost me more time to get it right, for which I'm not being paid, I'm not going to be the happiest person on earth. In a 'concept' show, an actor may want changes that are absolutely valid but which upset the balance of the total picture."

In other words, you may have the power to speak, but you may not be able to get anything done. However, there's still hope in the fitting room. Evan Ayotte: "Generally, the first place to begin an approach is after the show and tell, because the designer has just talked through his ideas. If that isn't possible, if you're going straight into a read-through without a break, then in the first fitting."

The costume fitting will put you into close contact with design and wardrobe staff, so wash and deodorize before you show up. Don't be offended that we mention so obvious a thing. Wardrobe people unanimously selected body odour (followed closely by bad breath) as the thing they hated most about having to deal with actors. We forget that the results of our emotional and physical work in rehearsal may be offensive to those who end up with their noses in our armpits.

Fittings are part of the rehearsal process and should be treated with the same seriousness. Don't be late. Evan Ayotte: "A fitting is not a break. There is a growing number of performers who feel that a fitting is a rest from rehearsal. It's not. The actor must be responsive to the needs of the production. The designer and cutter aren't wearing the costume. You have to tell them if it's uncomfortable."

Depending on time and budget, you may have to live with poor fit and discomfort. But you never have to compromise on health and safety. Stand up for yourself when any element of the costume, wig, mask, or footwear constitutes a health or safety problem. You shouldn't tolerate wearing material you're allergic to, especially if you informed the stage manager of your allergy during the first phone call. Wigs and headgear that don't fit properly or are too heavy can create headaches and neck strain; spirit gum can cause rashes. Masks that don't fit or that have inadequate eye holes can dangerously impede your vision. Uncomfortable, ill-fitting shoes can cause foot and ankle injury.

It's not always easy to call a time out to raise health and safety concerns. Public opinion, the law, and your union contract are on your side, but ultimately someone has to speak. Let it be you. Treat the matter as inarguable; just raise the problem as soon as you know about it and assume a proper solution will be agreed upon. If you're polite and firm, a reasonable management, director, or designer will acknowledge that something has to be done and you won't be treated like a diva. When people aren't reasonable, the pressures of time and budget will be raised, your team spirit and commitment will be questioned, or your complaint will be ignored. Suddenly you're on your own. Your fellow actors, who privately agreed that something must be done, don't support you in public. What do you do? Equity protects its members from health and safety violations, but if you are not a member, and repeated protests to higher authorities don't change things for the better, you have two choices: take what precautions you can and run the risk, or refuse to work until the problem is fixed. Refusing to work is your legal right, and you may have to exercise it.

Rehearsals

There are as many ways to approach a play as there are directors and actors. Most drama schools have their own strong method, and it comes as a shock to find that other people work in quite different ways. Keep yourself open to new ideas and new methods. If the director challenges you with a new approach, don't cut yourself off. Go with it. There is no right way of working.

There are directors who care only about the product. The process is up to you. In that case, work in whatever way you feel most comfortable. Don't expect other actors to work the way you do, but don't feel pressured to abandon your way of working. Many directors don't want to juggle a variety of approaches, and so they dictate their own. If you find after a good try that you can't work that way, don't attempt to change the director's habits. Don't fight him every inch of the way; use what you can of his method, and then work on your own to achieve what he wants.

Process and product are not necessarily related. We have been in plays where the rehearsal process was smooth, stress-free, exciting, and challenging, and the production was dreadful. We've survived rehearsals of trauma by the truckload, feuds, and factions, ending up with a thrilling, smooth-running show. Go figure.

The way to keep the process as painless as possible, however weird the approach, is to maintain a sensitivity in your work relationships with members of the cast and support staff. Be aware of technicians' needs. The support staff is proud of its role in the team. Lauren Snell: "Recognize the human being behind the function." Know when to joke and kibitz and when to keep your mouth shut.

Do your job the best way you know how. Lauren Snell: "The main thing that makes life easier for stage management is if the actor does his job well, if he is committed to the show. Spend time on the piece outside the rehearsal hall, come to rehearsal with fresh things. Work well with other members of the company. Try not to destroy all the props on the first day! There is something about a person who gives 100 percent of himself that sheds light on the whole process."

The rehearsal period is not an audition. You do not have to compete with the other actors, fight for recognition, or impress the director. You have enough on your plate doing what you're supposed to be doing. Concentrate on your character, its development and relationship with the other characters, and your own relationship with your workmates.

When you have a problem, who do you go to? Start with the stage manager. That's why she's there. Lauren Snell: "If actors go head to head artistically, I have some kind of guideline to follow, but if it is just personalities, count me out. Except that these things can escalate onto the stage. Then it's my responsibility. The ideal actor retains a professionalism and a commitment to the work that doesn't allow those things to happen." In most cases, you should be able to approach the director personally with artistic problems, but for a young actor who may be diffident about doing that, the stage manager is a bridge.

Personal problems between actors need not affect the working relationship. You can play a fight scene with a person you truly like; why not a love scene with someone you really hate? Some of our best work has been with people we wouldn't be seen dead with outside the job.

If the director suggests an "improvement" that you think is no good, what do you do? Try it. It doesn't work? Try it again. And we mean really try it — don't just give lip service to the suggestion. If it still doesn't feel right and you're First Burgher and A Floozy, our friends at the bottom of the hierarchy, you have to live with it. If you have more clout, you might be able to raise the matter later.

There is always something in a production that refuses to go right. You may eventually have to accept that it simply doesn't work and grit your teeth and do it. Acting, like politics, is the art of the possible. There will be inevitable compromises owing to lack of time, money, and (other people's) talent. We've said it before: Don't complain about things outside your control. Your job is to make what can work, work. You have only so much time.

Ah, time. That rare and precious commodity. Don't waste it. Be punctual. Learn your lines by the deadline. Do your homework. On the other hand, don't be afraid to ask or discuss. Never feel that you and your part are too unimportant. Just be sensitive to the needs of the whole group. Let the director judge whether you are wasting time. Believe us, he won't be shy about informing you.

Voicing safety concerns should never be considered time-wasting. Nor should insistence on rehearsing a potentially dangerous move slowly, step by step, until you feel secure enough to do it at speed. It isn't necessary to turn a concern into a five-act drama, but a request for enough time to practise the slap or the fall downstairs is only professional behaviour and not a waste of time. Daniel Levinson, president, Fight Directors Canada: "Actors have a professional obligation to be honest and forthcoming with the fight director and their colleagues about their stage combat experience, level of ability, and physical limitations. They are within their rights to withdraw from the fight if they feel that they are in physical danger, and should be encouraged to voice any concerns they have about their safety during the rehearsal process." In an Equity production, the theatre determines the need for a fight director. Even a single slap can be dangerous, and theatres can and do engage fight directors for an hour to work it out safely. When there is more extensive stage combat of any sort, Equity productions will have a qualified fight director to choreograph the routine and work with you in rehearsals, a fight captain to maintain the fight through the run, a fight call before every show, and a weapons handler, whose job it is to check and repair the weapons and lock them away every night. If you are missing even one of these, it is an added danger. Daniel Levinson: "Performers should always check their own weapons before each performance in the presence of the weapons handler."

When you are ready to go off book, be careful how you ask for a prompt. Some actors snap their fingers at the stage manager or ASM when they need a line. Don't. Ever. You can say "Line" or "Yes" or "Please" or "Damn it, what's the line?" or all sorts of things, but don't snap your fingers. It sounds rude and peremptory, and most stage management personnel dislike it. And we don't blame them.

Prop Perils

If, during the rehearsal process, you and the director agree that your character needs a particular prop, ask for it as soon as possible. Lauren Snell: "Stage management usually catches that sort of thing in rehearsal, but let them know just to be safe." Lin Joyce: "You have to phrase a request so that the person understands that they are your equal, your partner, not your personal valet. Always [make your wants known] in the form of a request, not a demand." But don't ask for a prop because you need a security blanket. Be sure it's your character that needs the prop.

As rehearsals progress, the workshops and Wardrobe will begin to produce the more important costume pieces and props to replace the mock-ups stage management collected for rehearsal. When you're presented with a prop, don't look at it suspiciously and ask, "Is this it? How am I supposed to work with this?" Lin Joyce: "Accept the costume or prop graciously; the costume or prop person who made it is usually there. Even if it's awful, try to restrain your glancing wit so that you don't destroy the person." Bob Baker, artistic director, Citadel Theatre:

"How would you like it if, after the read-through, a prop person approached you with his face in a grimace saying, 'Is that the way you're going to do it?' No one expects the actor to get it right first time. Don't expect any more from the support staff." Lin Joyce: "Remember, it's not finished. Hold off those cheap shots! Be willing to work with it for the balance of that day or the following day. Before saying anything, try to think through the problems so that they can be articulated clearly. 'Too small' — does that mean it's uncomfortable, it hurts, it restricts movement? Be specific. Also be super honest. If you are uncomfortable with something emotionally, say so. 'It makes me feel peculiar' won't make people think of you as a raving neurotic. You don't have to use things that make you feel terrible. There is usually a way of modifying it to make it OK."

NOTES

Notes are the director's criticisms and suggestions, based on a run-through. There are three things you never say in response to a note:

- "But I did that!"
- "But you told me not to do that yesterday."
- "I would have done that, but Miriam was late on her cue."

Never explain, protest, or whine. And never, never blame someone else, even if you are justified. Notes are not for debate. You may say that you don't understand, once, and expect a rephrased version, but that's about it. Notes are given at the end of the day, when people are tired and tempers are frayed.

If you really have a problem with a note, ask the stage manager or the director about it afterwards. If you get the same note repeatedly, it is probably because you think the director is saying one thing and he is actually saying something else. Ask for an analogy or an example or a different explanation or a line reading or anything. Otherwise, you both are wasting valuable time.

Traditionally, notes are given by the director to the actor, not by an actor to another actor.

Tech Week

Lauren Snell: "Tech week is hell for everyone. It is hell for the actor moving out of the warmth of the rehearsal hall onto a stage that looks nothing like those coloured pieces of tape on the floor." Lin Joyce: "By the time tech week arrives, the perfect actor is exercising the patience of Job." Lauren Snell: "Remember, rehearsals have gone on for two or three weeks; you are very familiar with the piece. The operators and crew have only had verbal briefings by the ASM, or have just been told to hit a button at a certain time. They don't really know what the piece is. They don't get to know until well after opening." Lin Joyce: "Techies are working like things demented. The gratitude of techies towards an actor with class is enormous and you develop a great company bond."

Of course they won't always get it right first time. God knows you didn't. Lin Joyce: "Even if they do get it right first time, it's only luck, and they'll screw it up the second time!" Lauren Snell: "There will be a day or two when changes happen constantly. The best rule is to continue to do what you have always done unless told to do otherwise. Don't change your timing to adapt to somebody else. They are changing, trying to adapt to you! You'll never meet."

Lauren Snell: "Keep a sense of humour. It is a trying week that doesn't have to be made worse by people having their biggest tantrum ever. But that is the week people do it." Lin Joyce: "If you do give in to tiredness and decide to have a tantrum, forget it, you've broken the bond. The crew won't accept tantrums from each other, and they won't accept them from a performer. If you do fall from grace, you must apologize publicly. Then you have a fighting chance of getting back into the crew's good books."

Lin Joyce again: "If you can only extend yourself to go beyond being patient and be grateful! It is so unusual for an actor to turn to a dresser and say, 'I'm really glad you're here.' Or to pass a lighting man in the hall and say, 'I know you've got about 250 cues; I think you're fantastic.' They need to hear it. The only recognition technicians get is from directors, stage management, and actors."

First tech day is dangerous. There is still a lot of work to be done on the set, and only the stage manager is in touch with all the departments. Today, she is in charge, more than the director. Kate Greenway, former stage manager: "Don't walk all over the set, open doors, and complain that there are no railings. When you arrive, sit in the house for the SM's ten-minute chat. She will warn you about incomplete and possibly dangerous spots. It's a work in progress — exposed cords will be taped, eventually; dark areas will have light. The crew are experts. Trust the stage manager to look out for your safety and health." Unfortunately, not all stage managers are as punctilious as Ms. Greenway. Make it your own responsibility to check the safety of everything you will be asked to do, in rehearsal as well as in performance. This needn't be confrontational, but you're the one who will fall down the hole where the stairs were supposed to be. Yes, that happened to one of us.

Make sure that all potentially dangerous moves, scene changes, special effects, etc. are gone through slowly and carefully before you do them in costume at performance speed. Moves in darkness must be rehearsed in light; explosions and gunshots must be demonstrated while you watch from the house; someone else must be hanged with the trick noose. Insist on more than one layer of safety; an actor was rushed to hospital from a Stratford production of *Julius Caesar*, stabbed in the lung despite protective padding and a retracting knife. It's your body; it's the only one you'll get. You can protect yourself without a major row. Don't say you *won't* do something, angrily; say you *can't* do it, regretfully.

A warning about costumes: during the tech dress, you will be sitting around in your costumes for ages. Do be careful of wrinkling, damaging, spilling coffee, and dropping cigarette ash. Someone who is already overworked will have to press, mend, and clean what you wrecked.

Be prepared to wait for no apparent reason. Lauren Snell: "In a Q to Q, it seems as if there are long periods where nothing is happening. But something is. People are adjusting sound and lighting levels, discussing cues, the necessity for cue lights, timing." Don't disappear — keep yourself available.

Props and costumes should arrive in time to be tried in performance conditions and improved, if necessary, before your first audience. Fall on everything with cries of joy. Wardrobe is working eighteen-hour days and needs all the praise it can get. Make notes as you use things on stage and find out the problems. List your wants in order of importance. Decide (1) what you can't do without, (2) what you really want, and (3) what would be kinda nice to have. Delete (3). Now look at (2). Now delete it. We're left with (1). Assuming there are no more than three things in (1), you can only be disappointed three times. That's reality. If you haven't received your requested item by opening night, you won't be getting it.

Being a classy actor has helped you get through the strains of rehearsal, but the benefits continue. Lin Joyce: "The support system network is strong and widespread. Directors ask stage managers all the time about actors — what are they like to work with, do they make trouble?"

Opening Night

If you are planning to give tokens of thanks and/or good luck, this is the night for it. (An exception: some actors prefer to give "Last Night" cards or tokens. That way you have time to think about the perfect trinket without pressure.) Never feel obliged to buy First Night cards or flowers or wine or anything else. If you want to, great. If not, no one will think the worse of you. However, if you give cards to your fellow cast members, you must also give them to the support staff. They had as much to do with getting the production on as you. In a theatre with a huge support staff, you don't have to give something to each person. A good rule of thumb is to give something to a department as a whole (e.g. Wardrobe, Props) and something else to any individual who specifically worked on your costume or prop. Remember to take extra cards to the theatre on opening night. You are bound to have forgotten someone.

Not everyone considers First Night to be Fun Night. Many actors prefer to treat it the way they treat any other performance, and you must respect that.

After the show, which we are assuming you have survived — most actors do — there is usually a First Night party. Although you are no longer on duty, as it were, be polite to the members of the public who have paid good money to see you. It is only common courtesy to listen civilly to whatever drivel is being aimed at you, and who knows, your patience may be rewarded. You might find yourself in a rousing discussion about the play and end up with an invitation to drinks or lunch or an afternoon aboard the family yacht. It's happened to us.

And speaking of drinks, try not to overindulge. You've got another show to do tomorrow.

The Run

And another. And another. The stresses of opening night now give way to the pressures of keeping the show running smoothly. You are required to be at the theatre at "the half" — half an hour before the show starts. Many actors arrive long before that, to give themselves time to let whatever has happened during the day wash away in the ritual of preparation.

In a room that is overcrowded and overheated (or underheated), dressing room diplomacy is a number-one priority. The authors, easygoing in the extreme at home, are Dobermans when their counter space is threatened. Woe betide the actor who invades our territory. If a box of tissues gets two inches inside our make-up area, it's straight for the jugular.

Actors prepare in different ways. If you like to do a full physical and vocal limber before you make up, find somewhere other than the dressing room to do it, or do it at home. The actor sitting quietly in the corner with a crossword and the daily paper may be preparing for the performance as well.

Some actors are superstitious. Some superstitions — the ones you believe in — make sense. Others — the ones you don't — don't. Whether it is quoting from *Macbeth* or whistling in the dressing room or having real flowers on stage or whatever, be diplomatic and patient with the actors who are affected by the superstition.

Wash your pits, brush your teeth. Remember, small hot spaces make for all sorts of nasty body odours, and that makes for rows in the weeks ahead.

Outside the dressing room, as part of your preparation, check all your props. Lauren Snell: "Lots of older actors check their own props. I used to find that quite irritating. I used to think, 'Why do they do that when they know we're doing it?' Now I realize that it's their way of going through it. They may have had an experience where something wasn't there." It's all in how you do it. Check at a time when the pre-set has been done. Never move a prop from where it has been set during the run. Let Stage Management know when things get worn or fragile. Stick to the same routine with a prop, so that the ASM knows she can collect it from the stage left prop table where you left it, instead of finding it behind the bin where you threw it.

You are getting bored with doing the show the same way night after night. Tough. You have a contractual obligation to perform the play as rehearsed. There is growth from continuing to think about the play, and an inevitable change as audiences differ. Lauren Snell: "As sound and lighting people become more familiar with the nuances of the show, their performances change as well." But, in essence, the production remains the same. Lin Joyce: "If something never worked and everyone knows it never worked, there is room within the performance to get it to work. An actor should go to the stage manager before trying something new. You never know if cues depend on it." In the same way, actors should expect to be told when Stage Management makes or authorizes changes. You have the right to expect everything on the set and on your costumes to remain absolutely unchanged, or be given the chance to see and work with the change ahead of time.

Whatever else you may want to change, never change fights! Daniel Levinson: "Stage combat is one of the non-negotiable elements in theatre. Once the fights are blocked and agreed on, there should be no changes. The fight(s) must be run before each show — any difficult or dangerous move, a hit, a jump, a blow — all these should be run. Not at full speed, but with the same intention and commitment that you'll have in performance."

It is the stage manager's job to keep the show going as it was directed. She is entitled to give notes to that end. Lin Joyce: "The perfect actor requests notes: 'Any notes for me?' It's best if it becomes an exchange. The stage manager can go into the dressing room after the show to ask for notes (torn costume, wobbly prop) and give notes in return." Lauren Snell: "Actors often resent notes. It's really hard giving them, Actors should know that. I'd rather have a show with a million cues than actors who I know are going to be hell on notes." Be gracious when receiving notes from the stage manager. All our advice for responding to notes from the director applies to those from the stage manager.

It is hard to be gracious when a technical error has made you look like a prime idiot in front of five hundred people. However tempting it is to blow a gasket at the nearest bystander, don't. Lauren Snell: "It is such a sensitive profession and so difficult to mend a breach. Count to ten. You usually blow up at the first person you see — the apprentice, then the ASM — and you're reasonably calm by the time you see the stage manager. If you've got a problem, don't walk up one side of the apprentice and down the other. It's not fair. At least the SM can defend herself if it's an unreasonable blow-up. And if it's reasonable, it's the SM who should be getting it anyway. It's nice if the operator who made the mistake goes down to apologize as well. But ultimately, it's the stage manager who must take the heat."

Try to accept the apology with good grace. It's not easy for anyone to admit he made a mistake. Don't make it any more difficult by being a Neanderthal.

In turn, if you do something wrong, whether to your fellow actor or to a support staffer, apologize immediately. It's gracious and grown-up, and it's the most effective way of defusing a potentially explosive situation. Lauren Snell: "It's gratifying to get an apology from an actor, but it's the information that's useful. 'I think I hit something in the blackout.' It's good to know that a actor doesn't panic in a crisis."

Try to anticipate problems. Lauren Snell: "It's helpful if an actor can show common sense in an emergency. If you know about crucial prop placement, you should think about what you'd do if it wasn't there one night."

All the problems of being the perfect actor are increased tenfold when you are on tour. Normally, you can get away from your co-workers, explore new places on your own once rehearsals are over, and have a life outside the theatre. On tour, you are trapped with a small number of people for weeks on end, and it takes all your tact, sensitivity, and class to keep a positive working relationship with them all.

Your Reward

What is the reward for being the perfect actor? Lin Joyce: "People cannot wait to work with you again! There is a star system inside the stage management and technical world. Our stars are the people we love and admire and who love and admire us."

Film and Televison – Extras

Oh, come on, who cares what Extras do? Extras Casting cares, gets reports, takes the flak, and won't call you next time.

One thing you can do to make your life more pleasant: Extras Holding generally starts off scruffy, but if everyone takes care, it won't be a dump by the end of the day.

The job experience is simpler, and you're lower in the pecking order, but the basics are the same as for Talent. You don't have much say in what happens, but you do have some. You'll be dealing with people with different titles sometimes, but it still boils down to Call, Arrive, Wardrobe/Hair/Make-up, Perform, Leave. Now read on.

Film and Television – Talent

Unlike the weeks of a theatre job, you rarely have more than a day or two on any film or television contract. Not much time to charm the socks off anyone. But plenty of time to screw up.

Wardrobe Call

When Wardrobe phoned, they probably asked you to bring your audition clothes and perhaps some alternatives. They have the right to do this, and you'll score big brownie points if you turn up with lots of choices. You'll save yourself sore feet if you bring your own shoes.

Be prepared to be there the full two hours of your call. Lots of actors, knowing that wardrobe calls are generally less than fifteen minutes long, book themselves doctor's appointments or lunch dates or auditions, and then are upset and anxious when the call drags on. Don't take the chance. Also, don't fume because you were called for two o'clock, arrived in plenty of time, and now have to sit around because everyone else was called for two o'clock as well. Think of it as a dentist's appointment, without the anxiety and with pay. That is the point, by the way. They are paying you for two hours of your time. So don't grumble, read a book. Or talk to the other actors: it's an excellent chance to break the ice.

Wardrobe call will be your introduction to some of the most helpful people on the set. It's part of their job to make you feel good about yourself. This does not mean that your costume will necessarily fit. As long as it looks all right for the camera and isn't too uncomfortable, accept the fact that sleeves will be shortened with safety pins. Find something to praise: complaints are not well received.

Wardrobe departments are notoriously overworked and understaffed and often deal with fifteen or twenty people at a time. Keep cheerful and relaxed. If a skimpy jacket is the worst thing you have to endure, offer prayers of thanks, not whines of discontent.

Call Times

No one likes getting up at oh-my-god o'clock in the morning. When the second or third AD phones with your call time, don't wail at the unreasonableness of the hour. At most, you may allow a slight, piteous whimper to pass your lips. Otherwise, it's a straightforward and cheerful, "Thanks, I'll see you then."

Shooting Day

Get there in plenty of time. You may have to search around for the exact location. The parking lot may be a quarter of a mile from the actual set. It may take you some time to find anyone who knows who you are, what you should be doing, and where you should be doing it.

Your first job is to find the AD who phoned with your call time and whose name you should have written down. Any AD will do in a pinch (they all have those walkie-talkie things and will get in touch with the one you want), but it's best to report to the person who made the first contact. That AD will get you to Wardrobe, Make-up, and Hair.

Wardrobe, Make-up, and Hair

Even at oh-my-god o'clock, you have no excuse for turning up without having brushed your hair and washed. Shave if you need to, don't put on any street make-up unless you're asked. Bring your own make-up just in case. If you have to be extra nice to anyone, these are the people who deserve it. They are artists in their own right, and yet are open to (well-chosen) comments or suggestions. They accept that you are more familiar with your own face and hair than they, and will ask about hair partings and make-up colours. Don't tell them what to do, but if they ask for input, don't be afraid to give it. Nicely.

If you're a man, they may want to trim your hair. Even if you could fake the look they want, even if the look is totally wrong for the period, you'll end up getting it cut just as much as they think is necessary. Relax; it grows back.

You are likely to be in costume for hours before you ever get onto the set. Don't wander about. You must be available and your where-abouts known at all times. Someone will show you where to wait.

And there you stay, unless you tell someone. Hurry up and wait is the order of the day. And it is bad manners to complain about it. Nadia Venesse, dialect coach: "I have never heard a principal player complain about having to wait — only the day players. You're being paid good money to read or do a crossword. Why complain about it?"

Rehearsals

There's one thing you can rely on in media work: you're on your own. You have been cast because you can deliver the goods: it's up to you to deliver them. If you are lucky enough to work with a director who is willing to talk and listen to the actors (like the directors we quote), you are ahead of the game. Most directors will give you technical direction and that's all. Accept the situation and give the director what you gave at the audition: that's why you got the job. If a director gives you a sug-gestion, follow it as if it were an order. Which it is.

Be particularly sensitive to the needs of the technicians. The techni-cian is king (only occasionally queen): be respectful, don't offer an opinion, pay compliments, and, if necessary, shine shoes. This doesn't mean you can't joke and kibitz. Just know exactly where your place is in the hierarchy. W-a-a-a-y d-o-o-o-w-n.

Even down here at the bottom, speak up when there is potential danger. Randy Butcher, stunt coordinator: "As stunt performers, we create an illusion of danger on the screen — not to say the actual performance of a given stunt isn't dangerous." And you're not a stunt performer. If something scares you, don't do it. ACTRA and the law help you protect yourself. A reasonable voice asking for a safer way will usually be listened to.

SHOOTING

You will be asked to do impossibly awkward things. If they are shooting someone's reaction to your words, you may be crouched out of frame, with your face squashed into the side of the camera, so that the person in frame will be looking in the right spot. Try to give full value to your off-camera lines; it's what you would like in return. If it is your shot and the other actor is sitting in her trailer, you may be doing all this great acting to the floor manager's hand, while someone drones the words at you. There is no point getting upset about either of these situations (or any other). You do what you are asked, promptly, efficiently, and without any game-playing.

If, for any reason, you are not having a good time, keep it to yourself. A set is a dangerous place to shoot your mouth off, no matter how quietly. Marc Green, sound recordist: "A mike is a very sensitive piece of equipment. I can eavesdrop so easily on actors. Whispers come through clear as anything!" Be warned.

YOUR WRAP

When you have finished (wrapped), make a point of going around to all the people who have had anything to do with you and thanking them for their help. Extras thank their AD and the casting director, if she's there. It doesn't have to be a big production number. "I'm wrapped now, so bye and thanks for everything." People appreciate being appreciated.

Commercials, Voice-overs, and Radio

There is something we should add about these three areas of work: Don't knock the copy. However inane or infantile you consider the script, keep quiet about it. Without exception in commercials, most of the time in voice-overs and frequently in radio, the person who wrote this garbage is sitting right beside you. Or at least within earshot. These scripts are not first drafts. They are the result of discussions, meetings, rewrites, client input, and several bottles of Prozac. And that is usually how they read. However, you have been hired to say the words, not comment on them.

A special word about commercials: Don't knock the product. If you are morally outraged by it, you shouldn't have auditioned for the commercial. No one is asking you to believe in the product. But they are paying you to be polite about it. Why antagonize a potential source of revenue?

Harassment

Everything we've said about health and safety concerns goes double for harassment. The law is on your side; in most cases a reasonable complaint will be dealt with. But it does need courage to speak out, so most people decide to keep quiet and not make waves.

Equity and ACTRA deal with harassment in detail on their websites. Non-union theatre and film workplaces are obliged to conform to their province's human rights codes.

We've heard the argument that acting and directing deal intimately with physical and emotional space, so the committed actor must expect treatment that would be unacceptable in the ordinary workplace. Nowadays, performers and engagers agree that sexual and personal harassment exist in our field and should not be tolerated.

Nudity and semi-nudity are part of our professional lives. *Professional* is the important word here. The director or stage manager has no God-given right to wander into a dressing room full of half-naked actors. This is your private space, and it's your decision whether or not you mind. If nudity or semi-nudity is part of your performance, the unions have detailed rules about auditions and rehearsals. Get to know the rules beforehand. If you feel uncomfortable, a reasonable director will listen to you. Union or non-union, it's your call.

None of this makes life easy for the person being harassed. You probably know what you should do: make it clear that the behaviour is unacceptable or offensive; if it continues, report it to the engager; if it still continues, and you're union, report it to Equity or ACTRA. Having the courage to start the process is never easy. There are people in the business who are notorious for their history of harassing, but no one has dared call them on it because of their position and prestige. However, there was a recent case where an actor won a complaint against a well-known director with a long history of harassing actors. The director was fined a considerable sum; the actor was vindicated. In our opinion, the very best production should not be paid for by the humiliation of the least of its team members.

The tiny time frame in media work makes it even more difficult to take action and easier to tolerate the innuendo or casual touching; two days, then it's all over. You may decide to bite the bullet, but you should report the incident to the union and your agent.

How, or even whether, you deal with this problem is ultimately up to you. The truth is, you may not be hired again by an engager you've complained about. But would you want to be? Blowing the whistle on someone won't make you unhireable; you won't be labelled a trouble-maker. Standing up isn't easy, but it can be done. And every time it's done, it sends a message to the other creeps.

There. The good, the bad, and the ugly. And you, the perfect actor. Any sane agent should jump at the chance of representing you. Let's go.

CHAPTER TEN

The Ten Percent Solution

"To manage men, one ought to have a sharp mind in a velvet sheath."
George Eliot

An actor-agent relationship is like a marriage. Like a marriage, you can only have one partner at a time, and like a marriage, you can only find out if it's good for you by trying it. And there's always the option of remaining single. Getting an agent may be a milestone in a career, but it's not necessarily right for you right now.

All we can do is discuss the problems and pitfalls, what you should expect, and your part of the deal. What you can't expect is your agent to get you work. An agent gets you auditions; you get the work.

What an Agent Does

The agent:

- Reads plays and casting breakdowns from casting directors.
- Puts the client's (actor's) name forward to casting directors, theatre directors, and producers for parts.
- Negotiates the terms of the client's contract.
- Counsels and advises a client on career decisions.

• Consults with a client on relevant financial matters.
• Deals with problems between client and management during work.
• Acts as an intermediary between client and management.

You have your agent to say the things you're too scared to say yourself. Shari Caldwell, Caldwell and Associates: "An agent is a necessary luxury, an intermediary, a buffer. Someone who stands between the actor and the engager without getting in the way."

Sandie Newton, Newton-Landry Management: "Your agent is a sounding board, a buffer, a control." For these services, the clients pay the agent a commission (normally 10 percent for stage and 15 percent for media work) of their gross professional income. You don't pay the commission on money paid for expenses (accommodation, travel, transport of pets). Actors should pay commission on a job to the agent who originally handled it, no matter how long ago the work was done. One of us was the voice of the Daleks on *Dr. Who* and paid that agent commission on video sales for thirty years.

People may suggest you also need a business manager and a publicist. Eve Brandstein, in *The Actor*: "Get a dog instead, it's better company."

What an Agent Doesn't Do

The Entertainment Industry Coalition includes ACTRA representatives, performers, agents, teachers, and casting directors. They hammered out the EIC Code of Ethics, which is the basis of their leaflet about scam agents. The leaflet warns:

• Agents do not advertise. According to the EIC Code of Ethics, talent and background agents cannot advertise to the general public.
• Agents do not provide photographic services or give classes. A reputable agent may suggest specific photographers or classes to you but cannot require you to use them.
• An agent cannot guarantee work.
• Agents are not casting directors. Casting directors are paid by the

production company. Agents earn commissions when their clients work.

- Agents specialize. Agents usually represent actors, extras, or models. Be wary if the agency claims to represents all three categories.
- A principal agent will rarely represent you if you have no experience or training.

We would add that the main exception to the above warnings are legitimate agents in smaller centres who, in order to make a living, have to handle every sort of performer and model work, teach classes, and arrange photo shoots. In that situation, you'll have to find out all you can about the agent, including how much work he handles, and not spend more than you can afford on services that may do you no good.

Extras Agents

If you have no experience and no training, a background agency will still take you on. In Vancouver and Toronto you need a background agent to work as an Extra. You still pay them 10 or 15 percent of your fees, and perhaps also a registration fee of seventy dollars or so. In Montreal, you can send your publicity straight to the background casting directors. Elsewhere, background casting is done by casting agencies or through open calls. In this chapter we are talking about talent agents.

How to Approach an Agent

Are they legitimate? In British Columbia, legitimate agents are registered; in Toronto, with one or two exceptions, they are EIC signatory or TAMAC (Talent Agents and Managers Association of Canada) members. Elsewhere, you have no guarantees.

The B.C. Ministry of Labour lists the province's registered agents (see Addresses). *The Actor's Organizer* lists agencies across the country, flagging TAMAC and EIC agents. *The Agents Book*, more Toronto based, lists only TAMAC and EIC agents, and includes advice about scam agents. Both books are available at TheatreBooks (see Addresses).

Your starting point is any legitimate agency close to you. It is not likely that an agent more than a couple of hours away will consider you unless you have a killer résumé. Don't approach the specialist agents unless you fit their focus. Apart from that, consider them all.

Getting an agent is like getting a job. You do your research, you send your photograph and résumé with a covering letter or you take in the promo package, you phone to set up an appointment, you follow up, and you keep trying. We got advice from several agents. One said: "The covering letter is as important as the résumé. Never use Dear Sir or Madam; you're saying you are doing a mass mailing, not applying directly to me. You should be doing research on the agent. Don't spell my name wrong." Try to get someone you have already impressed to contact the agent. Don't be shy about asking friends to recommend you to their agents. If you can mention a well-known name in your letter, and especially a current client, an agent will probably give you more consideration. Ask your teachers, if they are active in the business, and directors you have worked for.

Always say in your letter that you will follow up with a phone call. If your phone call results in no appointment, don't give up. Remember, agents receive up to a hundred photographs and résumés each week. Out of those, very few actors will be seen. Try again in a few months' time. The agent's situation may have changed by then. If an agent leaves the door open for you — "Why don't you call again next spring?" — take advantage of that. If you are coming in from out of town, write before you leave and phone after you arrive, if you see what we mean. As with all business calls you make, work out beforehand what you plan to say. And concentrate! You are often put on hold for so long that by the time the agent gets on the line, you have forgotten who you're calling and why.

Agents want to see your work. If you are in a show — workshop, showcase, school, professional — invite the agent to come to it. Be sure to give plenty of notice. If it is not free, offer tickets. Agents are busy and can't see many shows, but offering tickets gives you a reason to call and follow up on the letter. If you have a demo tape, you will want to drop it off with your promo package.

If you are lucky enough to get an interview with an agent, be prepared to audition or do a cold reading even if they've seen your work. As for any interview, come well groomed and presentable, in your own personal style. You should look your best, even if you are just dropping off your résumé. We know of at least one case where the agent was walking through just as the actor was handing her résumé and photo to the receptionist. The interview took place then and there. Don't expect that to happen, but go dressed for it.

Be on time (or phone as soon as you realize you are going to be late). Politeness and consideration are rare commodities in this business and make such a pleasant change. Be courteous to the receptionist. Many will pass on their comments before the agent even sees you. Actually, you don't know that it is the receptionist; it could be one of the agents. And even if it is "just" the receptionist, remember that today's receptionist is tomorrow's hotshot agent. You will probably have to wait, so use the time to get a feel for the agency. Chat to the receptionist if there is a break in the phone calls, look at the headshots of the agency's clients, check the bulletin board for the reviews of their work. Don't make a nuisance of yourself, just keep your antennae working.

Be prepared to be criticized. This is not personal and not for debate. Restyle your hair, lose or gain twenty pounds, shave the beard, get new photos, fix your résumé — it may sound abusive, but it is the agent offering free advice. Don't be offended. Don't feel that you have failed. Accept the comments and give them careful consideration. You may decide that the agent is all wrong, in which case, try another one. You may decide that the agent is right, in which case, restyle your hair, lose or gain twenty pounds, shave the … etc., and try again when you can show the agent the new you. In either case, follow the interview with a thank-you letter.

And stay in touch. Remember that the whole scene is fluid. New agencies are forming; agents are breaking away from the original group to set up on their own; actors leave agencies, creating holes that need filling; the industry's casting needs change as fashions in character types shift from year to year and season to season. Don't be discouraged. Circumstances change and persistence pays.

How to Choose an Agent

A large agency, with more than about three agents, tends to have a more extensive network of information and more contacts than a small agency. On the other hand, a small agency may be more inclined to hustle for you because you aren't lost in the crowd. A top-ranking, high-powered agency may be able to get you in to see important people — but a new agent may be more motivated to try.

Within most agencies, the individual agent has a separate roster of thirty-five or more clients and looks after film, television, and theatre. The larger agency may also have one or more specialists handling commercials or voice-overs for all their clients. An advantage to this set-up is that the actor has the use of someone who has special knowledge in a particular field. But it also means that, for that field, each actor is one out of maybe two hundred clients, and there is less chance of a personal commitment.

Who else does the agent represent? Find out from Face to Face Online, or ask the agency. If you know any of the clients, phone them up and ask their advice. Tread carefully in this area, and remember, what works for one person may not work for you.

Ultimately, what really counts is the single person who will represent you. Listen to your gut. Go by intuition. Go for the person who you feel is most concerned with your career, your problems, your success. Agents who feel wrong are like a pair of ill-fitting shoes: with time they get less comfortable, not more.

How an Agent Chooses You

Penny Noble: "Seeing the work is best. If I am familiar with their work in film, TV, or theatre, I won't need a demo tape. I very rarely interview before seeing their work. An exception to that is seeing a very full résumé with interesting work, or a recommendation of a casting agent. Even so, I will still want to see a tape before I make the final decision."

Kathy Gaitt: "We like to give them sides from a TV show or film. [Or] a demo from a finished product, not a demo from an acting class."

Dani De Lio: "I usually give them sides to put themselves on tape. If they come in with very little experience, that tape is a very important tool."

Brian Misener: "I prefer a demo reel, or seeing them in a show."

Sandie Newton: "I will choose on the basis of referrals and interviews. If the actor has no demo tape, I will ask for a monologue."

Lawrie Rotenberg: "I try to see their work. Film, television, live performance. A demo tape, if nothing else."

Shari Caldwell: "I won't audition actors. I like prospective clients with effective publicity to get in. It means their work-publicity philosophy is good."

Alicia Jeffery: "We generally don't interview people unless we've seen their work and been impressed by it."

Nancy LeFeaver: "I [might] ask a casting director if they wouldn't mind reading them at a prescreen and giving me the feedback."

What an Agent Looks For

Lawrie Rotenberg: "In general, it is a combination of gut feeling of talent and energy, and references. Saleability. Marketability. Do they fit into the market as it is? I have to consider my own needs. Are there conflicts on my roster?"

Penny Noble: "I look for the charisma, excitement. When you see it in an interview — the warmth and enthusiasm — it draws you."

Shari Caldwell: "I have all food groups on my roster, and I am careful to avoid conflict. Do I like the person?"

It would seem the ideal client has a strong commercial appeal that is easy to market, combined with that "certain something." Mind you, one agent's "certain something" is another agent's "yech, what's that?" Like your decision about your agent, like everything else in this business, your attractiveness as a client is judged as much on instinct as on information.

Agent-Client Relationship

The most important thing to remember is that your agent works for you, you don't work for your agent. You are paying for the agent's time and expertise and should expect value for your money. Respect the special knowledge the agent has, but remember that you are buying that knowledge. Too many actors are intimidated by their agents. Don't be. Shari Caldwell says, "You represent each other. Sometimes I represent the actor to the producer for the first time in negotiation, for example, and at times the actor represents the agent to the director and casting director. We are a team. We work together." The agent's reputation is on the line when you go up for a job. Sandie Newton: "If clients screw up, it is a reflection on the agency and the other clients it represents."

The agent-client relationship is a business arrangement. It must begin with discussing, defining, and agreeing on the areas of work and responsibility. The agent is acting on your behalf so you need to know this person is honest, forthright, and has your interests at heart. By the same token, you must not lie to your agent. Any gains made by lying to impress an agent are short-lived. Be frank about your ambitions. Discuss what you want your agent to do. Where you want to go. You and your agent should be on the same wavelength when it comes to the aim and thrust of your career.

Within the limitations of a business arrangement, there are great variations in an agent-client association. Shari Caldwell: "Friendship is fine but it only goes one way. The actor feels able to call on an agent for personal help, but the agent can't call on the actor."

Whether your relationship is close or formal, an open, honest connection is the most effective. Before you commit yourself to an agent, discuss where you want your career to go, what you want the agent to do for you, and how the agent will do that.

Career decisions are up to you, not your agent. Don't give your agent that power. In any case, most agents won't accept the responsibility. Penny Noble, Noble Talent: "I will give advice if it is appropriate to do so, but the decision is the client's." Sandie Newton: "Advise a client on a career move? We will discuss it together. I can give both a professional and a personal opinion, but I never make decisions without consulting a client." If you find you're consistently not taking your agent's advice, maybe that agent isn't right for you; you may want to think about a change.

The agent is a sounding board. Discuss the pros and cons of a career choice with your agent, who usually can predict and understand the consequences of that choice. You will find that simply talking it over with the agent will clarify the situation in your own mind.

Sometimes, all you need is someone to say "yes" to realize the right answer for you is "no." There is no need to assume that your agent knows better than you what's good for you. What you should expect is a more cool-headed, less emotional approach than you might have.

You should be able to voice dissatisfaction and concern. Although you must trust that an agent is working for you, you shouldn't be afraid to ask for an accounting of time and effort. And a good agent shouldn't resent the request. Cultivate your agent; get to know how your agent works. Can you call for a chat? Does calling every day break into the agent's routine? What hours does the agent work? A good agent shouldn't mind clients keeping in close touch. Call your agent after a job or an audition to keep the agent up to date and informed.

Good agents look after many careers; you look after only one. Believe us, no matter how much interest an agent shows in your career, no one is as interested in it as you should be (except your mother). And no one has as much to lose. This is a fact of life.

Agents want and expect their clients to form an active part of the relationship. Neither the actor nor the agent can sit and wait for things to happen. Certainly the agents we have spoken to all agree – it's your career and you are responsible for it. You are part of the promotional package. Ideally, the agent and the client are working with the same energy and commitment. The agent sells you; you sell yourself. Stuart Aikins, casting director, says there are actors who, "now that they have an agent, sit back and wait for the phone to ring. I don't believe that's the way love, life, or the arts work."

Here are some things agents want from the relationship. Sandie Newton: "I expect my clients to be professionals, dedicated. They should be spending the same amount of time and energy on their careers as I am."

Penny Noble: "I expect co-operation, enthusiasm. The recognition that every chance is precious. They should be accommodating, prepared to be inconvenienced. I expect them to be well prepared and do the best possible audition." Lawrie Rosenberg, The Talent Group: "I expect professionalism — the way they handle themselves, the tools they provide, their own approach and energy to the business. I want frankness, a career relationship. Sensitivity helps. Teamwork." Honesty. Dedication. Dependability. These qualities may sound like something out of a Boy Scout manual, but they are an integral part of the agent-client relationship.

Contracts and Power of Attorney

Whether you sign a contract or not, you do have a legal agreement with your agent. With or without a written contract, you must be perfectly clear who does what.

Is it necessary to have a written contract with your agent? Yes, according to lawyer Abe Greenbaum, in an article in *ACTRAscope*: "Authority for an agent to act is either by written contract or oral agreement.... Unless you contractually limit the scope of the agency, you may find that your agent does something of which you do not approve and you will have no legal recourse. With a contract, you will be able to specify [in] what kinds of matters the agent may act on your behalf (with or without your prior consent), what types of contractual relationships the agent may enter on your behalf and what, if anything, your agent may do with fees paid to you and sent to the agent.

"If you have no contract with your agent it will be very difficult to protect yourself if your agent does something wrong or something you feel was beyond the scope of your relationship. If there is no contract and you sue your agent, the court will look to industry practices of what agents do, and judge your case in that light."

Most agents who use contracts consider them more of a way to avoid misunderstanding than as a binding agreement. A contract is one way for an agent to pressure an ex-client into paying commission for residuals on work done before the split-up. Lawrie Rosenberg: "It's not much, really. Simply the sign of a relationship. I have never held anyone to it and will let people go." Says Christopher Marston, former executive director, Canadian Actors' Equity Association: "A contract with an agent is always dissoluble immediately. Termination terms should be reasonable — take legal action if you're worried." (In Toronto, call ALAS — see Addresses.)

The contract will normally specify that all your principal acting work goes through the agency and is commissioned. You may be able to agree that some work is handled by another agent, but that is rare.

If you have discussed every aspect of the arrangement and you feel comfortable about signing a contract that puts in writing what you have agreed to verbally — and nothing more — by all means, sign. Many agents use contract forms that are unnecessarily complicated. Go through any contract cause by clause; ask to take it home so that you can read it at your own pace. If you don't understand something, get it explained and have the explanation put in the contract. Or get it cut. The contract isn't graven in stone, and there is no future in agreeing to something like "abfamiliate the co-lessor in perpetuity," which may be garbage but may be a time-bomb. Look at the ACTRA Toronto website for a detailed discussion of the TAMAC contract.

Some areas you need to pay attention to are:

• Exclusivity
• Commission rates and what's commissionable
• Your obligations
• Assignment of the contract to another agent
• Dispute resolution (make sure it's in)
• Ending the contract
• Additional charges
• Power of attorney

Be sure you know what the agent will bill you for. The majority of agents we spoke to said that the actor pays for material supplies (photographs, résumés, voice tapes, demo tapes) and the agency pays for long-distance phone calls, postage, and courier services (unless — and they all added this — it is to send a photograph and résumé to a casting director because the actor forgot to take them to the audition).

Sandie Newton: "It is the client's job to supply the agency with the ammunition to sell her. On long-distance calls, I am usually representing more than one client, so the agency pays for it. But if I am specifically requested by the client to make the call, the charge goes back to the individual."

Some agents have started charging for services, such as the return of photos sent to casting directors, that used to be included in the commission deal. This is bad news, but worse is the handful of respectable agents who have started charging flat rate registration and administration fees.

Power of attorney is a contract where one person gives certain rights or powers to another person. The person given power of attorney is authorized to act as if he or she were the person who gave the power. This authorization can be as limited or as general as you allow. Your agent's power of attorney may be a separate form or it may be buried deep in a six-page agency contract.

Power of attorney, as used by agents, gives them the power to sign the client's contracts or cash cheques made out to the clients. Be sure you understand exactly what the agent's power of attorney covers. If you're not sure, take the form away and read it again. If it is still confusing, have a lawyer explain what it means. Ask ALAS (see Addresses) if you're in southern Ontario.

Power of attorney is a slippery thing. You may give it to your agent without realizing you've done so. The first time an agent signs a contract and you don't send her a letter to say she has no authority to do so, you have given her that power of attorney. The moment your agent endorses a cheque made out to you and deposits it in his client account, you have given away that power of attorney. In theory, the agent must supply the bank with proof of power of attorney. In practice, banks rarely demand any authorization.

In British Columbia, many agents don't ask for power of attorney to cash your cheques. They have the media cheques sent to the agency and you pay your commission when you pick them up. Elsewhere, it's usual to allow your agent this power of attorney. If you do, make sure the power of attorney agreement includes what happens next — where the money goes (into a separate client account), how soon you get it (within five business days), what gets deducted (contractually agreed fees and commissions). No power of attorney to cash cheques is needed for stage work since your fees are paid directly to you. You and your agent will work out how commission is paid.

Your agent wants power of attorney to sign your contract for the convenience of the producer. Take our advice and always sign your own contracts. You're unlikely to be cheated, but we have seen some really stupid mistakes on contracts signed by agents. If an error or omission slips through, it's your ass on the line, not your agent's.

Your powers of attorney need end dates. If you allow the agent to sign your contracts, that power of attorney ends when your agency contract ends. The power to cash your cheques ends when the residuals on work done through that agency end.

How Should an Agent Behave?

In 1989, the Talent Agents of Vancouver produced a code of conduct that was built on by the Entertainment Industry Coalition. Unfortunately, some of the best parts of the Vancouver code were lost in the hurly-burly of negotiation between groups with different agendas. Get a copy of the EIC Code of Ethics from the unions or service organizations and compare it with these extracts from the old code:

The Talent Agent shall:
- Conduct himself or herself with honesty, courtesy and good faith toward all parties;
- Represent Clients with integrity, honesty and confidentiality;
- Solicit prospective Clients only in an honourable, reputable and professional manner;
- Endeavour to obtain payment on behalf of the Client as expeditiously as possible.

The Talent Agent agrees to:
- Counsel or advise the Client in the advancement and promotion of his or her professional career;

- Be truthful and disclose all pertinent facts;
- Make every effort to negotiate above minimum fee for the Client;
- Inform the Client of the known terms and conditions ... and to obtain the Client's consent, before confirming or make binding any ... commitment on behalf of the Client;
- Advise the Client of all known information pertaining to each ... engagement;
- Seek out and confer with producers, engagers ... for the purpose of securing work for the Client;
- Maintain proper records. It will be the responsibility of Agents to define their services to their Clients and ensure that any Client is informed of their role in a business relationship.

The British Columbia Ministry of Labour now has regulations that govern talent agents (see Addresses).

We asked some Toronto agents what their clients should be able to expect from them. The words we heard most often were: availability, energy, frankness, interest, professionalism, sensitivity, leadership, guidance, time, effort, and dedication. (We should all be so lucky.)

Is Your Agent Working For You?

It's almost impossible to tell. The amount of work you do, even the number of auditions you go to, depends so much on whether the market happens to want you right now. Here are some areas where a bad agent may fall down:

- Can you reach your agent on the phone? Are your calls returned promptly?
- Do you feel encouraged and optimistic after talking to your agent? Or have you had to listen to your agent's problems?
- Do you seem to know more about what's going on than your agent does? Is your file kept up to date? Correct home and work addresses and phone numbers? Plenty of good-looking résumés? Are you warned when photos are beginning to run out?

- Can you ask who the agent is contacting on your behalf? What you are being put up for?
- Does your agent come to see your work in theatre and know when you are appearing on television?

And here's a suggestion from Bryan Misener with Characters Agency: "You need to sit down with your agent and ask her to set up meetings with the casting directors you haven't met yet. Ask why you haven't been in to see them. Depending on the answers you get, you can figure out where the agent stands with casting directors."

Well-respected Canadian film producers are not complimentary about Canadian agents. In Canada, they say, there are a handful of well-respected agents who are listened to for major casting. But unlike in the States, agents here rarely talk to producers. In the States, each agency will have someone bugging each production. Not in Canada; it's not a business here, it's a bureaucracy.

When to Leave Your Agent

All actors go through bleak periods. It can be comforting in such times to blame your agent for lack of work or work opportunities. It is not necessarily the agent's fault. You might not change your luck just by changing your agent.

Talk to your agent. Maybe she is still seeing you as you were when you joined the agency and doesn't recognize that you have matured. Maybe you should be going up for different roles. Maybe his roster of clients has changed and you have been moved into an unsuitable slot. Discuss your concern honestly and openly. It's possible that you can solve your problems without leaving.

If you have become very successful, you may want to move on to an agency with more prestige. Again, exercise caution. Shari Caldwell: "Changing agents after success is common, but it doesn't often help. A new agent always takes six months to work effectively for you. Being put up for casting doesn't differ much between agents." Brian Levy, casting director: "It is possible to outgrow an agency. But don't change agencies just for prestige. If your agent is getting you auditions, money, and billing, why move?"

How do you know when you have outgrown an agent? Is it wiser to stay with an agent who knows you, understands you, and has worked hard for you? Is your agent powerful enough to represent you now that you have become well known and sought after? Shari Caldwell: "Top agents represent stars, writers, and directors, and will hear of projects and have some say even before a casting director is contacted." It's fair to say you have to be pretty successful before you move in those circles, but even if you don't, it is reasonable to assume that a casting director will start by looking at casting suggestions from agents with the best reputations. However, Brian Levy says, "The prestige of the agency doesn't matter a bit. What does matter is the individual I'm dealing with. There are some agencies I won't deal with, but not because they are newer or smaller. It's because they give me hassles … and basically aren't pleasant to deal with."

How much does personal loyalty enter into it? Remember what we said earlier: however friendly you may be with your agent, essentially you have a business relationship. Any agent who cares about you should encourage you to move if you could do better elsewhere.

It's definitely time to leave if an agent is not representing you the way you want to be seen, if you're not being put up for parts where you feel you have a chance, or if your agent is repeatedly discourteous, unavailable, and unwilling to listen attentively. Talk it over and try to work it out first, but if it is impossible, make the break.

No matter how angry you are at your agent, leave the agency amicably; you may want to return someday. Slamming doors may feel great at the moment, but it could be damaging in the long run. Your offended ex-agent is under no obligation to pass on business calls once you've left.

It's legitimate to look for a new agent while still with the old one. It's sensible to try to solve the problem that's driving you out; it's ethical to explain the situation to new agents you talk to. To avoid accusations of poaching, the new agent may tell you she is potentially interested but won't make an offer until you're free.

Although it is certainly safer — and much less frightening — to have found a new agent before leaving the old one, it is often better to have no agent at all than one who is harmful to your career.

Think twice before moving. Remember Anon, in the *Penguin Dictionary of Modern Quotations*: "Changing agents is like changing deck chairs on the *Titanic*."

Is an Agent Necessary?

According to agents, the answer is a resounding "yes," as an access to media casting. According to actors, the answer is a resounding "sort of," as a buffer and negotiator.

In Vancouver, Montreal, and Toronto, and increasingly elsewhere, principal work on union film and television productions and commercials is closed to you if you don't have an agent. Casting breakdowns are sent to agents, and casting directors consider only the suggestions the agents make when they draw up audition lists.

Although more theatres are sending breakdowns to agents instead of relying entirely on general auditions and callbacks, few agents will be able to open many doors for you in theatre. Their strength is in getting information quickly and knowing everyone important. They can do this in the media, but you can do it as well as they can in theatre.

When you are a younger, less experienced, non-union actor, agents know your market value better than you do and have a better overall view of the business. Richard Curtis, in *How to Be Your Own Literary Agent*: "As my own client, I tend to be so flattered that someone wants to publish me, as to accept terms I would sternly reject if they were offered for one of my author's properties."

However, as a beginner, you are more likely to know about low- and non-paying jobs that will build your résumé. Your agent isn't likely to research work with no commission in sight.

Not having an agent loses you the advantage of that experienced eye, but it doesn't mean you aren't professional. It is possible to be a successful actor without an agent. You'll have to do all your own promotion and negotiation, but you'll have the pleasure of knowing that 100 percent of the fee you earn goes directly into your pocket.

CHAPTER ELEVEN

All for One, But Is It for You?

*"Yes, we must, indeed, all hang together,
or most assuredly we shall all hang separately."*
Benjamin Franklin

Canadian English-language performance is covered by the Alliance of Canadian Cinema Television and Radio Artists and the Canadian Actors' Equity Association. ACTRA governs film, television and radio; Equity governs live performance. Broadly, Equity is a professional association. ACTRA in B.C. (UBCP) is a trade union, but its status elsewhere is in the courts as we write. The difference, as far as we are concerned, is that professional association members can refuse to accept work but can't go on strike the way union members can. However, everybody calls them unions, so that's what we'll do here.

The unions negotiate with groups of engagers, developing and improving Agreements for each field of work. The Agreements come from many years of experience on both sides of the table, and set out the minimum standards of working conditions, hours, and pay. Non-union companies aren't bound by union fees and conditions but are influenced by them, especially in film and television.

The unions resolve problems between performers and engagers, run insurance and retirement plans, and generally promote performers' interests in the industry, and the industry's position in the economy.

If you have timed it right, joining the union opens up possibilities. As a member, you can call the union about all sorts of professional problems and have them solved or explained by people who are totally on your side and absolutely on top of the rules and customs of your work. As well as background information about contracts, RRSPS, and insurance, the unions will deal with your professional disasters.

After you have tried to deal with any situation yourself or through your agent (and that is an important first step), talk to the union. They will go to bat for you: in an emergency ACTRA can send people to your set, and Equity can be part of a company meeting, to make sure Management is living up to its side of the contract.

Every day, the unions win dollars for their members, negotiating better Agreements, being sure managements can pay their performers, and making sure they do pay.

ACTRA

ACTRA regulates English-language film, television, radio, new media, and other voice work. It was born over fifty years ago and changed again and again as the industry changed. It now represents actors through ten autonomous local branches, and has over twenty different Agreements with engagers. The British Columbia branch (UBCP) is a local union; there was a time when it looked like breaking away completely. Those problems were patched over, but tensions and crises continue. We will treat ACTRA as if it were a single organization, but UBCP runs its own house with similar services, sometimes bearing different names. All UBCP contracts are based on the Master Production Agreement, a fact that does not sit well with ACTRA National.

All ACTRA's contracts are based on Agreements negotiated with groups of engagers. They all cover these basic matters (and much more):

- Minimum payment — a higher fee may be negotiable for the work session.
- Licence to use material in specific markets or for defined periods.
- Minimum fees for use and re-use of material (residuals and royalties).

- Basic work conditions, hours, meal breaks, etc.
- Overtime, subsidiary payments, penalty payments.
- Bond to secure artists' payments.
- Engager contributions to health insurance and RRSP through ACTRA Fraternal.

Every Agreement says you must receive your money within fifteen business days of doing the job (about three weeks) or else the engager incurs a late payment penalty. (Non-union engagers pay when they're good and ready — or not at all.)

You can download a copy of any Agreement from the ACTRA sites. If you are a member of ACTRA, you can get a copy from your local ACTRA office. Take a look to see how much potential grief you are being saved once you're a member. Read it, if you are a member, to know what you and the engager are agreeing to when you sign a contract.

ACTRA on Set

ACTRA stewards are employees who are each responsible for the different Agreements. By visiting as many sets as they can, they head off problems before they affect the members. On Set Liaison Officers (OSLOs) are ordinary union member volunteers, selected and trained by ACTRA. OSLOs receive expenses and a daily fee, for which they monitor the set and call the steward when necessary. Any member can call the steward directly (the union guarantees anonymity) if an Agreement is being breached.

Don't phone the ACTRA national executive director about the lack of toilet paper in the washrooms, as once happened, when a reasonable request to an AD could solve the problem. But do use the union's power: we know of actors working in near-freezing temperatures who have been loath to complain, not wanting to jeopardize their jobs. The union can protect its members, but only if its members want to be protected.

Joining

Before you're a union member, you may work on an ACTRA production with ACTRA rates and conditions by buying a work permit. After your first permit for a speaking role on film or television, or a speaking or SOC (Silent on Camera) role in a commercial, you can apply for Apprenticeship. Apprentices pay $30 a year, as well as their work permit fees, and are treated as if they were full ACTRA members. You can join ACTRA once you have the qualifying number of credits. The conditions vary from branch to branch, and from time to time. Check with your local branch before you sign up as an Apprentice. ACTRA Apprentices may work in Equity productions as non-professionals but may not work in non-ACTRA film, radio, or television.

ACTRA and Equity have a Reciprocal Agreement: if you are already an Equity member, you may not do non-ACTRA film or television work. You must become an ACTRA member with your first professional media engagement, but you pay a reduced initiation, plus the half-year minimum dues. If your first engagement in ACTRA's jurisdiction is in an Extra category, or where the total fee is less than a hundred dollars, an Equity member may pay initiation fees and dues by installments.

ACTRA FRATERNAL BENEFIT SOCIETY

ACTRA Fraternal offers ACTRA members health and dental care insurance and RRSPS. The health and dental care plans supplement your provincial health plan, and the more you earn, the more they cover. Of course, the less you earn, the more help you need. But who said life was fair? You can buy extra coverage, but it's hard to make money from an insurance company.

You start your ACTRA Frat RRSP when you join the union. Each union engager deducts 3 or 4 percent of your fee, then adds its larger contribution, and sends the total to ACTRA Fraternal. You can also start a voluntary RRSP and make extra contributions.

ACTRA Performers Rights Society polices residuals and royalties here and abroad. ACTRA member or not, PRS will go to bat for you, although there are many occasions — when a production has been sold, for instance — where they can't do much. Their job will be much easier when and if Status of the Artist legislation gives performers legal ownership of their performances. If you think you're owed money, do make sure before contacting PRS that (1) you haven't already been paid,

(2) there isn't a five-year buy-out still running, (3) you weren't working as an Extra and (4) it really was you on the screen. Be cautious about claiming a residual unless you know the name of the program and where, when, and on what station it played. If you work on a non-union production, you won't see any residuals.

Canadian Actors' Equity Association

CAEA, better known as Equity, started life in 1955 as a branch of Actors' Equity Association (AEA) in the United States. It wasn't until April 1, 1976, that it separated from AEA and became a completely independent and autonomous body.

Equity has jurisdiction over live performance and represents five thousand active members, including dancers, singers, actors, presenters, puppeteers, stage management, directors, and choreographers.

There are two offices: the National Office in Toronto handles all items of national interest, as well as the day-to-day administration of members and theatres from Newfoundland to the Saskatchewan-Alberta border; the Western Office deals with the day-to-day administration of members and theatres from Alberta to B.C. and the Yukon.

Equity has over a dozen Agreements with groups of engagers, each dealing with the details of a different sort of work. Members can get the major Agreements on disk as the Agreement Switchboard, offering convenient computer access. Visit the Equity website to view the Agreements (some are downloadable) and to find out more about the union.

There are more similarities than differences between the Agreements, so we will look at actors working under the largest and most-often used one, the Canadian Theatre Agreement (CTA), which was negotiated with Professional Association of Canadian Theatres (PACT).

The CTA lays out hours of work, minimum pay and working conditions, plus rules, regulations and responsibilities for both artist and management.

Before a theatre may sign artists to contracts, it has to post a bond with the union. This cash or letter of credit is meant to guarantee that Equity members will receive two weeks' fees plus benefits in lieu of notice should the engager suddenly run out of money and close the show. A comforting thing, don't you think?

The Equity Deputy

All Equity productions have a deputy, elected by the Equity members of the company on the first day of rehearsal. The union says the deputy is "your representative and the direct link between the Equity members of the company and the Equity office." The union stresses that a deputy should never become involved in confrontation with management. The deputy is not an employee of the union, as the ACTRA steward is; he or she works with the stage manager to avoid potential infractions, and reports them to the Equity office.

The deputy represents the cast's interests, but is not responsible for the Equity members' dues-paying, timekeeping, or discipline. At the end of the contract, the deputy checks that all members, including stage management, have been paid in full, including travel money and any overtime owed, and, if all is well, signs the Deputy Release form to release the security bond the management posted with Equity.

Emergency Line

You don't have to be an Equity deputy to phone the Equity office. Any member can phone during business hours for help or information. You use the 1-800 line if you're out of town and calling the National Office, or call collect if you're out of town and calling the Western Office. For after-hours emergencies, Equity has a number where you can speak to a Business Representative. This is strictly for emergencies. Please don't use it to leave your change of address or find out information about your RRSP.

Non-professionals

Theatres using Equity contracts are allowed a certain percentage of non-union actors in a production — the richer the theatre, the smaller the non-union quota. Non-union actors get no advantage from Equity's minimum fees or conditions.

Joining

You can join Equity by being offered an Equity contract. The theatre may offer an Equity contract to whomever they wish; you may be offered a contract simply because the non-union quota has been filled. When you return Equity's copy of the contract, you apply for membership and pay $750 and a half-year's basic dues, currently $67.50. This is often paid in installments, by deductions from your weekly fee.

If you are already a member of ACTRA and have been offered work in an Equity production, you must join Equity and pay $67.50 basic dues. Your ACTRA initiation fee may be used to reduce your Equity initiation fee by up to 50 percent. If your stage experience is limited, Equity may allow you to register as an apprentice, but such permission is rarely granted.

Apprenticeship

Equity apprentices are part of the non-union quota in an Equity company. There is no minimum Equity rate for them, and they pay a fee that counts as a credit towards their union initiation. Apprentices need to earn three credits in thirty-six months. Once you have the credits, you may join Equity without a contract. Just inform the membership department, pay the balance of your money, and you're a member.

You may decide that the profession really is as dreadful as your teachers, parents, and this book have tried to tell you. If you give up the stress of the theatre (and join a bomb-disposal squad, for instance), you lose your credits and the money you paid for them.

At any time during your apprenticeship, you may accept an Equity contract and join that way, paying your initiation and a half-year's basic dues (less the apprentice credit fees already paid).

As an Equity apprentice you can accept non-union media and theatre work because you are still considered a non-professional. When you are working in your qualifying productions, you can be paid whatever the theatre chooses; you get no contractual protection, but you do get accident insurance from Equity while you're working.

The American Equity apprentice scheme guarantees classes and workshops, but in Canada all you'll have is the opportunity to work with a union cast and learn what you can. With rare exceptions, the Shaw and Stratford festivals being shining examples, you will simply be a gofer for anyone who needs help, on- or off-stage.

The one bright spot in those three years is that as an apprentice you may attend Equity auditions, thus losing out to a better class of actor.

Probationary Membership

This flexible form of membership was created originally to address the concerns of young actors who had been obliged to join Equity just after leaving theatre school in order to work for companies that had already filled their non-pro quota. Having joined Equity with no experience and too small a résumé, the result for the actor was a single job then never working again. Probationary membership allows the newbie actor to work as a full Equity member for the length of the engagement, with all the members' privileges and rights (except the right to vote), then revert to being a non-member once the contract is over. You pay for that flexibility with a non-refundable registration fee, but it's worth it. You get the full protection of the union while working as a probationary member. Once you're a non-member again, you can earn Apprenticeship credits while working in Equity companies, and even work completely non-Equity in amateur and community theatres.

Working Dues

As well as annual basic dues, you have working dues. The engager deducts 2 percent of your fee and sends it to Equity.

The RRSP and the Accident/Sickness Insurance Plan

You must apply for your Equity RRSP when you join: don't forget or you could lose your contributions. The theatre deducts 6 percent of your gross wage at source and sends it to Equity to deposit into your plan. You can make extra contributions if you want. The theatre also deducts and sends to Equity your insurance premium. While you are under contract and while you are travelling to and from an out-of-town job you are covered twenty-four hours a day, on or off the job site, for the medical, surgical, and job-loss results of accidents or illness. It doesn't matter whether the injury was job-related or you got hit by a bus on your day off. You're covered all the same.

Other Unions

We have added the following unions so that you won't feel like an idiot when the initials start to fly.

UDA

The Union des Artistes is the union that covers stage and media French-language work. The union has around six thousand actors, most of whom are based in Montreal. You join UdA by work permits — thirty of them — and by indicating that you can function in French. The reciprocal arrangements with Equity and ACTRA are rather complex.

Roughly speaking, ACTRA and Equity members may work in UdA jurisdiction (and vice versa) three times a year under courtesy work permits. If you want to know more about UdA, get in touch with their local offices (see Addresses).

IATSE

The International Alliance of Theatrical Stage Employees and Moving Picture Operators of the United States and Canada — IATSE (pronounced "eye-at-see" and also called IA) — is a union of nine hundred locals covering technicians, front-of-house staff, camera operators, costume designers, dressers, etc. Only larger Equity theatres are IATSE houses.

NABET

The National Association of Broadcast Employees and Technicians is a rival union to IATSE and started as a reaction to IA's nepotism. (Going to an IA meeting is like going to a family reunion.) Unlike IATSE, NABET is strictly a union for workers in the media.

Withdrawal

You can go on Temporary Withdrawal or Inactive Status if, for example, you have been going through a rough time and you're finding it hard to pay dues. You don't pay dues, you no longer have a vote, and you can't attend meetings, but you are still considered a union member. Which means you cannot, while on withdrawal, do any kind of theatre work. Or television. Or film. Or radio. Or anything. Union or non-union. Professional or amateur. Nothing. Nada. Nitchivo. The moment you act for the public, however far removed from union theatre or media it may be, you must reinstate yourself in the union, pay any outstanding dues, be under the relevant contract, and be paid for your services. We cannot make this point clear enough. Once you are a member of a performers' union you can never act for any company without the knowledge and permission of your union.

Kickbacks

A semi-professional theatre company offers you a part you would kill for, but hasn't enough money to pay you the appropriate guest artist fee. You're asked, as a personal favour by the producer, to make a "donation" of your fee back to the company.

A kickback occurs when the return of all or part of your fee is a condition of the engagement. Kickbacks are, in the authors' opinion, among the nastiest and most exploitive realities of this business. Agreeing to hand back some or all of your money is agreeing to theft. Not only does it cheat you, it cheats actors to follow.

Never, repeat never, allow yourself to be treated in this way.

From an Equity newsletter: "Don't be pressured by threats that another actor is at the door if you don't agree. Report the matter to Equity

— it will be dealt with confidentially. Once you have signed to perform, and the engager has signed to use you, you both have obligations to fulfill. Don't let a dishonest producer make a profit by taking your salary."

Under the Counter

ACTRA fined a dozen of its actors $2,000 each for working on a non-union film at a third of the proper minimum fee.

As long as you are not a union member, you are free to work for nothing, or, for that matter, to pay the theatre to let you work. It's up to you. But as Jimmy Namaro of Happy Gang fame said, "If you're good enough to play for people, you're good enough to be paid."

When you join a performers' union, you take on an obligation to defend the rights that people before you fought long and hard to obtain. If you find that difficult to understand, you are not ready to join a union. End of lecture.

Resignation

Now that you know all about the unions, how do you get out of them? Leaving ACTRA is easy enough. You simply resign, and it is as if you had never joined. You may rejoin at any time by going through the apprentice process or by asking for special consideration. You pay initiation fees like a new member. It is Equity's policy to discourage resignation. If you want to resign, you will have to apply to the Equity Council in writing for permission to give up your professional career.

The All-Important Question

Should you join the performers' unions? And if you should, when should you? (All right, that's two questions. So sue us.) The answer to the first question is reasonably straightforward. Yes. If you are serious in your desire to become a working professional actor, you will eventually have to become a member. Since its amateur beginnings, the business has grown and matured to become a complex structure with international connections.

It is theoretically possible to make a career as a performer without ever joining ACTRA or Equity, but in order to pit yourself against the best in the industry, to protect yourself against devious and exploitative engagers, and to get the most lucrative work, you have to join the unions. In the union you can have your complaints against management handled anonymously and you have knowledgeable people on your side. The union can only be as strong as its members, but it is bound to be stronger than an individual actor.

When to join is another question. All we can say is, not until you have to. Actors feel that by joining a performers' union, they have in some way "made it." Not true. It is better to have interesting credits on your résumé than simply union membership. By joining Equity and ACTRA early on, you cut yourself off from challenging amateur, semi-pro, and non-union professional experience early on in your career. Christopher Marston, former executive director, Canadian Actors' Equity Association: "Non-Equity companies may be useful to a new actor. They are likely to offer an actor bigger roles and more responsibility than an Equity company would. You have more chance to compare companies and ways of working. Media casting rarely depends on having ACTRA membership. If you're right for the role, they'll cast you." Bonnie Gillespie, casting director: "Consider your lifetime goals carefully before making big moves. Pro athletes train for many years as non-pros before they suit up professionally. Make sure you're ready for the big leagues, or you'll end up just warming the bench."

Please, don't rush this decision. Unions don't get you work. They protect against much of the exploitation of actors, but they don't get you work. Find out about the non-union opportunities in your area.

The Equity theatres probably have non-union general auditions for small parts. Outside Ontario there are masses of non-union commercials being done. Get in touch with provincial arts councils for lists of community and non-union professional theatres. Theatre Ontario has lists of professional theatres, union and non-union, across the country. Look in your area for amateur and community theatres and fringes.

Contact local university and college film courses. If you're in a larger centre, look for associations of independent filmmakers. Any new company that values commitment and enthusiasm will welcome and give real work to an actor even without a track record. Contacts you make when everybody in the group is struggling can stay with you throughout your career.

Before you decide to join, talk to union officers, or at least write to them. ACTRA has offices across the country (except in New Brunswick, Prince Edward Island, the Yukon, and the Northwest Territories), and Equity is based in Vancouver and Toronto (see Addresses). Union people are marvellously approachable and can give you all the information you need. Joining too soon can lose you work and money, and wreck your self-confidence.

Union Strength

Our Agreements spell out fair working conditions, and the union tries to see the Agreements are upheld. They are not always successful. Weak unions? No, weak membership. When you allow a rule to be broken and don't complain, the union can't police the rule, and it will die. If you disagree with a particular policy, get involved; run for office. It's the members who make the rules, the staff who enforce them.

If you want a strong union, you can have one. The strength of the union is the only protection you have against engagers abusing their power.

CHAPTER TWELVE

The Actor as Producer

"One must learn by doing the thing; though you think
you know it, you have no certainty until you try."
Sophocles

Provincial and federal government funding for theatre and the media is low, and what's worse, it's unreliable. Theatres that were the mainstay of the business are struggling to stay afloat. Funding for Canadian feature film production has not significantly increased the tiny number of Canadian films we see in regular release. Out of necessity, small, project-based, artist-driven productions have blossomed. The new breed of successful theatre companies does not need a season of plays or a building to present them in. Digital productions made in the filmmaker's home can rival the quality that comes from long and expensive post-production in traditional film.

A warning from Martin Scorcese: "You've really got to want to tell that story." That sounds obvious, but you'll be persuading all sorts of people to support your project, so you'd better have thought it through every which way and still be convinced. As Jaco Van Dormael (*Toto le Héros*) said of being a director, "You really have to be a maniac — to follow the same story for five years is like every morning you take the same piece of chewing gum to see if you can still taste it."

But you can do the show right here, as Mickey Rooney suggested. One or two people, often friends from drama school, can form a theatre company, a process often involving no more than giving themselves a cute name and opening a bank account. They work out a budget. They fundraise and apply for grants until they have enough money to mount the production. They rent a hall. They publicize. They do the show. They make a profit … break even … lose their shirts. The project is over. They start again. Indie films are the same, only more so. More planning, more begging and stealing, almost no chance of fame or fortune. Almost … As Samuel Beckett put it: "Try again. Fail again. Fail better."

Kathryn Stockwood, a Toronto actor, was star, writer, producer, and director of her short, *Gold 'n Solid*, in the 2004 On The Fly Festival. "When you're an actor," she says, "you're helping the director or the writer tell his or her story. But this was my baby."

trey anthony was playwright, producer, and star of *'da KINK in my HAIR*, which debuted February 2001 (during Black History month) at the Now Lounge in Toronto, and was a hit at the Toronto Fringe Festival, Atlantic Fringe, and NY Fringe through 2002. In 2003 it was staged at Theatre Passe Muraille, was picked up by Mirvish Productions and had a very successful run, including eight hold-over weeks, followed by a U.S. production in Fall 2005 and a tour to England in Fall 2006.

If you want to hire union members, or if you are a member and want to set up an artist-driven production, both unions advise talking to them well ahead of time. Why not? They've seen all sorts of productions similar to yours and you might as well avoid other people's mistakes and find out if your project can fit union requirements. Equity and ACTRA have policies for small producers and artist-driven productions that recognize the limitations of budget and project. If your production meets specific conditions, you can pay less, or nothing at all, and get some breaks on working conditions.

You can organize your production in different ways, to suit your circumstances. You can be a traditional producer, find all the funding, cut all the deals, take all the profit, and bear all the losses. That's what Sandra Shamas does, producing herself in a successful series of her own one-woman shows. You probably want to organize yourself so that you qualify for one of the Not Ready for Prime Time options if you're going to engage union artists.

You can organize a co-op. ACTRA and Equity have guidelines to make it easier for members to show that they are sharing all the risks and profits, and so don't need the protections given members against greedy producers. Even if you're not a member, check the union websites for their co-op agreements. Union co-ops demand detailed plans — non-union work is freer and easier. If you choose not to follow the union guidelines, you'll find it easier to make stupid mistakes and lose all your money.

How you set yourself up affects the finances, and it affects the way you feel as a producer and as an actor.

Producing gives you control, but it's not easy. Sandra Shamas spoke of the difficulty of producing your own show: "My producer is not a very nice person [but] my artist is a little flaky, she wants everyone to like her." Being a producer means paying the bills and taking the blame. It does not necessarily mean doing everything yourself, although it may feel like that. Most small-scale, project-based, artist-driven productions are run just like the standard establishment theatre or production company. There is a hierarchy: a few people make the decisions, the rest carry the decisions out. At best, the other people involved share the producer's excitement and understand their contracts, written or not.

In a co-op, all the people involved in the making of the film or play have a stake in the project. They are equal partners in a business and have a say in how the business is run. They share in the profits and are liable for the losses. Co-op decisions are voted on by the co-op members, who also decide their own voting procedures. The whole process can be cumbersome and time-consuming, but it can also be the most rewarding way of being in charge of your own art. There is little we can control in this business. Co-ops are a way of creating and taking control.

Mickey and Judy didn't plan: in film reality, they could solve each problem as it came up. This makes for good screenwriting, but in real life it makes for ulcers. And failure. Go to an expert. You'll be improvising quite enough as a self-producer or a co-op member: get an expert to clear away as much uncertainty as possible before the deadlines begin to roll. Get professional advice from your lawyer and tax preparer before committing to incorporation or to a co-op. If you're in Ontario, ALAS offers nearly free advice from experienced arts lawyers. Talk to UBCP or Equity about your project. Way in advance. You're not making a commitment yet, you're just borrowing some experience.

How much planning you do is your choice, but we based these points on the co-op advice you can get in detail from the unions — not all these points will apply to your case, but think about them to be quite sure. Get a framework organized in advance, even if the details change. In a co-op, there's no one else to blame. Everyone is the producer, everyone shares the responsibility, just as everyone shares the profits. If you're a self-producer, read this anyway: these are decisions you'll have to make sitting down with yourself. Start early. Grants routinely take a year before you get the money; theatres are booked in advance.

Sit the group down with pen and paper and make some decisions:

How do you make decisions?
Is everything decided in huge meetings? If the DOP and the director dig in their heels, who wins? Is there voting, who votes, what's a majority?

How do people join the group?
How do they leave? Can you sack them?

Who is going to do what?
Exactly. Offstage stuff as well as the casting. Everyone should have a detailed written job description. Are people wearing too many hats?

How do people work elsewhere?
You'll find it easier to get people to commit if they can take time out to make more certain money, at least in the early weeks. Clearly, it's too late to beg off as the audience files in, or as the borrowed equipment is being unloaded on set.

Who gets blamed?
If a group member is doing the job properly, the production should take the blame. That means insurance. Or accepting the risk.

Who gets what?
Members of a union co-op agree to share profit and loss; every-

one else gets to negotiate. Sponsors, tradespeople, facility rental, Fringe organizers, the crew — everyone would prefer something up front. Cash is always acceptable, but promises of exposure, a share in the profits, or a pittance now (with more later) are all possible.

And when do they get it?

If your brainchild is organized and efficient, people will be more likely to wait. Set an exact time for payment, soon enough to be attractive, late enough to be realistic. Scheduling is all. When is the money coming in? Who gets first shares? After what running costs?

Who winds up the group?

And who owns what at the end, including the things you buy and the things you create? You have a script, you have a production, you have tape. You have a set, you have costumes, you have supplies. Agree who controls them. In writing. Can the writer take back her script? Can you recast the Fringe show and take it on tour? Who sells the short film to the big network next year?

What are your liabilities?

Members of any group, but especially one formally set up like an ACTRA or Equity co-op, may be individually liable in the case of a judgment against anyone acting for the group. If your treasurer-person can't add, or skips off with the loot, and suppliers are unpaid, you may get stuck with the bill. If someone in the audience falls and sues, you may have to pay the doctor. If the script offends someone, you could be named in the suit. Is there insurance? Who and what does it cover?

Now, finally, the production:

What are we doing?

Are you aiming at a full-scale production, or just a few days at the Fringe? Do you want the tape for your reel, or are you aiming at the festival circuit? Knowing where you're headed is you key to getting grants and corporate support, but it will also keep you on track. You can always change your mind, but you can only go in one direction at a time.

Who's got the money?

Or who will give you the help, which amounts to the same thing. What do the money people want to see? Exactly what are your donors ready to give you? What hoops do you have to jump through?

And last but not least:

Who is going to keep the books?

Everyone in a group production should get to check the books, but only one person should fill in what was bought and what was earned. Everyone in the group needs a copy for tax time.

Who's writing this down?

Get it in writing. From the beginning, get it all written down. Your memory won't hold up. The arguments will be too long to record, but at least have records of the decisions. Even though you'll change them over and over, write them down so you'll know the current version. Too much trouble? When an argument breaks out hard up against a deadline, you'll be glad you have it in writing that Mary was to order the lights.

Be careful about a production that calls itself a co-op but is actually a producer and a group of volunteers. If you don't sign an agreement before you start work, you may find that Joe is making the decisions, Joe is directing and talking to the press, and you are buying your costume, working eighteen-hour days, and housing the cameraman. If the film is a success, Joe's career takes off, and you get an honorarium and no publicity. If it's a failure, the laboratory can legally chase you, as the only member of the group with any money, and sue you for their bill.

After all this foundation work, dreary as it is, remember what Thomas Edison had to say: "Opportunity is missed by most people because it wears overalls and looks like work."

CHAPTER THIRTEEN

The "T" Word

"The art of taxation consists in so plucking the goose so as to obtain the largest amount of feathers with the least possible amount of hissing."
Jean Baptiste Colbert

Tax. There, we've said it. That wasn't so bad, was it? And neither is filling in a tax form. If you have been conscientious throughout the year, income tax is a breeze. If you haven't been, it's more of a Force 9 gale, but it only gets worse if you put it off. Canada Revenue Agency (formerly Revenue Canada) loves to jump up and down on people who don't file, even if the tax in question is laughably small.

You have to make a return if you have tax to pay, or if you need to pay CPP contributions (that is, if you earned over $3,500 in self-employment), or if CRA tells you to. You will never gain by putting off filing. If you owe tax, there is interest and a late filing penalty, calculated on what you owe. If you don't owe any tax, you are cheating yourself out of the GST credit and any provincial credits paid to low income earners. You are also buying trouble with your Home Buyers Plan and the Tuition and Education credit, if any.

You can do your own tax. Believe us, it's not brain surgery. You can use the regular income tax form, which you get from the post office in the spring, or a thirty-dollar tax software program, or an online program, which is often free. Tax programs can be set to lead you gently through a Q & A session, transferring your answers to the proper places on the forms. Doing your own tax from the beginning, while things are simple and amounts are small, makes it less likely you'll be ripped off by a shark, or mismanaged by an incompetent, in years to come.

With enough patience, a calculator, and a stiff scotch, anyone can work through a tax return. However, if this chapter is already making you queasy, you can get your tax done for you for $200 and up. Way up. You'll save money if you use this chapter to get things organized ahead of time. Not all accountants are tax preparers, and not all tax preparers know anything about performers. Ask around; look for names in the union newsletters and performer notice boards. Find someone who will work with you as a partner. "I have no use for bodyguards, but I do pay two highly trained certified Public Accountants," Elvis Presley.

As an actor, union or not, you are self-employed, unless you work in Newfoundland. If you do other work as well, you may also be an employee. The ordinary tax form has places to enter both sets of income.

When you are an employee, your employer is legally obliged to deduct tax from your pay before you get it, along with CPP and EI payments.

As a self-employed person, you don't need to have tax deducted from your pay. You have to pay your own CPP with no contribution from your engagers, and you may not have EI deducted, nor can you claim EI benefits based on your acting work. (Canada is the only country we have found worldwide where acting income doesn't qualify you for unemployment benefits.) If you earn enough to have $2,000 of federal tax due, the tax man will send you a note telling you to pay next year's tax in advance, by installments. You'll have to make about $14,500 after expenses before worrying about this.

Remember that this is just general advice. We have been tax preparers for twenty-five years, but we don't know your special case. Call CRA's local Business/GST number for information. Call an artist-friendly tax preparer: it's amazing what you can get explained by booking a half-hour chat. Check out canadianactor.com, taxxman.ca, and the Equity site, all of which have tax information.

Keep records of everything, incoming and outgoing. Keep a diary of all your professional appointments and engagements. Keep receipts of all your purchases, personal and professional. Keep the pay slips from all your jobs. Although CRA requires only very few receipts attached to your return, you must have evidence available of every single outgoing expense and incoming fee. If your return is challenged seriously, the simple fact that you have kept detailed records will count in your favour.

How you keep your records is up to you. The authors use their own Tax Kit, of course (see details at the end of the chapter). You can use any stationery store system you like or have around. Cheaper than accordion files, but less convenient, are big envelopes, labelled and punched and put into a three-ring binder. If you want to fill a pillowcase all year long, and sort the receipts out at the end of the year, that is up to you. Whatever works best. (We do not recommend the pillowcase method ourselves, but then we're just a couple of old fuddy-duddies.) Whiz-bang spreadsheet programs and PDAs have a steep learning curve, and they are capable of doing much more than you need. If you aren't already keeping your records in pen and pencil, they won't help you. Use the simplest method that works for you, and use it regularly.

The ideal receipt has on it the name and address of the store, your name and address, the date, the purchase, the amount, how it was paid (cash, credit card, etc.), and the salesperson's initials. Under $30, say, ordinary cash register receipts are all right. Scribble "$12.75 make-up" on the receipt right away, and you won't have a pocket full of anonymous litter when you get around to clearing it out. The more information you have on a receipt, the less likely it is to be challenged. Credit card slips, bank statements, and cancelled cheques are worth keeping for cross-checking, but don't rely on their being accepted in place of real receipts.

You may not dump your tax information even after your return has been okayed by CRA. Books and records must be retained for six years from the end of the year you filed the return. If you want to destroy them any earlier, you must get written permission. CRA can audit four years back, or as far back as they like if they suspect fraud. After six years, breathe a sigh of relief and chuck it.

Canadian residents are taxed on their world income. That includes cruise ships — the fact that they're in international waters makes no difference. Around February or March, your Canadian employers must give you a T4 with all the details, but your professional engagers may or may not give you a T4A. There are two copies of the T4 or T4A for you, and a third copy is sent to CRA. If you get a T4A, your gross income should be in Box 28, Other Income. If you don't get a T4A for a gig, write to the engager so they'll know where to send the T4A. That may not help, but your copy of the letter will avoid possible hassles with CRA. If they don't send it, you'll be relying on your own records.

With or without an official statement, you have to declare all your income, worldwide. Don't try to save tax by hiding some of your professional income. You can't be sure your engager didn't send CRA their copy of your T4A, even if your copies didn't reach you. Every year, CRA penalizes people who thought their income would stay under the table. Attach whatever statements you have received to your tax form, and add a list of all your other income for the year. Identify the sheet with your name, the tax year, and your SIN, and lay out your engagers and the totals from your pay stubs before deductions.

Now comes the fun part: deductible expenses. The basic rule is you deduct anything you spent as part of your acting business. You will be astonished and delighted at what you are allowed to deduct, as long as the items are properly receipted. Where getting a receipt is difficult — pay phones, bus and subway fares, parking meters — use your work diary. CRA will accept a reasonable deduction without receipts, based on your notes at the time. It may seem a petty amount to worry about — a quarter for a phone call — but it is amazing how quickly those quarters add up.

You can download the Business and Professional Guide from the CRA site, or get it mailed to you, and use Form T2124 to show your income and expenses. You may need to add an extra sheet for expense details. Or you can simply list your expenses on a sheet with your name, SIN, and the tax year on top. The tax return has slots for gross and net Business Income.

The following expense headings are the ones we use. It really doesn't matter as long as they seem logical and you don't keep changing your classifications:

Advertising and Promotion: Résumés, photographs, postcards, flyers, online casting membership, CDs, tapes, videotapes.

Agent Commission: The whole schmear. Including the expenses you are billed for, and the agent's GST.

Bank Charges: Only if you have an account just for business. Same goes for credit card charges.

Business Meals: Claim 50 percent of "a reasonable amount ... for food beverages, or entertainment incurred in earning income." For example, you can entertain directors you want to work for, actors you're working with, writers who will tell you about their new play. Include any home entertainment — keep all those supermarket receipts and liquor bills. Staple the party receipts together with a list of who was there. You must be able to show the meal was arranged with the express intention of talking business. Set up the meal by letter or email and keep copies. You can claim restaurant meals for yourself if you are caught between appointments, or if you are away from your hometown on business. Make a note on the back of the receipt and put enough details about the conversation in your work diary to show it was a professional expense.

Business Use of Home: You can claim the expense of using your home as your principal place of business to rehearse, store books, do administration, teach, exercise, and more. You don't need a separate room; it doesn't have to be devoted solely to business purposes. Don't believe anyone who says otherwise — this is laid out in CRA information and has been cleared in detail, face to face, with high-level CRA honchos. Add together all your general household expenses: your share of the rent, utilities, mortgage interest, property tax, insurance, cleaning. Divide by the proportion of your home you use for business, by area or room count (whichever gives you a better deal). If you use a space half the time for personal and half for business reasons, count it as half its area. This is a huge deduction, and you can carry it forward if you are not allowed to use it this year.

Car: Not nearly as tricky as some people think. Calculate what percentage of your yearly mileage is business use. Claim that percentage of your total operating expenses. What expenses can you claim? Everything: gas, oil, servicing, insurance, licence, motor leagues, repairs. How do you decide what percentage to use? CRA wants you to keep a log book in the car. Enter the mileage on January 1, then write down the beginning mileage of each trip and what you did. Enter your mileage on December 31, get out your handy-dandy calculator, add up all the business miles, and work that out as a percentage of the total miles you have driven. It's worth doing: the figure will be higher than you guess.

Because your home is your main base of operations, unless you have an office elsewhere, any trip for a business purpose is deductible. Travelling to and from an employed job is not deductible.

Dressing Room Supplies: The duplicates you buy to have at the theatre or in your on-set bag. Towel, deodorant, paper tissues, contact lens supplies, tampons, shampoo, soap, etc. And all the bits and pieces you need to perform in often temporary spaces. No fair carrying your toothbrush back and forth.

Hair: 100 percent of styling and cut for a specific role. Be reasonable about general styling. Maintaining our appearance is part of our job, so some expense is allowable.

Local Transportation: Claim the taxi if it was necessary; use transit transfers as receipts. Ask for a receipt for your transit pass or bulk tokens, and claim a reasonable business proportion.

Make-up: In the past, which is where CRA lives, actors bought make-up from theatrical make-up suppliers. People have been challenged on large sums for regular make-up from drugstores. If, like most actors, you buy your make-up from your local Pharmaplus or equivalent, write the uses of the make-up on the back of the receipt.

Office Supplies: Tape, pens, computer supplies, staples, address stamps, hole punch, liquid paper, calculator, erasers, etc. Large equipment like a computer will go under Capital Cost Allowance (see below).

Out of Town: Don't believe anyone who says CRA allows you an out-of-town per diem without receipts. Not true. You may get away with claiming an amount for each out-of-town day, but if you're audited, you won't be allowed a penny of it without receipts. The rules in the States, under the IRS, are quite different. Normally, if you keep your home base, you can deduct the extra expenses of being away from home to work, or train, or to look for work. Claim your rental and hotel costs. Of course, if you are subletting your home apartment, the tax man will expect you to declare the rent you get as income. Remember, you're not living at home, so taxis are more freely allowable. You'll eat out more, so claim your restaurant costs under Business Meals.

Postage and Stationery: Get receipts. It's more convenient to buy stamps in bulk, but you can get a receipt for even a single stamp. Some people include postage and stationery in Office Supplies. Up to you.

Professional Development: Claim for books, plays, accent tapes, etc., and any research expenses. Deduct classes for general professional improvement, as well as for a particular role, and for business-related courses like tax counselling and entrepreneurship, too. Split classes and research into two categories if the total is high; list the teachers separately if it's still big enough to invite questions. A proportion of your gym membership should be allowed, but be prepared to be challenged.

Professional Dues: Equity, ACTRA, UDA, etc. Only the yearly dues, not the initiation fee, which is an Eligible Capital Expenditure — look at your Business and Professional Income Tax Guide. Membership in societies, theatres, and any other organization that is professionally useful.

Professional Gifts: First night cards, flowers, booze. If you get a single receipt for thank-you cards for a group of people, make sure to list their names on it.

Professional Journals: All journals, periodicals, and magazines, as long as they are work-related. You may possibly be allowed part of the cost of magazines and newspapers that are not wholly related to your career but have arts sections or theatre and film reviews.

Professional Tickets: Any play or film you attend, and by extension any concert, opera, or ballet. Not football; not Jell-O wrestling. Unless they're on your résumé.

Telephone: Deduct 100 percent of business long-distance calls, not the basic service charge. If you have a cell phone, pager or a second line for business, claim the whole shot. We haven't seen any problems from claiming voice mail and other services, although to be safe you might take just a business proportion of those costs.

Travel: All your travel costs on professional out-of-town trips, except anything your engager should pay for. To be safe, book your business appointments ahead of time, to show the intention of the trip.

Wardrobe: Claim for repairs, laundry, dry cleaning. Current rules on wardrobe have been tightened up with two poorly written paragraphs in IT525. We advise you to claim wardrobe as Capital Cost and be very sure it was bought and used for business purposes only.

All clear? Feeling strong? Some complications, some solutions:

Capital Cost Allowance (CCA): If you buy any item of enduring value — computer, oboe, car — you can't deduct the whole cost in the year you bought it. You can claim CCA, a percentage of the cost, in any year you continue to own it. You have to fill in the CCA form in the CRA Business and Professional Guide, which gives you all the information you need and more. If the item cost less than $200, people are normally allowed to simply deduct it as an expense.

Losses: Don't worry if your expenses exceed your acting income. Just enter a negative net professional income. When you add up all your income (net self-employed, employed, and the rest), your negative acting income will reduce the total. The tax man will look oddly at you if you claim to have lived for a year on a net income of $417, and you may be asked to show outstanding loans or withdrawal from savings. New businesses don't expect to make a profit immediately, but beware of the impatient auditor. If you show a professional loss for a number of years, you may be asked to prove that you are running a business with the intention of making a profit. Fail to prove that and your losses will be disallowed. Keep financial records, career particulars, and a detailed work diary, and you should be safe.

Medical Expenses: Have their own schedule. CRA allows fees paid to a range of medical practitioners, counsellors, dentists, and registered nurses. There are some differences between provinces (naturopaths are an example). Drugs are allowed if they are prescribed by a medical practitioner and supplied by a pharmacist. Three percent of your net income is deducted from your medical claim. ACTRA Fraternal and Equity send you a receipt for the medical part of the premiums paid from your acting fees. This is claimed as an ordinary professional expense, not subject to the 3 percent deduction. If you pay a premium for your provincial health care, that is not deductible. Go figure.

RRSPs: Save some money and cut your tax bill. Tax deferral is a wonderful thing. Withdraw what you need if you're having a poor year and pay tax on it then, if necessary. You won't find a better home for your spare cash than the Equity and ACTRA Frat RRSPs. Their rates are highly competitive and you're not locked in. But it is a retirement plan. Stick windfall cash into your RRSP as soon as possible and leave it there as long as you can. Let compound interest work for you: your $2,000 graduation present will grow to $128,000 by the time you retire.

GST: You don't have to register if your world-wide self-employed income before expenses is less than $30,000 from all sources, but if you do, you'll get back all the GST you pay on those expenses. You can't lose money on this deal. After you register and give your engagers your GST number, they pay you an extra 6 percent of your fees. Remember to tell the payroll services you are registered, so that you'll be paid GST on the current residuals for past work. You make a GST return annually, in most cases at the same time as your income tax return. It asks for just four figures: your professional income, the GST on it, your expenses, and the GST on them. You pass on to CRA the GST you were paid, minus the GST you paid the stores, which can amount to a substantial savings. If your expenses are relatively low, you'll save even more by opting to use the Quick Method. Simply send CRA 3.3 percent of your total self-employed income up to $30,000 (4.3 percent on anything over $30,000).

Audit: There are actors who can't say the word without breaking out in hives. In fact, CRA can't possibly check everyone's return, so in 99 percent of the cases they enter your figures, check your arithmetic, run some cross-checks, and pass you for now. They have set their computers to flag suspicious returns for more attention. If your income or expenses were wildly different last year, for example, they will pull your file to look for an explanation. If there's no explanation, or they don't buy your story, they'll ask you for more information. CRA doesn't pick on actors, but it has six thousand auditors to carry out its stated policy to check up on the self-employed as a group. They can pick on anyone for any reason, or no reason at all, just to keep us on our toes. They trust us to tell them about our incomes, but they only trust us so far, and then we have to prove our story. We call this an audit, although technically it isn't. A full audit can involve some days of CRA staff camping out in your office going though the whole year and demanding explanations for everything. The best way to avoid this is to have satisfactory answers to their initial questions. If the axe does fall, get professional help. Ease the shock at tax time by having tax deducted by payroll, if you're in a long enough theatre job. Or do it yourself: open a savings account and stash away 10 or 15 percent of every cheque when you pay it in. That should be enough to cover your bill and give you a little refund. Add another 5 percent to be sure of your GST bill if you're registered.

We've had to be general and cautious in this chapter; if you need help with your specific problem, call us — (416) 960-9272. The TaxXman will answer quick questions in return for an Actors' Fund of Canada donation, sell you a Tax Kit (which you can also get from Theatrebooks in Toronto or Bizbooks in Vancouver), or do your tax return country-wide, by mail, fax, and email.

Final Warning: Everyone will give you free advice about income tax and GST. Don't believe them. Don't believe us, necessarily. Don't even believe your tax preparer, until you've been shown why something is so. CRA will send you full information and will try to answer your questions in their office or on the telephone. Look for their local Business number, not General Enquiries, for answers about self-employment.

CHAPTER FOURTEEN

Grownups

*"If you're old enough to be an actor, you're old
enough to know better."*
John Bjorgum

Young actors pride themselves on being outside the common herd. As the years go by, we continue to be outside but are no longer so happy about it. The Applebaum-Hébert Report: "[Artists strive to be different but] they want to be integrated into the society they live and work in." Christopher Marston, when executive director of Canadian Actors' Equity: "It's a rough life, not only because of psychological pressures of work and job-hunting, but also because of being outside the mainstream of society." Not fitting into the normal categories is romantic, until you are turned down for a credit card or a bank loan or a mortgage. Then those dull, pedestrian categories start looking pretty good. How can actors reconcile an artistically satisfying profession with the real world?

The Actor and the Establishment

Actors are stuck with the "rogues and vagabonds" myth. No matter how grownup our behaviour is, we suffer from society's view that we are not quite trustworthy. Some of our bad press is justified. Most of us are poor and nomadic — not something designed to endear you to the local bank manager. However, much of our bad press comes from ignorance and misrepresentation. The general public reads the *National Enquirer*, not the Equity newsletter.

Norman Bethune said: "An artist makes uneasy the static, the set and the still." Members of the Establishment don't like us. We don't fit on their forms. Society is run for the benefit of the average, so we are bound to have some problems. We can only fight their misconceptions by showing our best Establishment face when we need to.

When dealing with a bureaucrat, dress the part. Pretend it's an audition for the role of a business executive. Get all your facts together before you start. Treat the bureaucrats as people and they may return the compliment. If they don't, it is always possible to go higher. "We are having a problem dealing with this," you might say, "I wonder if I could talk to your supervisor?" Shoving your file down the clerk's throat is more satisfying, but only in the short term.

Filling in forms is like writing a résumé or having a job interview. Avoid lies, but put the best face on things you can from their point of view. Don't attempt to write last year's eight engagers in that little space on the form. Probably all they want is "self-employed" and your income, near enough. If you have had as many apartments as job rejections, use your parents' address. When dealing with banks, you should enter your gross income.

However, it is not your income that is the main concern. Anyone lending you money wants an assurance that they will get it back. You need a credit rating, and to get a credit rating you need a credit rating. Catch-22? Not necessarily. Just prove that you are an excellent debtor. (Unfortunately, a student loan won't count.) Take out a small bank loan secured with an equal amount frozen in a term certificate. Be frank with your bank manager about why you want this. Pay it back on schedule. Bingo, you've proved you can handle credit responsibly. It will cost you the difference in interest rates between the term certificate and the personal loan, so keep the term down to six months or so.

Insurance rates for the contents of a house or apartment can be slightly higher for actors. Quite reasonably. Insurers love couch potatoes who go away once a year and have a non-smoking, teetotaller accountant look after the place while they are gone. The best we can do is to ask different insurance brokers to quote for the same coverage, and find the company that gives us the best rates. ACTRA Frat has negotiated good house and car insurance rates for ACTRA members.

The Actor and the Bureaucracy

EMPLOYMENT INSURANCE

Acting work, by and large, doesn't qualify you for EI benefits. You don't pay the premiums, you don't get the coverage. But if you worked enough hours as an employee in the fifty-two weeks before you claim, you do qualify. As soon as your employment ends, take your Records of Employment in to a Service Canada Centre and put in your claim. When you list your last work, don't include self-employment however much they insist. It doesn't count, and it has caused trouble in the past. You have to be available for work and looking for work, and you have to declare anything you earn while you're drawing benefits. Your benefits will be a percentage of your average earnings over the last twenty-six weeks and they start two weeks after you make your claim.

Being self-employed does not disqualify you, if you have the qualifying hours. If they disagree at the counter, ask the clerk to check and, if necessary, insist on seeing a supervisor.

Human Resources and Social Development Canada (HRDSC) will give you information about appealing the counter clerk decision, but it's easier and quicker if you can win a good decision at the beginning.

GRANTS

There is no shame in going after a grant you deserve, unless you prefer to be poor. Even in these fiscally prudent days, governments show some awareness of the importance of the arts to society. Grab what you can. The traditional starving-in-an-attic thing doesn't produce art, and eating regularly doesn't equal selling out.

Getting a grant needs plenty of lead time. Find out what might fit your project, get the detailed information from the grant-giver. Talk to the administrator to get advice about the real ground rules. If you can interest this gatekeeper in your project, you can get unexpected help with new rules and changed opportunities. The administrator can't help you apply, but when your first application fails, which it generally does, the administrator you've cultivated will often go through your application and point out its weaknesses.

Every province has grant-giving agencies. Write to your local arts council and check out their websites (see Addresses) to find out what sort of grants your province provides. If the money is there, you might as well be the one to receive it. Your provincial arts and culture department may know about city grants and local, private grant-giving foundations, as well. Six provinces that we know of publish booklets or newsletters that may give you useful local knowledge. Talk to your university about their foundations and bursaries; check this site for other resources: http://ca.dir.yahoo.com/Arts/Organizations/Foundations_and_Trusts/

The Canada Council for the Arts is a federal body with grants for actors with at least two years professional experience who are Canadian citizens or permanent residents. Professionalism is defined as having had specialized training, being recognized by your peers, showing a commitment to devote more time to one's artistic activity if financially feasible, and having a history of public presentation.

Provincial Health Care Plans

Each province has its own health insurance scheme, with its own rules and regulations; check yours for its out-of-town coverage. Any province that charges premiums has a premium assistance scheme. This is a provision for lowering (sometimes to zero) premiums for low-income subscribers. That's us, folks. Their form asks for last year's income and your projection for this year. Some provinces ask for proof, in which case a copy of the tax assessment you were sent from CRA, or your tax return, should do the trick. Don't bother to explain the impossibility of the projection of future earnings. Just put in a reasonable figure.

The Actor and Other Work

Most actors do more than act. They have to, if they want to eat. What sort of job do you want? How do you go about finding it?

Secondary employment can be a touchy subject. Some actors hate to admit they need to work outside the profession. Somehow it smacks of failure. Rubbish. It would be wonderful if your acting income alone could support you, but in all likelihood it won't. Statistics Canada tells us that among professionally active actors around half make some money from a job outside the business and half get money from a non-acting job in the business. A quarter have a regular full- or part-time job. Don't be ashamed to acknowledge your second job. It is allowing you some freedom from financial anxiety and giving you the ability to concentrate on your profession rather than on your survival.

The other job you do doesn't have to be secondary. Genie Award–winning actor Thomas Peacocke happily admits that his main profession and great love is teaching (he is in the Department of Drama at the University of Alberta). That does not stop him from performing on stage and in film and television. You don't have to swear an oath to put acting first. You decide. It's your life.

Most people, though, think of other jobs as a way of supporting their acting habit. The standard secondary jobs for actors are those that allow flexible hours for auditions: office temping, telephone marketing, catering, bartending, waiting tables, house-cleaning, painting, renovating. Work is available in these areas all the time. Find a job that suits you, and show you're reliable so you can go back when you need it again.

Although it is easy enough to phone up a temp agency or answer an ad for telephone marketing, the best way to find secondary employment is to use your networking skills. Try your fellow actors. They know the employers who positively like actors and are prepared for you to be off to audition at a moment's notice. ACTRA and Equity have secondary job information, and companies occasionally advertise in the Equity newsletter as well as on the actor notice boards around town.

Do you want a job totally outside the profession or one connected with it? An outside job is likely to be better paid, but an inside job keeps you in touch. Don't assume that an employer in the business will be more sympathetic to your actor's scheduling problems. The authors' teaching, private coaching, and writing do not pay hugely, but we stay in the acting community. Stephanie Gorin was an actor when she worked as a receptionist for Mirvish Productions, and she has now become a noted casting director.

Your second job may become more important and consuming than your acting. If your second job gives you an excitement, an interest, or a security that you need and want and that you do not get from acting, go for it. Why not? There is no rule that says you can't change your mind. Leaving acting and taking up beekeeping full time is not an admission of failure. It is a mature decision arrived at after careful thought.

Or it should be. Don't let a particularly bad bout of unemployment get you so depressed that you throw your career over in a fit of despair. Sit down and assess your situation. If the acting minuses now outweigh the acting pluses, it may be time for a change. Pack up your skills and knowledge and experience, and use them elsewhere. No decision is irreversible. You may want to try something else for a while and come back to acting later on with a whole new set of experiences to enrich your work. If you don't come back, that's all right, too.

Don't be panicked into giving up because of a short-term disaster. The Actors' Fund of Canada is a charity that offers emergency cash to anyone in the performance industries. Get their application, make your case, and if you meet the criteria, they'll give you enough cash to pay next month's rent or otherwise get you out of a temporary hole. They are industry professionals, so they know your situation, and they will get money to you in less than a week, or as little as twenty-four hours in an emergency. They will buy you time to get your feet under yourself again.

The Actor and the Dry Spells

Leslie Nielson: "Doing nothing is very hard to do … you never know when you're finished." Any actor will tell you that the hardest part of an actor's work is being out of it. When you are under contract, your energy is greater, your capacity to appreciate and enjoy life is increased, and you generally function at a higher, more intense level of awareness. Being out of work brings with it anxiety, stress, depression, and that awful feeling of having been found out. After all, if you were any good, you'd be working, right? Intellectually, we know that is rubbish, but it haunts us all the same. The longer unemployment lasts, the more reinforced the belief becomes, and the harder it is to lift yourself out of the mire of self-pity and boredom. Please break away from your sense of failure. Failure isn't missing the target; it's shooting yourself in the foot. As long as your publicity is going out and you give a good account of yourself at auditions, you're a success waiting to happen.

What can you do right now? The first thing to do is ... anything! Just get off your butt and do something active to keep your energy up. Take a class, play squash, write letters, make phone calls, get in touch with your agent, read some new plays, work on your audition material, do some vocal exercises. There are dozens of ways to focus your mental and physical energy.

Create your own projects. If no one is offering you work, make your own. You don't need thousands of dollars to invest in an idea. Organize a showcase production with a group of like-minded actors. Develop a show for one of the fringe festivals. Write a script for a television or radio show. Research what the show wants and submit it to the script consultant. These projects may not earn you any money, but they will keep the creative juices flowing. With your own production, people will see your work and you will build new relationships. In the case of a writing project, you may open up a whole new work area.

The Actor and a Personal Life

Everyone needs the support and understanding of loving friends and family. Actors often get neither. Even when your nearest and dearest support you, it is rare that they understand you or what you do. Parents are always delighted when you get work, even if it's not a "real job," but can't understand why you won't leave the set a couple of hours early to attend your favourite cousin's wedding.

In one-to-one relationships, actors have a notoriously bad track record. (We're going to call the other person in your life your "mate." There is a married connotation, but it's also the British for "pal." If you can think of a better word, please let us know. We'll use it in the next edition.) We don't have actual statistics, but from looking around at people in the business we see that long-term relationships are the exception, not the rule. Certainly, actors have no less desire for a steady, loving pairing than the rest of the world. Why, then, is it so difficult for us to succeed?

Separation is a major pressure. Most actors go where the work is. In the authors' first twenty years nominally together, we were apart for a total of ten. However, separation in itself is not the problem. There are airline personnel and travelling salesmen and truck drivers whose relationships are able to withstand the distances. Combine physical separation with an intense working relationship, though, and you have the formula for trouble.

A group of people, many of whom are total strangers, act out the most personal, intimate, and emotional moments in human experience. Working associates who were introduced yesterday watch and offer comments as you expose the tenderest and most vulnerable parts of your psyche. Just another day down at the acting factory. To deal with this situation, you quickly develop a group identity and loyalty with bonds as strong as those in the most tightly knit family. In fact, *family* is a word actors frequently use to describe their working team. When this feeling is combined with the absence of your mate, the sense of separation is vast.

Actors can find it difficult to separate the professional and the personal. Before you become more experienced in the ritual of meetings and leave-takings, it is easy to believe that your group will remain close and special friends long after the final curtain or the wrap party. It won't. Work relationships have a limited shelf life, but while you are working, they can be extraordinarily close, and that closeness can endanger more important relationships. ("Tell me, Sir Henry, did Hamlet ever sleep with Ophelia?" "Always in my companies, dear boy, always.") Onstage love and lust can easily travel off the stage. The emotions are real and intense, but rarely long-lasting. In the process of finding that out, people get hurt. Be aware that you may damage a long-term relationship if you cannot recognize the boundaries of a professional one.

Having a mate in the business has advantages. At least your mate will understand what you are going through when the audition you did was lousy, or the engagers decided to cast a known quantity, or the writer changed the sex of the part. Not necessarily, though — professional jealousy is a fact of life. We know it is ridiculous to be angry when your mate gets an audition or a job offer and you don't. It is unlikely, even if you are a gay couple, that you would be up for the same part, but knowing that doesn't help much. Early on in the authors' relationship, jealousy was a big problem. Whether we are wiser now or just older and tireder, we realize what a waste of energy it is.

Work is involving. So is unemployment. If you are depressed about being out of work and your beloved is complaining about billing on the contract, you are going to find it hard to summon up much compassion. Even when you are both working, fascination with your own work makes it difficult to open up to your mate's. When you are both out of work, a whole new set of tensions enters the equation. One of you is "up" and doing the rounds, and the other has hit a bad slump and deeply resents any activity more positive than turning over in bed. All you can do is reach out to the other person. Self-absorption is death.

Having a long-term mate outside the business should make life easier. Another source of income, a different schedule, a different set of priorities so that things stay in proportion. But it's not all good. Few people outside the profession can appreciate the stress and worry, the highs and lows that are our daily companions. However sympathetic and understanding your non-actor partner tries to be, you find it easier to communicate with actor friends, people who've been there. Your partner feels isolated, not allowed into one of the most important parts of your world.

Sometimes an actor pairs well with a stage manager or a technician. The competition and jealousy are reduced (but not removed), and the sympathy is increased by knowing some of the problems first hand.

Living Life

Your career is not your whole life. Concentrating solely on acting destroys you not only as an actor but also as a human being. Eve

Brandstein, from *The Actor*: "Postponing your life until you 'make it' is one of the saddest decisions an actor can make. This is your life now, right now. This is not a rehearsal."

Don't mix up who you are with what you can do. Soprano Measha Brueggergosman: "Once you start to equate your self-worth with the … success of the sound of your voice, you're stepping down a very dangerous road."

A career is not a substitute for family and friends. You should not put the people around you on hold. You need not give up music, politics, social issues, sports, philately, or soap-making for your career.

Actors who are interested in nothing but acting are lifeless, boring, and deadly — on stage and off. As people, we need a broad base of passion and interest to keep us fully alive. As actors, we need a rich, complex life from which to draw. Otherwise, our acting is a puny imitation of the real thing: it's like watching an episode of "National Geographic" compared to visiting the Arctic.

You have to keep on at extending and improving yourself. All we have is what we are. If you feel good about yourself you can handle all the unpredictables that professional life will throw at you.

Envoi

"It's a good answer which knows how to stop."
Italian proverb

We could go on forever. Each time we start to write "The End," we remember another problem you're bound to face or another question you're likely to ask. However, if this book is to remain not only easy to read but also easy to carry, it is time to call a halt. Besides, if there are no surprises in store, why enter into this glorious, absurd adventure?

"The wise man learns by example, the fool by experience." There has got to be a bit of the fool in any actor, so we willingly allow you to make your own mistakes and learn by them. Perhaps you will be writing the sequel to this.

In the meantime, we wish you courage, good luck, and good management.

Addresses

Every contact here was checked directly, but details change. Call ahead and check for yourself before wasting a lot of time or money on out-of-date information.

National

Academy of Canadian Cinema and TV
172 King Street East, Toronto, ON M5A 1J3
Tel: 416-366-2227
www.academy.ca

Actors Fund of Canada
1000 Yonge Street #301, Toronto, ON M4W 2K2
Tel: 416-975-0304 or 1-800-399-8392
Fax: 416-975-0306
contact@actorsfund.ca
www.actorsfund.ca
Charity for anyone in the performing arts.

ACTRA (Alliance of Canadian Cinema, Television and Radio Artists)
625 Church Street, Toronto, ON M4Y 2G1
Tel: 416-489-1311 or 1-800-387-3516
Fax: 416-489-1435
apg@actra.ca
www.actra.ca

ACTRA Fraternal Benefit Society
1000 Yonge Street, Toronto, ON M4W 2K2

Telephone: 416-967-6600 or 1-800-387-8897
Fax: 416-967-4744
nelson@actrafrat.com (Member Services)
benefits@actrafrat.com (Benefits)
www.actrafrat.com

ACTRA PRS (Performers Rights Society)
625 Church Street, Toronto, ON M4Y 2G1
Tel: 416-489-1311 or 1-800-387-3516
Fax: 416-489-1040
prs@actra.ca
www.actra/control/prs.ca

Canadian Association of Fringe Festivals
344 Bloor Street West, Suite 507, Toronto, ON MSS 3A7
Tel: 416-966-1062
www.fringetoronto.com

Canada Council for the Arts
Arts Award Service
350 Albert Street, Box 1047, Ottawa, ON K1P 5V8
Tel: 613-566-4414 or 1-800-263-5588
Fax: 613-566-4390
Theatre Section: (613) 566-4414 Ext 4480 or 1-800-263-5586
Fax: 613-566-4410
www.canadacouncil.ca

Canadian Conference of the Arts
130 Albert Street #804, Ottawa, ON K1P 5G4
Tel: 613-238-3561
Fax: 613-238-4849
info@ccarts.ca
www.ccarts.ca
An umbrella organization for arts groups across the country.

Canadian Theatre Review
University of Toronto Press, Journals Department
5201 Dufferin Street, Toronto, ON M3H 5T8
Tel: 416-667-7810
Fax: 416-667-7881
journals@utpress.utoronto.ca
www.utpjournals.com
Articles on theatre themes, new play scripts, national news.

Centre for the Study of Black Cultures in Canada
York University
4700 Keele Street, Toronto, ON M3J 1P3
Tel: 416-736-2100
www.yorku.ca/aconline
Online sites for film and theatre.

Dancer Transition Resource Centre
250 The Esplanade #500, Toronto, ON M5A 1J2
Tel: 416-595-5655
Fax: 416-595-0009
nationaloffice@dtrc.ca
www.dtrc.ca

Equity (Canadian Actors' Equity Association)
44 Victoria Street, 12th Floor, Toronto, ON M5C 3C4
Tel: 416-867-9165 or 1-800-387-1856
Fax: 416-867-9246
commdir@caea.com
www.caea.com
Has links to other professional associations and professional theatre managements

PACT (Professional Association of Canadian Theatres)
215 Spadina Avenue #210, Toronto, ON M5T 2T7
Tel: 416-595-6455
Fax: 416-595-6450

info@pact.ca
www.pact.ca

Playback
366 Adelaide Street West #500, Toronto, ON M5V 1R9
Tel: 416-408-2300 or 1-888-BRUNICO
Fax: 416-408-0870
lgibb@brunico.com (Circulation)
www.playbackmag.com
TV/film production news.

Playwrights Guild of Canada
54 Wolseley Street, 2nd Floor, Toronto, ON M5T 1A5
Tel: 416-703-0201
Fax: 416-703-0059
info@playwrightsguild.ca
www.playwrightsguild
Reading room and national office. Publishes *Canplay*, a playwrights' view of theatre.

TAMAC (Talent Agents and Managers Association of Canada)
10 St. Mary Street #306, Toronto, ON M4Y 1P9
Tel: 416-963-0100
tamac@canadafilm.com
www.tamac.com

Telefilm Canada (Head Office)
360 St. Jacques Street #700, Montreal, Quebec H2Y 4A9
Tel: 514-283-6363 or 1-800-567-0890
Fax: 514-283-8212
info@telefilm.gc.ca
www.telefilm.gc.ca

TheatreBooks
11 St. Thomas Street, Toronto, ON M5S 2B7
Tel: 416-922-7175 or 1-800-361-3414

Fax: 416-922-0739
action@theatrebooks.com
www.theatrebooks.com
Carries books on all the performing arts. Ships across Canada.

UdA (Union des Artistes)
1411 boulevard Rene Levesque Ouest, Bureau 400, Montreal, Quebec
H3G 1T7
Tel: 514-288-6682 or 1-877-288-6682
Fax: 514-285-6762
www.uniondesartistes.com
Francophone performers' union.

Alberta

ACTRA
Calgary Branch
#304, 1300 – 8th Street S.W., Calgary, AB T2R 1B2
Tel: 403-228-3123
Fax: 403-228-3299
jblaney@actra.ca
www.actracalgary.com

ACTRA
Edmonton Branch
#302, 10324 – 82 Avenue, Edmonton, AB T6E 1Z8
Tel: 780-433-4090
Fax: 780-433-4099
skilley@actra.ca
www.actraedmonton.com

Alberta Community Development
10405 Jasper Avenue, 7th Floor, Edmonton, AB T5J 4R7
Tel: 780-427-6530
www.ed.gov.ab.ca

Education, touring and financial assistance for individuals and organizations.

Alberta Playwrights Network
2633 Hochwald Avenue SW, Calgary, AB T3E 7K2
Tel: 403-269-8564 or 1-800-268-8564
Fax: 403-265-6773
admin@albertaplaywrights.com
www.albertaplaywrights.com

Theatre Alberta
11759 Groat Road, 3rd Floor, Edmonton, AB T5M 3K6
Tel: 780-422-8162 or 1-888-422-8160
Fax: 780-422-2663
theatreab@theatrealberta.com
www.theatrealberta.com
Performer and theatre service organization. The library has fourteen thousand plays and theatre-related titles. Alberta residents can telephone-order scripts to be mailed to them.

British Columbia

ACTRA/UBCP (Union of BC Performers)
856 Homer Street, #300, Vancouver, BC V6B 2W5
Tel: 604-689-0727
Fax: 604-689-1145
info@ubcp.com
www.ubcp.com

ACTRA Fraternal Benefit Society
301-856 Homer Street, Vancouver, BC V6B 2W5
Tel: 604-801-6550 or 1-866-801-6550
Fax: 604-801-6580
afbswest@actrafrat.com
(also see UBCP Member Benefits Trust)

B.C. Film Commission
865 Hornby Street #201, Vancouver, BC V6Z 2G3
Tel: 604-660-2732
Fax: 604-660-4790
info@bcfilm.gov.bc.ca
www.bcfilmcommission.com

Biz Books
302 Cordova Street West, Vancouver, BC V6B 1E8
Tel: 604-669-6431
Fax: 604-669-6432
info@bizbooks.net
www.bizbooks.net
Specializing in the performing arts.

CBC
700 Hamilton Street, Box 4600, Vancouver V6B 4A2
Tel: 604-662-6000 or 604-662-6127 (Radio Drama)
Fax: 604-662-6335 (Radio Casting)
www.cbc.ca/bc
Radio drama, but no TV casting department.

Duthie Books
2239 West Fourth Avenue, Vancouver, BC V6K 1N9
Tel: 604-732-5344
Fax: 604-732-5314
info@duthiebooks.com
www.duthiebooks.com
Bookstore with excellent performing arts section.

Equity — Western Office
505 Hudson House, 321 Water Street, Vancouver, BC V6B 1B8
Tel: 604-682-6173
Fax: 604-682-6174
woffice@caea.com

British Columbia Arts Council
800 Johnson Street, 1st Floor, Victoria, BC V8W 1N3
P.O. Box 9819 Station Provincial Govt., Victoria, BC V8W 9W3
Tel: 250-536-1725 or 250-536-1727 (Professional Performing Arts)
Fax: 250-387-4099
BCArtsCouncil@gov.bc.ca
www.bcartscouncil.ca
Grants programs and complementary services.

BC Ministry of Labour — Child Employment
4946 Canada Way #210, Burnaby, BC V5G 4J6
Tel: 604-660-2097
Fax: 604-660-7047
www.labour.gov.bc.ca/esb/chldflm

BC Ministry of Labour —Talent Agents
4946 Canada Way #210, Burnaby, BC V5G 4J6
Tel: 604-660-2097
Fax: (604) 660.7047
www.labour.gov.bc.ca/esb/talent

Playwrights Theatre Centre
398 Cartwright Street #201, Vancouver, BC V6H 3C8
Tel: 604-685-6288
Fax: 604-685-7451
plays@playwrightstheatre.com
www.playwrightstheatre.com

ReelWest Magazine
4012 Myrtle Street, Burnaby, BC V5C 4G2
Tel: 604-451-7335 or 1-888-291-7335
Fax: 604-451-7305
info@reelwest.com
www.reelwest.com/magazine/mag.htm

Telefilm Canada (Western Office)

609 Granville Street #410, Vancouver, BC V7Y 1G5
Tel: 604-666-1566 or 1-800-663-7771
Fax: 604-666-7754
info@telefilm.gc.ca
www.telefilm.gc.ca

Theatre B.C.
P.O. Box 2031, 150 Commercial Street, Nanaimo, BC V9R 6X6
Tel: 250-714-0203
Fax: 250-714-0213
info@theatrebc.org
www.theatrebc.org
Community theatre umbrella organization.

UBCP Member Benefits Trust
300 - 856 Homer Street, Vancouver, BC V6B 2W5
Tel: (604) 685-1678
Fax: (604) 685-1478
www.mbt.ca

Manitoba

ACTRA
245 McDermot Avenue #203, Winnipeg, MB R3B 0S6
Tel: 204-339-9750
Fax: 204-947-5664
manitoba@actra.ca
www1.actra.ca/winnipeg

Manitoba Arts Council
93 Lombard Avenue #525, Winnipeg, MB R3B 3B1
Tel: 204-945-2237 or 1-866-994-2787 (within Manitoba)
Fax: 204-945-5925
info@artscouncil.mb.ca
www.artscouncil.mb.ca

Projects grants, bursaries, artists-in-schools.

Manitoba Association of Playwrights,
100 Arthur Street #503, Winnipeg, MB R3B 1H3
Tel: 204-942-8941
Fax: 204-942-1555
map@autobahn.mb.ca
www.autobahn.mb.ca/~map

New Brunswick

New Brunswick Arts Board
634 Queen Street #300, Fredericton, NB E3B 1C2
Tel: 506-444-4444 or1-866-460-2787
Fax: 506-444-5543
www.artsnb.ca
Financial assistance to artists for development, travel, artists-in-schools.

Newfoundland

ACTRA
Newfoundland/Labrador Branch
685 Water Street, P.O. Box 575, St. John's, NL A1C 5K8
Tel: 709-722-0430
Fax: 709-722-2113
newfoundland@actra.ca
www1.actra.ca/stjohns

Newfoundland and Labrador Arts Council
P.O. Box 98, St. John's, NL A1C 5H5
Tel: 709-726-2212 or 1-866-726-2212
Fax: 709-726-0619
nlacmail@nfld.net
www.nlac.nf.ca

Direct grants, loans, loan subsidies, and awards.

Writers' Alliance of Newfoundland and Labrador
P.O. Box 2681, 155 Water Street #102, St. John's, NL A1C 6K1
Tel: 709-739-5215
Fax: 709-739-5931
wanl@nf.aibn.com
www.writersalliance.nf.ca

Nova Scotia

ACTRA
Maritimes Branch
1660 Hollis Street #103, Halifax, NS B3J IV7
Tel: (902) 420-1404 or 1-877-2872 (in Atlantic Canada)
Fax: 902-422-0589
maritimes@actra.ca
www.actramaritimes.ca

Playwrights Atlantic Resource Centre
RR #2, 1333 Upper South River, Goshen, NS B0H 1M0
Tel: 902-783-2084 or 1-877-845-1341
Fax: 902-783-2948
parcoffice@ns.sympatico.ca
www.playwrightsatlantic.ca

Telefilm Canada (Atlantic Office)
1717 Barrington Street #300, Halifax, NS B3J 2A4
Tel: 902-426-8425 or 1-800-565-1773
Fax: 902-426-4445
info@telefilm.gc.ca
www.telefilm.gc.ca

Writers' Federation of Nova Scotia
111 Marginal Road, Halifax, NS B3H 4P7

Tel: 902-423-8116
Fax: 902-422-0881
talk@writers.ns.ca
www.writers.ns.ca

Ontario

ACTRA
ACTRA Toronto Performers
625 Church Street, 1st and 2nd Floors, Toronto, ON M4Y 2G1
Tel: 416-928-2278 or 1-877-913-2278
Fax: 416-928-2852
info@actratoronto.com
www.actratoronto.com

ACTRA Ottawa Branch
Arts Court, 2 Daly Avenue #170, Ottawa, ON K1N 6E2
Tel: 613-565-2168
Fax: 613-565-4367
ottawa@actra.ca

ALAS (Artists' Legal Advice Service)
Tel: 416-367-ALAS (2527)
www.artistslaw.org

AMIS (Acting and Modelling Information Service)
c/o Theatre Ontario
215 Spadina Avenue #210, Toronto, ON M5T 2T7
Tel: 416-977-3832
Fax: 416-408-3402
info@amisontario.com
www.amisontario.com
Volunteers from the entertainment industry answer your questions.

Al & Malka Green Artists' Health Centre

Toronto Western Hospital
399 Bathurst Street, 3rd Floor, West Wing, Toronto, ON M5T 2S8
Tel: 416-603-5263
www.uhn.ca

Canadian Film Centre
2489 Bayview Avenue, North York, ON M2L 1A8
Tel: 416-445-1446
Fax: 416-445-9481
info@cdnfilmcentre.com
www.cdnfilmcentre.com
Student production projects for actors and directors.

CBC (Canadian Broadcasting Corporation)
Box 500, Station A, Toronto M5W 1E6
Tel: 416-205-3311
Talent Resource Centre: 416-205-7201, talent_resources@cbc.ca
Radio Drama Casting: 416-205-6011
www.cbc.ca/toronto

Centre for Indigenous Theatre
401 Richmond Street West, #205, Toronto, ON M5V 1X3
Tel: 416-506-9436
Fax: 416-506-9430
citmail@indigenoustheatre.com
www.indigenoustheatre.com
Aboriginal theatre training centre. Full-time seven-week intensive course: apply in February.

Cinematheque Ontario
2 Carlton Street #1600, Toronto, ON M5B 1J3
Tel: 416-967-7371
Fax: 416-967-9477
ccummings@torfilmfest.ca
www.e.bell.ca/filmfest/cinematheque

CLASP (Community Legal Aid Services Program)
4700 Keele Street, York University, Osgoode Hall, Toronto, ON M3J 1P3
Tel: 416-736-5029
Fax: 416-736-5564
www.yorku.ca/osgoode/clasp
Claims of under $6,000 only.

Dance Ontario
55 Mill Street, Case Goods Building #304, Toronto, ON M5C 3C4
Tel: 416-204-1083
Fax: 416-204-1085
contact@danceontario.ca
www.danceontario.ca
Newsletter, directory. Audition notices for members.

Dance Umbrella of Ontario
490 Adelaide Street West #201, Toronto, ON M5V 1T2
Tel: 416-504-6429 or 1-800-919-5019
Fax: 416-504-8702
www.danceumbrellanet
Management and resource centre, On the Move seminar series,
newsletter.

Equity Showcase
651 Dufferin Street, Toronto, ON M6K 2B2
Tel: 416-533-6100
Fax: 416-533-2449
mail@equityshowcase.ca
www.equityshowcase.ca
Classes in theatre skills, special events, Showcase Production series.

Galbraith Photo Digital
24 Carlaw Avenue, Toronto, ON M4M 2R7
Tel: 416-465-5466 or 1-800-561-5466
info@galbraithphotodigital.com
www.photodigital.com/galbraith

Has a mailing service across Canada for photo reproductions.

LIFT (Liaison of Independent Filmmakers of Toronto)
171 East Liberty Street #301, Toronto, ON M6K 3P6
Tel: 416-588-6444
Fax: 416-588-7017
office@lift.on.ca
www.lift.on.ca

Ontario Arts Council
151 Bloor Street West #500, Toronto, ON M5S 1T6
Tel: 416-961-1660 or 1-800-387-0058 (in Ontario)
Fax: 416-961-7796
info@arts.on.ca
www.arts.on.ca
Supports theatre organizations and new works by emerging companies
and co-operatives.

OMDC (Ontario Media Development Corporation)
175 Bloor Street East, South Tower #501, Toronto, ON M4W 3R8
Tel: 416-314-6858
Fax: 416-314-6876
mail@omdc.on.ca
www.omdc.on.ca
Media-related background and current information.

Performers for Literacy
2 Carlton Street #1304, Toronto, ON M5B 1J3
Tel: 416-410-4193
Fax: 416-979-1144
info@pfl.ca
www.nald.ca/pfl

Samuel French
100 Lombard Street (lower level), Toronto, ON M5C 1M3
Tel: 416-363-3536

Fax: 416-363-1108
www.samuelfrench.com/store
Large stock of mainly standard plays, very cheap.

Telefilm Canada
474 Bathurst Street #100, Toronto, ON M5T 2S6
Tel: 416-973-6436 or 1-800-463-4607
Fax: 416-973-8606
info@telefilm.gc.ca
www.telefilm.gc.ca

Theatre Ontario
215 Spadina Avenue #210, Toronto, ON M5T 2C7
Tel: 416-408-4556
Fax: 416-408-3402
info@theatreontario.org
www.theatreontario.org
Performer and theatre service organization. Publications, professional
coordinator. TAAS.

Toronto Arts Council
141 Bathurst Street, Toronto, ON M5V 2R2
Tel: 416-392-6800
Fax: 416-392-6920
mail@torontoartscouncil.org
www.torontoartscouncil.org

TAAS (Toronto Association of Acting Studios)
(see Theatre Ontario)

Toronto Alliance for the Performing Arts
215 Spadina Avenue #210, Toronto, ON M5T 2C7
Tel: 416-536-6468 or 1-800-541-0499
Fax: 416-536-3463
www.tapa.ca

Toronto Film & Television Office
City Hall
100 Queen Street West, Main Floor, Rotunda North, Toronto, ON M5N 2N2
Tel: 416-392-7570
Fax: 416-392-0675
filmtoronto@toronto.ca/tfto
www.toronto.ca/tfto

Toronto International Film Festival Group
2 Carlton Street #1600, Toronto, ON M5B 1J3
Tel: 416-967-7371
www.bell.ca/filmfest

Toronto Reference Library
789 Yonge Street, Toronto, ON M4W 2G8
Tel: 416-395-5577
www.torontopubliclibrary.ca
Huge collection of plays and performer-related materials including videos.

UdA
Francophone performers, Toronto Bureau
625 Church Street #103, Toronto, ON M4Y 2G1
Tel: 416-485-7670
Fax: 416-485-9063
www.uniondesartistes.com

Prince Edward Island

Council of the Arts
115 Richmond Street, Charlottetown, PE C1A 1H7
Tel: 902-368-4410 or 1-888-734-2784
Fax: 902-368-4418
info@peiartscouncil.com

www.peiartscouncil.com
Individual grants, workshops, and travel and study grants.

Confederation Centre Public Library
P.O. Box 7000, Charlottetown, PE C1A 8G8
Tel: 902-368-4642
Fax: 902-368-4652
ccpl@gov.pe.ca
www.library.pe.ca/libraryfinder
Large selection of Canadian plays.

Quebec

ACTRA
1450 City Councillors Street #530, Montreal, QC H3A 2E6
Tel: 514-844-3318
Fax: 514-844-2068
E-mail: montreal@actra.ca
www.actramontreal.ca

Playwrights Workshop Montreal
4324 boulevard St. Laurent, Montreal, QC H2W 1Z3
Tel: 514-843-3685
Fax: 514-843-9384
playwrights.ca

Quebec Drama Federation
460 St. Catherine Street West #807, Montreal, QC H3B 1A7
Tel: 514-875-8698
Fax/Hotline: 514-875-8873
quebecdrama@bellnet.ca
www.quebecdrama.org
The Hotline has details of anglophone theatre currently running. QDF
Updates has news of anglophone theatre and classes.

UdA
580 avenue Grand Allée Est #350, Quebec City, QC G1R 2K2
Tel: 418-523-4241
Fax: 418-523-0168
www.uniondesartistes.com

Saskatchewan

ACTRA
Saskatchewan Branch
1808 Smith Street #212, Regina, SK S4P 2N4
Tel: 306-757-0885 or 1-800-615-5041 (Prairies)
Fax: 306-359-0044
mburns.actra.ca
www1.actra.ca/sask

Saskatchewan Arts Alliance
#205A, 2314 – 11th Avenue, Regina, SK S4P 0K1
Tel: 306-780-9820
Fax: 306-780-9821
info@artsalliance.sk.ca
www.artsalliance.sk.ca

Saskatchewan Arts Board
2135 Broad Street, Regina, SK S4P 1Y6
Tel: 306-787-4056 or 1-800-667-7526 (toll-free in Saskatchewan)
Fax: 306-787-4199
sab@artsboard.sk.ca
www.artsboard.sk.ca
Individual grants for theatre training.

Saskatchewan Film Pool Cooperative
1822 Scarth Street #301, Regina, SK S4P 2G3
Tel: 306-757-8818
Fax: 306-757-3622

web@filmpool.ca
www.filmpool.ca
Source of non-union film casting information.

Saskatchewan Playwrights Centre
P.O. Box 3092, Saskatoon, SK S7K 3S9
Tel: 306-665-7707
Fax: 306-244-0255
sk.playwrights@sasktel.net
www.saskplaywrights.ca

Yukon

Yukon Arts Centre
300 College Drive, P.O. Box 16, Whitehorse, YT Y1A 5X9
Tel: 867-667-8575
Fax: 867-393-6300
info@yac.ca
www.yukonartscentre.org
Theatre and gallery spaces, artists in schools, subsidized theatre space
for local artists.

Yukon Arts Advisory Council
Tourism & Culture, Cultural Services — Arts Section 3
Box 2703, Whitehorse, YT Y1A 2C6
Tel: 867-667-8589 or 1-800-661-0408, local 8589 (in Yukon)
Fax: 867-393-6456
arts@gov.yk.ca
users.yknet.yk.ca/dcpages/bertonhouse/about

Glossary

Terms in small capitals are also listed as separate items.

Acting Coach: A teacher hired by a production company to assist the actors on set.

Actor-proof: The play will work, however bad the acting. The prop cannot be broken by an actor.

Actor Role: Media classification, 10 lines or fewer.

AD: (1) In theatre: ARTISTIC DIRECTOR. (2) In film or TV: Assistant Director. First AD, second AD, third AD, etc. are union-defined non-technical positions.

ADR: Automatic (or Additional) Dialogue Replacement. In POST-PRODUCTION, taping lines, new or already recorded in the shooting, to fit the existing visuals. Also called looping OR POST-SYNCHING.

Advance: (1) Casual sales, not subscription tickets, bought before the day of performance or before a touring company arrives to play an engagement. (2) Salary paid before it is due.

AEA: Actors' Equity Association. American stage union.

AFTRA: American Federation of Television and Radio Artists.

Agency: (1) Actors' agent's office and company. (2) The advertising agency that devises a commercial and then hires a PRODUCTION COMPANY to make it.

Alternative: Of theatre companies: not in the mainstream. Politically and/or artistically progressive.

Ambience: (1) Media slang for haze produced by smoke machine. (2) ROOM TONE. Media term for subliminal sound on a "silent" set.

Apron: In PROSCENIUM theatre, stage area downstage of the proscenium arch.

Arena Stage: (1) The stage runs through the middle of the room; the audience is on two sides. Has come to mean: (2) Theatre in the round.

The audience is on all sides.

Artistic Director: AD. Head of theatre organization (but see Producer). Decides plays and guest directors, casts and directs plays, deals with crises, is responsible for artistic policy.

Artistic Producer: See Producer.

ASM: Assistant stage manager. Without whom theatre would die.

Available: (1) Of light: natural light or regular indoor lights, un-augmented by film or television lighting. (2) Of an actor: not Working.

Back Light: In Media Three-Point Lighting, the light shining on the far side of a person, to lift them from the background.

Background Performer: Extra, Background. Media category of player with no individual dialogue or characterization.

Barn Doors: Opaque panels hinged at the sides of a lighting instrument, to block off the edges of the beam of light. Shutters.

Batten: (1) Pipe to which lights and scenery are attached in order to be flown. (2) Wood, often a two-by-four, used to weight the bottom of a soft flying piece.

BCU: Big Close-Up. A tight shot. The face fills the screen.

Best Boy: Chief assistant to the head Gaffer. Best-boy Grip does the same job for the Key Grip.

BG: Background. Media jargon. Setting, not Background Performers.

Billing: Definition of where, how, and when one's name is to be used in advertising a show.

Bit Part: Small role, especially in media. "He does a bit part, your role is interesting, I have a cameo appearance."

Blacks: (Soft blacks) Black drapes hung to hide part of backstage.

Blow: Forget one's lines, ruin a crucial moment.

Blue Screen: Television technique enabling an actor to be recorded in the bare studio and shown, for example, being charbroiled in a Mayan temple. Often green.

Board: Notice board where theatre calls and company and union messages are posted

Book: Script. The spoken words, not the lyrics, of a musical.

Book Show: A musical with a plot.

Boom: The long arm that places the microphone close to the actor but off camera. (Generally.)

Box Office: (1) Ticket-selling department. (2) The gross takings from ticket sales.

Breakdown: Details of the characters the CASTING DIRECTOR is trying to cast. Sent to agents for suggestions from their rosters.

Bus-and-Truck Company: A production touring to second-class dates, the company and costumes in a bus, the scenery in trucks.

Business: (1) The entertainment or performing arts industries. (2) A series of actions, often comic, e.g. setting table, lighting cigarette, falling on bum. "Great bit of business, dear! Never do it again." (often abbreviated to "biz" in either sense.)

Buy-out: Allows a media ENGAGER to pay, up front, at a discount, for various future uses of a program without residual payments.

Call: Call time. The time your services are needed. Wardrobe call, half hour call, train call, etc.

Callback: A second or later audition for the same job. Theoretically the odds improve as callbacks multiply.

Cameo: Small part with big potential for being noticed. Any small part played by a big actor.

Cans: Headphones.

Cart: Audio cartridge, cassette tape.

Cash Extra: Non-ACTRA BACKGROUND PERFORMER. Makes the same as an ACTRA member Extra on ACTRA sets, or else minimum wage. Paid by cheque, generally.

Casting Couch: Sexual harassment of actresses. And actors.

Casting Director: Hired by a production company to suggest actors who will be auditioned. Sends out BREAKDOWNS to agents, who submit suitable actors' names.

Cheating: Appearing to look at one's fellow actor but actually facing slightly downstage (or toward the camera) to enable the audience to see one's face or actions better.

Chew the Scenery: Overact, ham it up.

Clapper Board: SLATE, sticks. A small blackboard, or high-tech equivalent, on which is recorded details of the shot to identify the film or tape later in the editing room.

Clapper Loader: The crew member who fills in the slate, and who often also loads the camera with film.

Client: (1) Company whose products are being advertised. (2) An actor, director, etc. on an agent's ROSTER.

Cloth: Painted canvas flying piece with BATTENs top and bottom.

Cold Reading: An audition with little or no time to work on the script.

Commercial: Of theatres: supported by ticket sales alone, with no grants or donations.

Commission: The 10 or 15 percent of a performer's fees paid to agents for their services.

Comp: Complimentary ticket. Free ticket or pass given to the cast for guests. (See PAPER.)

Company Manager: On tour, the MANAGEMENT's representative. Deals with transport, accommodation, salaries, and much, much more.

Concession: Permission by the union to set aside part of the normal union contract to make a deserving ENGAGER's life easier. Hrrmph.

Conflict: The situation where a performer may not appear in a commercial for a competing range of products while an earlier commercial is still current.

Continuity: (1) Especially in out-of-sequence film shooting, matching the positions, colours, etc. of things at the end of a shot with the same things at the beginning of the next shot. (2) Person responsible for such matching.

Continuity Extra: BACKGROUND PERFORMER brought back to be, for example, a regular patron of a bar. The performer must be available for all calls during the full duration of filming.

Costume: Clothes worn by the actors. Clothes carried but not worn are PROPS. Clothes on the set but not carried or worn are DRESSING. The basis of many a craft union problem.

Cover Shot: SAFETY. An extra shot taken after a good take, "just in case." Occasionally = MASTER SHOT.

Crab: Of a camera: to move across the action, e.g., along the baseline of a tennis game while looking at the net.

Craft Services: The job, and hence the people doing it, of providing snacks and coffee on a set.

Credit: (1) A part played, appearing on a résumé. (2) BILLING, in the MEDIA.

Crossing the Line: Shooting the action from different sides. Without an intervening shot, the audience sees the movement reverse itself.

CTA: Canadian Theatre Agreement.

CU: Close-up. A head (and shoulders) shot.

Cue Light: The most common visual cue in theatre. Can be "red-warn, green-go" or "on-warn, off-go."

Curtain: On any stage, the end of the show. From traditional PROSCENIUM theatre.

Cut: (1) Stop recording the action. (2) Change instantly from one shot to another. (3) Edit. (4) Take out (dialogue, your best scene, etc.).

Cyc: (Pronounced "sike.") Cyclorama. Curved surface of cloth or cement around the entire back of the stage or set, on which sky effects and slides can be projected.

Dance Captain: Often a senior chorus member. The person who maintains the choreography during the run and often acts as assistant choreographer through rehearsals.

Dark: Describes a theatre with no show in performance.

Dead: Of any space, having no echo at all.

Defer: Contractual agreement to delay part of a fee until the project has started to make some money.

Demo: Demo tape. A videotape, CD, or DVD with five to eight minutes of representative media work, to send to potential ENGAGERS. See Chapter 4, "Show and Tell."

Deputy: Elected member of a theatre cast who maintains liaison between Equity and the management.

Dialogue/Dialect coach: A professional who advises performers on a specific regional accent, for example.

Director: Decides how the scenes should be read and arranges the production schedule. Directors may also have the authority to make decisions about the script, costumes, sets, and choice of performers.

DLP: Dead-letter-perfect. Knowing all one's lines. "I was DLP on the bus but now it's gone."

Dolly: Wheeled platform for camera. "Dolly in/out," to follow the action by moving the camera forward and back.

DOP: Director of Photography, Cinematographer. Supervises the lighting and camera style in TV or film shooting. May also operate a camera ("lighting cameraman").

Dormancy: A fee paid to an actor whose commercial has been re-aired after having been off the air for a period of six months or more.

Double: (1) A performer dressed and made-up to resemble another actor. (2) In MEDIA, twice the union minimum fee. "Double double" means the RESIDUALS are also at double.

Dramaturg: *or* Dramaturge. One who may recommend plays to the AD of a theatre and work with playwrights on new scripts, research periods and styles, etc.

Dresser: In theatre, a person, often from maintenance WARDROBE, who helps actors into and out of costume.

Dressing: Object on the set for its appearance only, not for use.

Drop: Canvas or fabric flown piece without rigid framework.

Dub: (1) In video, to make a copy of a tape, or such a copy. (2) To record new sound, e.g., English over original Urdu.

ECU: Extreme Close-up. Shot showing eyes to mouth or less.

Edit: Put film or TV shots or radio segments together to form the final product.

Effects: FX. Technical tricks, sight or sound (SFX), to enhance a production.

Eighty-six: To cut, turn off, stop using, dispose of something. The alleged reason for the expression is worth asking about.

Engagement: A paying acting job.

Engager: In media work, a person or company that hires and pays actors.

Ensemble: A cast working as equals. Sometimes including the stars.

Establishing Shot: Sets up the situation for the audience. Snow falls: it's winter. Big Ben rings over a street with carriages: it's Victorian London.

Executive Producer: In film, above the producer, although sometimes only as a name to attract backing.

Extraordinary Risk: Hazardous work (what in media might be called a stunt) that Equity requires be acknowledged in a contract. Such risks receive better-than-usual insurance coverage.

Eye Line: In media, where someone is looking. Conventionally, heroes look slightly down when talking to women.

Fake: (1) Ad lib, having forgotten something. (2) Give a sufficient impression of doing something (writing a letter, cutting off your children's heads) which would in reality take too long or otherwise be awkward.

Favoured Nation: Contractual provision, now forbidden by Equity, in which the actor is guaranteed that nobody else in the cast is making more money. (See Most Favoured Nation.)

Feature: Film made to be shown in cinemas.

Featured: Prominently billed under the first billing.

Fill Light: In media Three-Point Lighting, throws light into the shadows caused by the Key Light.

First Tier Recoupment: Agreement that deferred fees will start to be paid as soon as the project has any income.

Flag: Panel held or on a stand; translucent to soften the light or opaque to cut the spread of light. Cf. Barn Doors.

Flat: A piece of scenery, usually rectangular, four to eight feet wide. Traditionally in theatre a wooden frame covered with canvas but now, following television's lead, often covered with Masonite.

Floor: The film or television studio itself, not the control room.

Fly: To raise scenery by ropes. "The flies": space above the stage where such scenery hangs; "Flying piece": scenery flown as a unit.

Focus Puller: Watches the action and changes the camera's focus to pre-set marks.

FOH: Front of house. The audience part of a theatre, and its staff.

Foley Artist: Adds sound to recorded scenes, in Post-Production, to replace or enhance existing sound like footsteps, locks, and fight noises.

Frame: The imaginary line around what will be seen on screen. "In frame," "out of frame," "frame it tight."

Freelance: Not on a staff contract. Brought in for a specific job.

Fringe: (F. theatre, f. festival) Experimental, Alternative theatre. From the Edinburgh Fringe Festival, where such productions are mounted around the main festival of more Establishment works.

Full House: No seats available. Except for the Box Office's little pets.

FX: Effects. Lighting or sound (SFX).

Gaffer Tape: Two-inch-wide adhesive cloth tape, like duct tape, without which media and theatre production would founder.

Gaffer: Media head electrician, responsible for lights, etc.

Gel: Transparent coloured sheet put in front of a lighting instrument. From "gelatin," now replaced by scorch-proof plastic.

General Manager: Administrative boss of theatre. Over office, box office, and custodial staff. Nominally under the ARTISTIC DIRECTOR. Typically negotiates actors' contracts.

Get-in: The process of moving a touring set, costumes, and properties from the trucks to the stage for the coming performance.

Glossy: Actor's eight-by-ten-inch publicity photograph.

Gobo: Perforated opaque screen inserted in the focal plane of a lamp to cast shadows of, e.g., tree branches on the stage.

Go-see: An audition-type tryout for models or EXTRAS to judge their suitability.

Greasepaint: Still means stage make-up generically, but in fact it's now more often lighter water-based pancake make-up as used on television and in the street.

Grid: Gridiron. Beams over the stage, carrying the pulleys of the flying system.

Grievance: Formal complaint filed by ACTRA against an ENGAGER. The first stage in the arbitration procedure.

Grips: Media carpenters and roustabouts. Head is KEY GRIP.

Guest Artist: Equity members may work for non-union companies only by permission under a GA contract.

Head Shot: GLOSSY. Actor's eight-by-ten-inch publicity photograph.

Hold the Book: To prompt, especially when running lines.

Holding Area: Extras Holding. A place for BACKGROUND PERFORMERS when not required on set.

Honey Wagon: Trailer divided into make-up and dressing cubicles. Each has its own separate lavatory facilities. Hence the name?

Hot: Of a set: currently being used, not to be struck. Or loaded with explosive effects ready for use.

House: The audience, and also the auditorium. "Open the h.": allow the audience in.

House Seats: Good seats held by a theatre until the last minute, to be able to offer them as a courtesy to professional visitors.

Industrial: (1) Stage show for dealers and salesmen, entertaining the audience and extolling the product. A modern medicine show. (2) Television production for IN-HOUSE use, for training or morale.

Industry: The acting business, particularly the film part of it.

Ingenue: Pretty young actress who plays innocents. Such a part, e.g.,

Lisa in *The Simpsons*.

In-house: (1) Not intended to be seen by anyone other than the engagers' client's employees. (2) Done by someone in a permanent staff position.

Iron: Fireproof curtain lowered at the front of a PROSCENIUM stage in case of fire, to cut the actors off from the audience, which is exiting in safety.

Jobbed-in: A FREELANCER added to a company to do a specific job.

Jurisdiction: The particular range of work and the particular geographical area a union has responsibility for and power over.

Juvenile Lead: Male ingenue, e.g., Bart in *The Simpsons*.

Key Light: In media THREE-POINT LIGHTING provides highlights on actor's face.

Key Grip: Head of department doing moving and building on media set.

Klieg Light: An early trade name (from Herr Kliegl, the inventor) for a carbon arc light.

Late Payment: The union-prescribed penalty when media fees aren't paid on time. Sometimes collected.

Lavalier: Small condenser microphone pinned on chest or hung around neck.

Lazzi: Commedia del Arte term for a standard piece of business.

Left: Stage left: actor's left, facing the audience. Camera left: actor's right, facing the camera. Draw a moral, if you like.

Legs: Narrow drapes at the side of the stage, masking the wings from the audience's view.

Libretto: Book or text of a musical comedy.

Lime: L-Light. Powerful movable spotlight. Now normally an electric arc light.

Live: (1) Not recorded. (2) Carrying electricity. (3) Of a studio, etc., full of echo.

Live on Tape: Live to tape. Recorded and then shown without editing, as if it were being transmitted live.

Local Jobber: Someone who is not, never has been, and does not want to be a professional actor, who signs an affidavit to that effect and is hired by an Equity theatre as part of the non-professional quota.

Location: A media shoot away from the home studio.

Looping: POST-SYNCING. ADR.

LS: Long shot. The picture shows a full-length standing figure, up to a full landscape.

LX: Electrics.

Management: Theatre administration.

Master Shot: The overall picture of the action. Close-ups and reaction shots are cut in to the master shot.

Media: From "electronic media." Radio, film, and television, as opposed to stage.

Method: Acting technique in which the actor aspires to completely identify with the part. Lee Strasberg's development of Stanislavski's counter to the style of acting popular in Russia at the turn of the century.

Mic: Mike. Microphone.

Monologue: One person speaking. An audition speech is a special sort of monologue. A one-person play is a monodrama.

MOS: "Mit-out sound." (From European film directors in early Hollywood?). Mock-German description of scene shot for visuals only.

Most Favoured Nation: Undeservedly reviled contractual provision, now forbidden by Equity, in which the actor is guaranteed that nobody else in the cast is making as much money. See FAVOURED NATION.

MS: Mid-Shot. Shows the human body to waist level.

Noddy: The familiar shot of the interviewer "reacting to" words off-screen. Recorded afterwards, it means the guest can be edited unobtrusively.

Non-professional Affidavit: See LOCAL JOBBER.

Non-signatory: Productions not signed to a union Agreement, operating without union restrictions and not allowed to hire union performers.

Nut: The weekly cost of running a show. To "make the nut" is to break even for the week. The story is that the innkeeper would keep the axle nut from a travelling show's cart until he was paid in full.

Negotiate: Not getting everything you deserve from someone who thinks you are getting too much.

Off Book: Knowing one's lines well enough to need only occasional prompting.

Off Camera: Off screen. In television and film, heard but not seen. As opposed to ON CAMERA.

On Air: Broadcasting.

On Camera: In view of the MEDIA audience.

On Hold: Being presented. Casting directors may ask shortlisted performers to keep dates reserved pending possible hiring. Only a courtesy thing: the unions say it cannot be binding.

Out of Work: Not presently hired as an actor.

Overscale: Of a MEDIA fee, more than the union minimum. From the States, where the minimum is admitted to be the norm.

Pan: (1) To rotate a camera on its mounting. (2) To give a production a bad review.

Paper: "To p. the house." To give away complimentary tickets to boost the apparent size of the paying audience.

Patch: Connect lighting circuits to the dimmer board so that one dimmer controls a group of lights.

Per Diem: Payment made to actors working out of town to cover hotel and meals.

Permittee: Actor not a full member of ACTRA working on an ACTRA contract with a WORK PERMIT.

Personal Manager: Agent.

Post-production: After the filming or taping is over, choosing the best parts of the takes, adding music, and POST-SYNC, to turn the raw performance material into a saleable product.

Post-sync: (LOOPING, ADR) Adding dialogue, synchronized with the originally recorded words where necessary, after the main filming or taping is finished.

POV: Point of view. The camera shows the scene as if through a particular character's eyes.

Practical: Describes something that actually works, is not a fake. Practical gun, knife, staircase.

Pre-screen: Casting directors may hold general auditions before the full casting process starts, to show the range of available talent.

Principal: A major character (various union definitions).

Print: (1) "Print that." A take noted to be a good one. From earlier film days, when processing obviously bad TAKES was expensive. (2) Print work. Still photography for advertising.

Print Work: Still photography used for print advertisements in magazines, flyers, etc.

Producer: One who puts together the major elements of a show and arranges the financing. In various versions of the title (e.g. ARTISTIC PRODUCER), a combination of a theatre's ARTISTIC DIRECTOR and GENERAL MANAGER. In English theatre = a director.

Production Company: In media, the concern actually making the film or television show which other people may have conceived and commissioned.

Production Stage Manager: PSM. In large theatres, head of stage management department.

Profession: The people involved in the acting business. The business itself.

Programming Agent: In a big AGENCY, your own agent, rather than the agency's specialist in, say, commercials.

Prompt: To give an actor a line he has forgotten. Rarely found in performance since the end of PROSCENIUM theatre. The hardest job for an ASM in rehearsals.

Prompt Book: The master copy of the script; "the Bible." Records final decisions on lines, moves, and business, with cues for lights, sound, etc.

Prop: Property. An object, not furniture, on a set to be used. Often a fake. Personal props (cigars, whip, copy of *Buglestone Chronicle*, etc.) remain with the actor or are returned to him at the end of the show.

Proscenium: Prosc. The wall between the stage and the audience in traditional theatre buildings. "P. theatre": such a theatre. "P. arch": the frame of the traditional stage picture.

Pro-rated: Partial payment, proportionally reduced for partial work.

PSA: Public Service Announcement. A TV or radio advertisement for a charity or other good cause. By agreement with ACTRA, performers may be allowed to waive their fees.

Put-in: The rehearsal, rarely more than one, preparing for a change of cast, when a replacement performer or an understudy takes over.

Rake: The gradient of a stage so that the rear is higher than the front, giving better acoustics and SIGHTLINES.

Regional Theatre: Once, a theatre serving a large area by touring, etc. Now, the major professional not-for-profit theatre in an area. In the US, any not-for-profit theatre outside New York City.

Repertoire: (1) Past seasons' plays, which characterize the theatre. (2) The organization of a season so that a cast rehearses a group of plays, which it then performs in rotation.

Repertory: (1) Now synonymous with and replacing REPERTOIRE. (2) In the UK, a theatre producing a number of plays in an announced season.

Resident: R. company: One with season-long occupancy of the same building. R. designer, etc.: A staff position, not a freelancer JOBBED IN.

Residuals: USE FEES. Television fees paid for the use made of the final product. In addition to the SESSION FEE, paid for the work done. Residuals are paid in advance for a period of use in a specified market and may continue for many years. Thank God.

Resting: Word that non-professionals use to describe actors' being OUT OF WORK.

Résumé: One-page summary of actor's experience, skills, physical type, etc.

Retake: In the media, to record a SHOT again.

Review: Drama critic's version of what happened on first night.

Revolve: Rotating platform, on the stage or set into it. They never work.

Right: (1) Stage right: actor's right, facing the audience. (2) Camera right: actor's left, facing the camera.

Draw a moral, if you like.

Risk Performance: Under ACTRA, a part requiring a performer to do something or be somewhere he or she considers dangerous. If declared in advance, a reason for negotiating OVERSCALE; if not, a valid reason to refuse to do the work.

Roll: Start camera or tape recorder working.

Room Tone: AMBIENCE. Media term for subliminal sound on a "silent" set.

Roster: List of the performers, writers, etc. that an agent represents.

Rounds: 'Doing the r.' The process of self-publicity. From New York practice of physically visiting agents, casting directors, etc., trying to catch a word of encouragement.

Run: (1) To rehearse a whole section without stopping. (2) "To r. lines": to practise scripted dialogue without moves. (3) The number of consecutive performances of a play.

Run-through: An attempt to rehearse a whole section without stopping.

Rushes: Dailies. A viewing of film recorded during a day's shooting to assess its quality.

Safety: Benevolent media lie: "That was perfect — let's do another TAKE, just as a safety."

SAG: Screen Actors' Guild. American film union.

Saint Genesius: Patron saint of actors.

Scrim: An open-weave material that appears solid from the lit side but disappears when the scene behind is lit instead.

Season: (1) A group of plays announced in advance. (2) A number of episodes of a series, shot as an administrative unit.

Second Unit: Film crew for atmosphere and crowd shooting. Often shoots STUNTS and special effects and material found necessary in POST-PRODUCTION

Session Fee: Paid for the work done in recording the action. Often followed by BUY-OUT or RESIDUALS

Set: (1) In film and TV, the place where the acting takes place. (2) In theatre, the construction on the stage.

Shooting Ratio: Between the amount originally shot and the final length of the edited film or videotape. Often high in productions with animals and children

Shot: (1) What is to happen between calling "action" and "CUT." (2) The type of picture the camera is set up for; close-up, long-shot, etc. (See LS, MS, CU, BCU, EC.)

Showcase: A stage production where all or most of the profit for the people involved, especially the actors, is in demonstrating their skills to people who may hire them.

Shutter: BARN DOOR. Hinged panel in front of the light cutting off edge of beam.

Sides: Originally theatre, now mainly media. Only those pages of the script that have a particular character's lines.

Sightline: An imaginary line from the eyes of someone in a theatre audience to a part of the stage. Particularly, the line after which you can be seen coming onto the stage. Important in planning sets and blocking so that the action can be seen, and in designing auditoriums so that all seats can have a good view.

Signatory: An engager who has agreed to hire actors only under the terms of an agreement negotiated with a performers' union.

Slate: (1) Use the CLAPPER BOARD to identify a shot. (2) Identify yourself and your agent before a taped audition.

SOC: Silent on Camera. In commercials, a performer with no lines, but a developed character.

Socko: A comedy hit. From the Greek comedy actors' low soft shoe, "soccus."

Soubrette: Heroine's best friend.

Spelvin: (George S., Georgina S.) Fictitious name used in a theatre programme to conceal the fact that an actor is playing two roles. In the UK, Walter Plinge.

SSE: Special Skills Extra. BACKGROUND PERFORMER hired to use unusual physical abilities, e.g. scuba diving, not amounting to STUNT work.

Stand-In: EXTRA hired to replace a PRINCIPAL PERFORMER while the lighting is being set.

SRO: Traditional but rarely used sign outside theatres: Standing Room Only.

Stage: (1) Theatre acting area. (2) Theatre work as opposed to MEDIA.

Stage Manager: SM. She Who Must Be Obeyed. Administers rehearsals, including breaks and overtime reports, passes on show's needs to technical departments, and compiles the prompt copy. Maintains liaison between actors and management. After opening, maintains the director's show. In US, may also cast and rehearse understudies and replacements.

Stagehand: One who changes scenery and does other physical jobs backstage.

Statutory Holiday: Forget it. You don't rehearse on Christmas Day but otherwise it's business as usual.

Steadicam™: Patented camera mount giving hand-held manoeuvrability with close to studio smoothness in movement.

Steward: ACTRA employee who polices productions, or is at least available on the phone in case of trouble.

Stock: A theatre that produces different plays successively without a substantial dark period or lay-off between.

Story Day: In film, TV, the passing of a day in the narrative, as opposed to time passing in the production process.

Story Board: The high points of a film or TV story, shown in sketches with key dialogue.

Strike: (1) Taking down a set at the end of a scene or more permanently when the run of a play is over. (2) In the sense of industrial action, almost unknown. See Chapter 10, "All for One…"

Studio: (1) Small theatre space, often a simple room with movable seating. (2) Indoor media space devoted to recording and broadcasting.

Stumble-through: An early attempt to get through a section of a play without stopping. The director wants a RUN-THROUGH but the SM knows the actors aren't up to it. A stagger-through is worse.

Stunt: In MEDIA, a hazardous or physically demanding action requiring experienced, qualified performers. Stunt performers receive higher fees and more consideration in production. (See RISK PERFORMANCE, EXTRAORDINARY RISK.)

Stunt Coordinator: Choreographer of stunts. Gives stunt performers direction and advises on safety throughout the performance. Usually responsible for providing or sourcing any specialized equipment required.

Stunt Double: A stunt performer dressed and made-up so that it appears that the actor did the stunt.

Succés d'Estime: Everyone likes the show. No one pays to see it.

Tableau: Frozen stage action. In Victorian theatre, the main curtain would be raised briefly after the end of an act to show the next exciting second.

Tabs: Main curtains in a PROSCENIUM theatre. Perhaps from TABLEAU.

Tail Slate: SLATE at the end of a TAKE, instead of at the beginning as usual.

Take: (1) Short for "double take," a familiar comedy routine. (2) In film or TV, an attempt to record a sequence. ("Pouring the milk, take twenty-seven.")

Talent: Performers, in the MEDIA. Often not including BACKGROUND.

Talent Agent: Agent, personal manager. Person representing and paid by a roster of CLIENTs.

Talley Light: Red light on top of whichever TV camera currently has the picture on screen.

TBA: To be announced. Also TBC (to be confirmed), TBD (to be determined).

Teaser: Wide, short curtain hanging above the stage to mask the FLIES and light BATTENs.

Technical Director: Similar to PSM but more linked with craft departments and less with actors.

Theatre: (1) Live performance, no matter where it is staged. (2) A theatre management.

Three-Point Lighting: Standard MEDIA lighting consisting of BACK

Light, Fill, and Key Light. The key light produces highlights on your face, the fill lightens the shadows from the key, and the back light separates you from the background.

Thrust: The stage extends forward so that the first rows of the audience wrap around it.

TK: TC, Telecine. Transferring film or projected stills to videotape.

Tormentor: The most forward wing flat or leg, closest to the Proscenium.

Tracking: Moving the camera parallel to the action. On tracks, hence the name.

Trades: American expression for periodicals dealing with news of productions now being planned or in process, casting, etc. Nearest equivalent here would be *Canadian Theatre Review*, *Playback*, *Equity News* (see Addresses).

Trap: Trap door in the stage. Various designs, all dangerous.

Traveller: A stage curtain, generally large, that opens from the middle out.

Triple Threat: A performer skilled in acting, singing, and dancing.

Twofer: Bargain ticket — two fer the price of one.

Type: Informal classification of the sorts of parts an actor could play.

Typecast: Given a part for which one is obviously suited.

Underdress: To wear a (part of a) costume under another, to speed a quick change.

Understudy: Actor ready (more or less) to take over a part in an emergency.

Unemployed: Not currently under contract as a performer.

Up Front: Paid in advance.

Upgrade: In Media, to be moved to a higher category of performance, often on set. One may be booked for an Actor role and subsequently upgraded to a Principal, or hired as an Extra and given lines, promoting one to Actor.

Use Fee: Residual. Part of an ACTRA Media fee, calculated by reference to the potential audience for a production. Paid in addition to Session Fee.

Voice-over: Off-camera speaker heard over action on screen. Also, loosely, narration over background sound on radio.

Voucher: A slip given to a Background Performer working under ACTRA rules, to be filled in and signed at the end of the day.

Walk the Stage: Uneven lighting is often seen and corrected by the theatre designer's having an ASM or convenient actor move about the acting area.

Walk-in: More or less unofficial equivalent to a complimentary ticket. The FOH manager may walk a person past the ticket-taker and allow the use of seats unoccupied close to curtain time.

Walk-on: Under Equity, a theatre Extra, with no personal characterization. Talks in crowds, may have one individual line.

Walk-through: A tentative run-through with limited objectives. See STUMBLE-THROUGH.

Wardrobe: (1) The clothes you wear as costume. (2) The rooms where the clothes are made, repaired, and stored. (3) The people who do the work on the clothes.

Weather Day: If a shoot is to occur outdoors, an alternative shoot day in the event that the shoot must be rescheduled due to weather conditions.

Window Shot: The last shot of the day. "Win do we go home?"

Wings: Space at the side of a stage, nominally out of the audience's sight. The FLATS meant to conceal this space.

Work Permit: A fee paid to ACTRA when a non-member of ACTRA is hired for a union production. This can also serve to record a job as part of the performer's qualifications to join ACTRA. (See Chapter 10, "All For One…")

Working: Under contract as an actor.

Workshop: (1) A minimal production of a play, to improve it before public showing. (2) A class with some practical component.

Wrangler: In MEDIA, person responsible for animals; originally horses, now also children, etc.

Wrap: MEDIA talk for "finish with": You're wrapped. That's a wrap. Wrap party.

This glossary is wrapped.

Bibliography

Benson, Eugene and L.W. Connolly, eds. *The Oxford Companion to the Canadian Theatre*. Don Mills: Oxford University Press, 1989.

Brandstein, Eve with Joanna Lipari. *The Actor: A Practical Guide to a Professional Career*. Plume, 1987.

Callow, Simon. *Being an Actor*. London: Penguin, 1995.

Charles, Jill. *Actor's Picture-Resume Book*. Theatre Directories, 1991.

Directory of Community Theatres in Ontario. Theatre Ontario.

Dunmore, Simon. *An Actor's Guide to Getting Work*. London: A & C Black, 2001.

Engel, Lehman. *Getting Started in Theatre*. MacMillan, 1973.

Hooks, Ed. *The Audition Book*. Backstage Books.

Johnson, Denis. *Up the Mainstream*. Toronto: University of Toronto Press.

Jordan, Alan. *Acting on Acting* (video). Morningstar Entertainment Group.

Joseph, Erik. *Glam Scam: Successfully Avoiding the Casting Couch and Other Talent and Modeling Scams*. Los Angeles: Lone Eagle Publishing Company, 1994.

Mattis, David. *Rising Stars Guide for Showbiz Kids and their Parents*. Crown.

Mayfield, Katherine. *Smart Actors, Foolish Choices: A Self-Help Guide to Coping With the Emotional Stresses of the Business*. Backstage Books, 1996.

Messaline, Peter and Miriam Newhouse. *Tax Kit 2000+*.

Monroe, Paula Ann. *Left Brain Finance for Creative People: A Money Guide for the Creatively Inclined*. Napierville, IL: Sourcebooks, 1998.

Newhouse, Miriam and Peter Messaline. *The Canadian Performers' Tax Kit*.

Newhouse, Miriam, Margaret Bard, and Peter Messaline. *"And Do You Have Anything Else?": Audition Pieces from Canadian Plays*. Toronto: Simon & Pierre, 1991.

Nowacin, Angela. *Modelling: A Guide to Working In Canada*. Toronto: Stoddart, 1994.

Ropell-Baruchel, Robyne. *The Stage Mom Survival Guide*. ACTRA.

Silver, Fred. *Auditioning for the Musical Theatre*. Penguin, 1988.

Strategies: The Business of Being a Playwright in Canada. Playwrights Union of Canada.

Tarling, Bill. *In the Background: An Extra's Handbook*. Toronto: Simon & Pierre, 1996.

The Actor's Organizer. TheatreBooks.

The Agents Book. Theatre Ontario.

The Indie Theatre Producers Guide. Toronto Theatre Alliance.

Wallace, Robert. *Producing Marginality: Theatre and Criticism in Canada*. Fifth House, 1990.